INTO
THICK
AIR

INTO THICK AIR

BIKING TO THE BELLYBUTTON OF SIX CONTINENTS

JIM MALUSA

Sierra Club Books
San Francisco

Text copyright © 2008 by Jim Malusa
Illustrated maps copyright © 2008 by Neil Gower

Published by Sierra Club Books,
85 Second Street, San Francisco, CA 94105

Sierra Club Books are published in association with
Counterpoint (www.counterpointpress.com).

SIERRA CLUB, SIERRA CLUB BOOKS, and the Sierra Club design
logos are registered trademarks of the Sierra Club.

The Sierra Club observes all regulations governing the use of public lands in all of its outings and other sponsored activities.

Book and cover design by Blue Design (www.bluedes.com)
Front cover photo © Dugald Bremner/National Geographic/Getty Images

Library of Congress Cataloging-in-Publication Data:

Malusa, Jim
    Into thick air : biking to the bellybutton of six continents / Jim Malusa.
       p. cm.
    Includes bibliographical references.
    ISBN-13: 978-1-57805-141-0 (pbk.)
    ISBN-10: 1-57805-141-X (pbk.)
  1. Malusa, Jim, 1957—Travel. 2. Voyages around the world. I. Title.
    G440.M27A3 2008
    910.4—dc22   2008003813

Printed in the United States of America on Cascades Enviro 100 acid-free paper, which contains 100 percent post-consumer waste, processed chlorine free.

Distributed by Publishers Group West
12 11 10 09 08
10 9 8 7 6 5 4 3 2 1

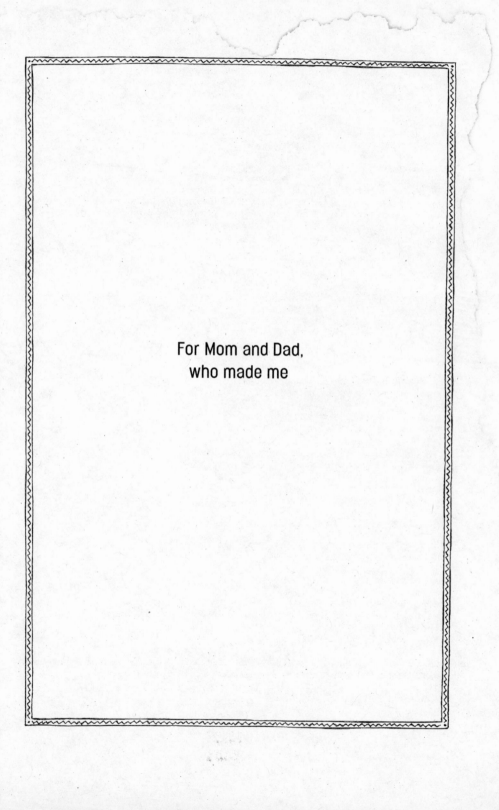

For Mom and Dad,
who made me

CREDITS FOR REPRINTED MATERIAL

CONTENTS

SOUTH AMERICA

AFRICA

NORTH AMERICA

*I turned down into the valley,
wishing to examine the bottom, and
a little curious, too, to indulge the
fancy of taking a ride below the
proper level of the earth and ocean.*

—Arthur Woodward, *Camels and
Surveyors in Death Valley*, 1861

*Get a bicycle. You will not regret it.
If you live.*

—Mark Twain, "Taming the Bicycle"

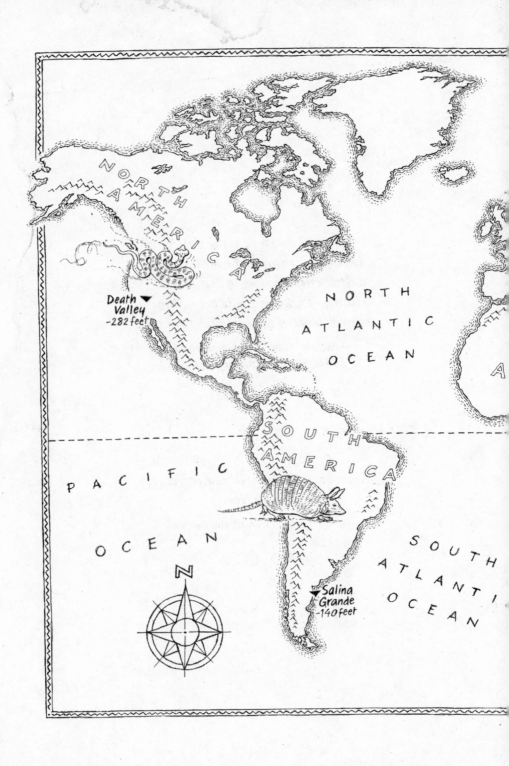

Death
Valley ▼
-282 feet

NORTH
ATLANTIC

OCEAN

PACIFIC

OCEAN

SOUTH
AMERICA

N

▼Salina
Grande
-140 feet

SOUTH
ATLANTI
OCEAN

A

ROPE

Caspian Sea
-92 feet

Turpan
Depression
-500 feet

Dead Sea
-1350 feet

Lac Assal
-505 feet

ASIA

INDIAN

OCEAN

AUSTRALIA
Lake Eyre
-49 feet

THE ANTI · SUMMITS OF THE WORLD

*One of the advantages of cycling
is that it automatically prevents
a journey from becoming an
Expedition.*

—Dervla Murphy, *Full Tilt: From
Ireland to India with a Bicycle*, 1965

An Odd Character
in the Bush

THE CLOSEST I'VE COME TO AN EXPEDITION was my honeymoon, six months on bicycles with no particular destination. Fate had dealt our little team two leaders and no followers. We survived because Sonya and I were linked not only by marriage but also, for better or worse, by physiology. We had ants in our pants. Like dogs sticking their heads out of car windows, we liked feeling the world go by. All we really needed was a map.

I'm a sucker for a pretty map, and a few years after the honeymoon I received as a gift *The Times Atlas of the World*. It was the size of an oven door, and with a little free time and just one beer it was easy to picture places where rain hardly ever falls or snow comes in August, where people love Jesus or bend toward Mecca. To my eyes, the best map of all was a colored topographic plate labeled "China, West."

I found it one evening while Sonya fiddled with her flute. Staring out from the center of the map was the yellow oval of the Takla Makan desert, a thousand miles across and rimmed with ice-mountains colored frostbite gray. The towns were arranged like the pearls of a necklace, evenly spaced along the foot of the mountains. They were oases, and the one called Turpan sat within a deep green oval. That shade of green appeared nowhere else on the map, because no other place was like Turpan—it was sunk five hundred feet below sea level.

I urged Sonya, a geologist by training and disposition, to sit down and take a look at the great green dimple in the desert. What in the world, I mused, were those Turpanians doing down there?

Sonya, who fears nothing but sunburn, took a look. "It could be thrusting," she said with admirable if misplaced focus on the geologic situation at hand. "Or it could be a sunken block." I said that I meant the people, not the hole. "Who knows?" she said—and that was mystery enough. Three years had passed since our honeymoon, and we had the itch.

I picked an excessively scenic route via Kazakhstan and Kyrgyzstan—the back door to China, over the mountains. After one year and several hundred dollars in phone calls to secure the "invitation" each visa required, we flew from our Arizona home to the other side of the earth. With us in the plane were two boxes, and in the boxes were our bicycles and camping gear.

The pedaling made us happy, and the people saved our necks. The mountains were gorgeous and brutal. On our bikes, we were exposed to the winds, the wilds, the works, and this vulnerability pulled kindness from everyone. We lived on flatbread and woolly cheese lumps and fermented mare's milk proffered by Kyrgyz herders wearing coats that were little more than sheep turned inside out, with the original owners evicted.

Three weeks skinnier, we reached the 12,400-foot pass into China. The atlas was right: it was August and snowing. Back in Arizona, we'd imagined summer flurries to be refreshing. We hadn't counted on freezing.

Far below was the Takla Makan, a glowing pool of warmth. The tourist literature insisted that Takla Makan meant "Go in and you don't go out." I wanted in. People say terrible things about deserts; they give them frightening names like Hell Hole and Satan's Armpit. But to a man standing in a frozen mud rut, going down made perfect sense.

Turpan was a hot and cheerful oasis of not-too-serious Muslims. They placed their faith in fruit. Their grapes and melons were a kind of miracle, grown not with rain but with meltwater from glaciers 18,000 feet above the town. Water was carried from the foot of the mountains in a subterranean waterworks of man-high tunnels dating from the glory days of the Silk Road. This liquid catacomb beneath the driest place in China was meant to last forever. The tunnels didn't lose water to the desert sun; they were immune to sandstorms; gravity delivered the water to irrigation ditches running along the streets. At day's end, when the donkey carts loaded with raisins quit stirring up the dust, the locals hauled their beds from their mud houses and parked them beside the canals, for the cool of the indigo sky and a little water music.

The surrounding desert was nearly rainless yet vaguely aqueous, with nude mountains of paleo-lake sediments sliced by erosion until they looked like shark's teeth, and sand dunes as black as a swamp.

No signs announced our elevation. Perhaps it was just the thick air, but pedaling below the usual level of the sea gave me the juvenile but real pleasure of breaking rules. One day Sonya and I lunched on noodles at a cafe that was no more than a grape trellis and tables with a view of the Tien Shan mountains. The name means "heavenly," but when I looked up at the dirty glaciers I was thankful for our deliverance from those cold and windy cracks.

Down was better than up, and it was only a matter of time before Turpan's burnt hills and friendly desolation gave me an idea: why not visit the lowest points on the planet? The bellybutton of each continent. The scheme had two golden attributes: I wouldn't need insulated underwear, and I could ride my bicycle.

It was a wonderful and unlikely scheme. Most everyone has such a plan tucked into his or her imagination, including the Turpan watermelon vendor who fancied himself emigrating to the United States and triumphantly returning five years later, quite wealthy yet still pious. The odds were not in his favor, but that really wasn't the point. It was the plan that counted, the pleasure of possibility.

Which is why, upon our return to Arizona, I looked up the lowest place below sea level on each continent. It was easy: each pit was marked on the National Geographic Map of the World. Turpan isn't the nadir of Asia— that would be the Dead Sea, on the shaky Israel-Jordan border. The beach of the Dead Sea is 1,350 feet below sea level, the lowest you can go on earth without a submarine or a flashlight.

I discovered that a good bit of Australia drains not to the ocean but into a sump called Lake Eyre, just 49 feet below sea level. In Europe, the lowest you can go is minus 92 feet on the Russian shore of the Caspian Sea. Salina Grande is sunk 140 feet in the center of South America's Valdez Peninsula, in the Patagonian Desert of Argentina. North America's basement, Death Valley, goes deeper, 282 feet below sea level, and only 700 miles from my home in Tucson. And Africa bottoms out at minus 505 feet on the shore of Lac Assal, in the wee country of Djibouti.

I was alarmed that I'd never heard of Djibouti but happy to see that Antarctica's depression is buried under 15,000 feet of ice. I scratched it from the list. I didn't mind a risk so long as it was a warm risk. Way down in the pits, closer to the core of things, I imagined therapeutic sunlight and oxygen galore. Yet nobody, so far as I knew, had ever reached all the world's depressions—or at least they weren't talking about it. The idea of climbing the Seven Summits, highest on each continent, inspired a race to the top of the world. The Six Sumps were forsaken, the opposite of success, and it was easy to understand why. Take your choice: climber or lowlife.

Because of my desire to go down rather than up, I didn't bother looking for money from the sort of sponsors that offer financial encouragement to people with more lofty aspirations, willing to hang from a cliff on an alloy claw the size of a cricket. For the next few years I kept taking freelance work as a journalist or botanist. My plan languished on a back burner, where it did not seem so absurd. I was not alone in this regard. "On my tenth birthday a bicycle and an atlas coincided as gifts," wrote the Irish cyclist Dervla Murphy in *Full Tilt*, "and a few days later I decided to cycle to India. . . . However, I was a cunning child so I kept my ambition to myself, thus avoiding the tolerant amusement it would have provoked among my elders."

But, unlike Murphy, I didn't grow up aiming for the bottom. As a boy I'd looked up—to big people, big machines, big mountains. I'd become a fairly regular guy, married to the opposite sex and settled in a brick house a mile from my high school. I lacked the usual excuses for wandering the globe.

"I decided that travel was flight and pursuit in equal parts," mused Paul Theroux while taking the choo-choo out of the "gray sodden city" of London, bound for *The Great Railway Bazaar*. Theroux fled bad weather, or the end of his marriage. The weather in Tucson was fine and my wife had not left me. I wasn't battling addiction, and my parents had failed to abuse me as a child. My exceedingly ordinary life might have depressed me if I suffered from depression, but I didn't. I just wasn't a quest kind of guy.

And then the phone rang with an unusual proposal. It was the year the Internet began gobbling up print magazines, much to my disgust. Yet I listened carefully when an editor I knew well from the Discovery Channel's computer venue, Discovery Online, tossed out her idea of a trip for an intrepid reporter.

"We'll equip you with a laptop, digital camera, and satellite phone, then send you far away, to some undisclosed destination that not even you know." The story would be in my efforts to find my way home over the course of a month. The electronics would allow me to transmit dispatches and pictures from the road for posting to their website. "We'll call it *One-Way Ticket to Nowhere*," she said with guarded enthusiasm. "Think about it."

I thought about it. I thought that if I were on the road for a month, I'd rather be freewheeling with my bicycle than hoping for the goodwill of whatever tribe Discovery decided to drop me into. There would still be dangers, including the chronic threat to a bicycle traveler of being mistaken for a Mormon missionary, but I came up with a counteroffer: I'd gladly go to an obscure locale, so long as I chose it. How about Lake Eyre, the lowest point in Australia? I'd ride my bicycle, which guaranteed that I'd meet the locals—I'd just be able to escape if necessary. If all works out to everyone's pleasure, I added hopefully, I'll take a pit trip every year, one to each continent.

She bought it—not the whole menu, just Australia for a start. Success there, she hastened to point out, may or may not lead to the other depressions; six years was a very long time in the publishing business. I agreed: I would travel in my archaic mode, and the computer would relentlessly connect me to my editor. The burden of technology was lamentable but bearable. I'd written for years on a computer and I thought it merely an ambitious typewriter, probably radioactive. I'd risked the Internet at the public library, diligently checking on the claims of rampant pornography.

And I guessed I wouldn't need to lug a satellite phone—surely there were phones everywhere in Australia.

Or were there? My notions of Australia were a grab bag of hard fact and harebrained rumor. So far as I knew, it was a gigantic and lonesome island that long ago had wandered far away from the other continents. Fate had dragged it to the southern hemisphere, where everything is backward—sun in the north, constellations upended, New Year's in the dead heat of summer.

I was reasonably sure that two sorts of people lived there: sunburned Brits, guzzling immense cans of Foster's beer, and grub-eating Aborigines playing classical tunes on a kind of bassoon. The British had taken over the places most like Britain and the natives got the good parts, where they hunted with boomerangs the Tasmanian devils and wallabies and other creatures pouched and hopping weird. There were crocodiles too, I recalled, long and quiet, like canoes with teeth and hunger.

Most of Australia, however, wasn't right for crocodiles. It was a desert, a bloody red desert with a huge rock stuck in the middle.

I may have had a few details wrong, but that was my Australia. It was an image based solidly if not proudly on *National Geographic* specials and Saturday morning cartoons, a memory buttressed by *National Lampoon* satires and the *World Book Encyclopedia*. Such visions were tough to dislodge by truth alone.

Yet even the most elementary research revealed that there would be no oasis of grapes and canals at the bottom of Australia. The *World Book* described Lake Eyre as a "strange lake," roughly in midcontinent, that had recently covered 6,000 square miles, but because it was in "an extremely hot region" it was currently "just a vast salt pan." Nobody lived there.

If Lake Eyre was dry and lonely, it seemed proper to start my ride at a place that was wet and busy. That would be the city of Darwin, on the tropical northern coast. I guessed it was sweating with jungles and swimming with crocodiles, and although this sounded awful I wanted to see for myself. From Darwin to Lake Eyre it was a straight shot south into the arid heart of Australia. Heading south was no small bonus: the sun would be at my back, not in my face.

It was around fifteen hundred miles from the wetlands to the salt pan, the last two hundred miles along a dirt road with its own name, the Oodnadatta Track. This was likely too far to cover in the thirty days Discovery had given me, but I figured I could hitch if needed—if anyone ever came along.

Seeking fresh information on my route, I wrote to a Margaret Day of the Bicycle Federation of Australia. Within a month I'd received Ms. Day's kind reply, in an envelope plastered with kangaroo and pygmy possum stamps. "Water supplies are essential as you already know. Small towns/petrol station outlets are about 100 to 120 kilometers apart along the road so supplies are not too much of a problem if you can eat basic food. Flies could be a worry so a net for your face is a possible solution. Road trains travel hard and fast so just get off the road when they are around. If you camp, be sure to get well off the road in an invisible place, as there can be an odd character in the bush. You will see the most beautiful stars at night."

That was enough. No mention of Lake Eyre, but I figured I would see for myself. I bought a ticket across the sea and the equator. I began to hoard Australian lore, concentrating on the presumably true stuff. After two months I recklessly considered myself a regular Aussie expert. I felt sorry for the nineteenth-century explorers who failed in a fatal way. I read Robert Hughes's *The Fatal Shore*, the story of the British flotillas of convicts and their wardens who founded the "thief-colony" that became today's Australia.

The Fatal Shore was a gift from my neighbor, Mr. Rodgers, whose only obvious connection to the southern hemisphere was a tremendous Australian eucalyptus in his front yard. It gave welcome shade from the early sun on the morning I hollered for Sonya to come and help heave-ho the bicycle box into the back of our station wagon.

It was a lousy time to leave my wife behind, a spring day with bees wobbling in the orange blossoms. But I had Australian questions without proper Australian answers. I wanted to know why there were no Australian restaurants in Tucson. I wanted to know who lived in Oodnadatta, a dot on the map where I imagined a single waterhole and one man kicking and swearing at forlorn livestock. And I wondered what was beyond the smallest town, out in the desert, under the big sun.

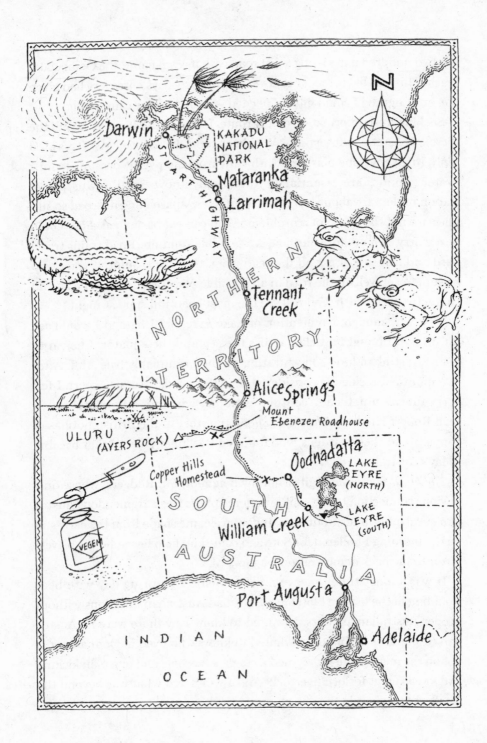

AUSTRALIA

Bicycling around outback Australia is for masochistic people. I wouldn't recommend it to my worst enemy.
—Jens Holtman, Big Red Tours

CHAPTER 1

Tucson to Darwin

A Wonderful Place to Bring Your Ex-Wife

MY MOTHER could not bear to see me off at the Tucson airport. She worried, and those worries would become flesh and blood if she saw me vanish into the sky. The best I could do was a farewell phone call.

"Mom, it's only Australia. It's like England, but drier. Tea time in the desert. The police don't carry guns—they just say, *Please behave*."

"I don't want to cry in the airport, Jimmy."

I reminded her that I'd avoided death all of my life—but it was no use. I took a little jet to Los Angeles International, where I switched planes for a whopper, a flying village. Less than a mile west was the edge of the continent and the challenge of not drinking myself silly with complimentary booze during a fifteen-hour night flight over the Pacific Ocean.

I lost the challenge and woke to the sun pouring in the north windows. Yesterday the sun had been in the south, and the switch was incandescent proof that the earth was round and we'd crossed the equator in the night. The big jet tilted and the island nation appeared. Banks of clouds politely parted, opening like louvered blinds, and sunlight striped the surf bashing the shore of prime Sydney real estate. The city was shiny wet after a night storm, and it pressed up to a narrow bay with blue inlets tucked into low hills.

The customs man at the Sydney airport wore stiff shorts and black socks. I thought: *If that's his uniform, I must be in Australia.* The bike box I left at the airport for the next day's flight to Darwin. In Sydney I was to rendezvous with a man who was critical to the success of my trip. He was not a desert survivalist or a crack shot or a crocodile hunter. He knew how to connect my computer to Australian telephones.

I caught a ride into the city, found a hotel, and walked downtown under a milky sky. On a Monday morning in the financial district the women wore freckles and cell phones, and the men were buttoned into gray flannel suits. I happily crunched through the fallen sycamore leaves—it was autumn here, not spring—past a newspaper stand with headlines announcing "ENGLAND ON BRINK OF MAD COW SLAUGHTER!"

On the fifteenth floor of a building modeled after an ice-cube tray, I found Andrew Hobbs at a steel desk connected by data and electrical cords to a hole in the plasterboard wall. After the perfunctory mutual inspection of our hardware, he handed me a discreet black nylon sack and said, "You'll be needing these." This had the effect of making me want to call him Agent Hobbs; surely it was a very important bag.

Inside were the assorted hookups for various species of telephones I might find in the Australian hinterlands. As with the genitalia of insects, there had to be a precise plug for each socket, or the connection would fail.

I thanked Hobbs and hiked over to the Australian Museum. As a curious and cautious tourist soon to be set loose in the outback, I was drawn to a desk near a sign reading "Search and Discover," and at that desk sat the master of biological advice, Michael Harvey. I told him my camping plans.

Mr. Harvey stated the facts: "If you pick up a snake in Australia, chances are it's a venomous snake. Most are elapids—front-fanged—and only twenty to twenty-five species will kill you. Of course, if you get the antivenin you should survive. If not, you're dead."

Mr. Harvey was twenty-six, looked younger, and made me wonder if the older naturalists had expired. In particular, herpetologists are famous for ignoring their own advice: don't touch the snakes. Like gun collectors, herpetologists feel the urge to occasionally handle the deadly object of their desire.

"The elapids you might worry about include taipans, brown snakes, tiger snakes, death adders, copperheads, and black snakes. Death adders have a habit of sitting very still and not getting out of your way. Please watch where you put your feet."

Mr. Harvey opened an atlas that showed I'd be out of the range of the northern death adder after a week or so on the road. Unfortunately, I'd then enter the range of the desert death adder.

MOST OF AUSTRALIA is desert and most of the desert is without Australians. They cling to the southeastern coast and the island of Tasmania, where the climate is agreeable to rose gardens and tea cozies and the long-term survival of very white people. A minority bask in the Indian Ocean glow of the southwest coast and the city of Perth, but between Perth and other Australians is the Nullarbor Plain. Valiantly searching for a kind word to say about this featureless tableland, one guide to "Outback Tourism" wrote, "Once a seabed, now home to the hairy-nose wombat, the Nullarbor (no trees) Plain is the world's largest continuous limestone area."

The only Australian city more remote than Perth is the northern port of Darwin. Judging from the Northern Territory Holiday Guide, Darwin is the luckiest place on earth, where "at one time of the year soft balmy breezes rustle the ever present canopy of palm trees, while at another, Nature's light shows produce dramatic skies." Enticing propaganda, and I went for the bait. I'd be going during the "dramatic skies," not knowing that this includes hurricanes. Australians knew: the morning flight out of Sydney held maybe two dozen international suckers like myself, clutching our Holiday Guides. There were far fewer locals, and many empty seats.

That was OK. "All forms of velocity are forms of vitality," wrote Nabokov, probably while on a train. Anything that moves will do the trick, from bicycle to jet. I had my maps, my camera, and a window, and this was a kind of bliss. The delightful surge of takeoff lifted me above the fungal haze of humidity and exhaust and the yak-yak of billboards. Below me, highways wiggled out of the city and into the Blue Mountains, to valleys stopped up by hydroelectric dams. Beyond the mountains the trees grew scarce and the land yellowed with wheat.

Onward, at nearly the speed of sound. The roads and the farms and all human geometries petered out and the color of the earth deepened to the red of clotted blood. It was sand, heaped in long low dunes, and between the dunes lay skinny clay pans, shining like minnows. The Simpson Desert. To the south was a sprawl of dry channels leading to the long-ago sea that became Lake Eyre. The lake was too distant to see anything but the glare off its skin of salt. It was more phantom than lake.

A thousand miles without a single town: Australia is like that. Even after we crossed the Tropic of Capricorn and the trees returned, humanity did not. The creeks swelled into great loopy rivers. The trees became a forest fringing the rivers, and between the forests were smooth grassy flats ponded with floodwaters.

The engines shushed and the jet eased closer to earth. The road came into view, my road, the only paved highway through a 1,500-mile-wide swath of Australia. Imagine flying from Los Angeles to Memphis and passing over a single highway. In Australia, that highway runs coast to coast, from Adelaide to Darwin on the shore of the Timor Sea.

The northern coast is not a rainforest but a tropical savanna, seasonally soaked and, according to the *World Book* climate map, Always Hot. It wasn't hot in the profoundly air-conditioned terminal of Darwin International Airport, where I assembled my bicycle in ignorance of the heat fog outside. A minute after I pedaled out I knew why the sternest warning in the Holiday Guide was "Your skin needs a lighter moisturizer than usual." You cannot apply moisturizers to sweat.

I rode out of the airport and into a traffic circle. No sign said: Darwin, that way. Worse, the traffic circle had by design no stop signs or signals, no chance to pause. I made several tours of the circle, leisurely pursued by cars brazenly driving on the wrong side of the road. They wanted me out of the traffic circle, but I was stuck in the spin cycle. So I simply rode off into the roadside shrubbery.

An embarrassing start, but riding alone means never having to say you're sorry. I mopped my brow and studied my free tourist map. A few miles later I rested at the Darwin Lawn Bowling Club, confident I was on course. Gentlemen in proper white outfits rolled midget bowling balls without paying the least attention to the four-foot-long lizard in the adjacent field. "What's that? It's a goanna. Quite common, mate."

By the time I reached my hotel, I understood that this tolerance of the native fauna extended only so far. Although Darwin is on the sea, nobody will get in the water. The beaches were deserted.

"Darwin's a wonderful place to bring your ex-wife," a rugby-looking fellow told me. "Take her for a swim, and if the crocs don't get her the jellyfish will." He sniffed and pulled at his mustache, which was the size of a rodent.

I met him at the Green Room, the lounge at the Hotel Darwin, where we swilled Victoria Bitter under the anemic breeze of a ceiling fan. He worked for the *Northern Territory News*, whose current headline declared, "UFO STUNS 14 AT DARWIN PARTY!"

Yet it was true: three weeks earlier, a girl had fallen from a fishing boat into the trailing tentacles of a box jellyfish. Mysteriously equipped with eyes but no brain, it kills like a drunk driver, by blunder, except the box jelly uses a neurotoxin capable of shutting down a life within a few minutes. By the time the girl was pulled aboard it was too late.

I stayed away from the sea. The Green Room would do for acclimating to the tropics. There was no air-conditioning. The hotel was one of the few buildings to survive both the Japanese bombardment of World War II and a 1974 cyclone that flattened Darwin. The new city was Valu-Lodges and Muffler Stops, and this made the Green Room's louvered windows and jungle garden irresistible. I settled into a chubby rattan chair and sampled an exotic item on the menu, "Nesting Crocodiles." My waiter placed it before me with a polite bow and said, "The trick with crocodiles is to eat them before they eat you."

The same sort of black gossip infects Arizona—rattlesnakes cozying up in your sleeping bag and tarantulas jumping like popcorn. Funny, but it's never happened to me. I remained an Australian skeptic. It was easy: I'd yet to spend a night outside.

And I'd never seen a crocodile. I'd only read *Crocodiles of Australia*, whose authors describe a 16-foot-long, 1,800-pound specimen named Sweetheart, "a cunning, patient, ruthless, fast and highly agile predatory killer." He enjoyed a hearty and varied diet, taking an occasional cow or fishing boat.

Yet Sweetheart never snacked on the people inside the boat. Hardly anyone is eaten by crocodiles in Australia. They die the usual way, with seized hearts or corroded livers or busted in car smashes. According to my semiprofessional calculations, hungry crocs eat only 0.000018 percent of Australia's populace annually—about one person a year.

Trouble is, 100 percent of the victims go dreadfully. Before leaving town, it seemed wise to join the other tourists and visit Crocodylus Park. It was feeding time, when very large reptiles were suddenly transformed from inanimate logs into a blur of teeth. They snapped up chicken carcasses so quickly that the multinational audience was left gasping what sounded like *"Schneider mitzel!"* and *"Sacre la mamma mia!"* American alligators were compared to the native crocodiles, and the former were found lacking in grit and spunk, a "rather slow and dumb animal." Both species have the winning physical characteristic of all crocodiles, alligators, gavials, and caymans: a trick nostril-to-lung passage that allows them to breathe when their mouth is open underwater.

If I'd been here during the last ice age (and the Aborigines were), I would have had more to worry about, namely *Quinkana fortirostrum*, a crocodile that was completely terrestrial. All I had to do was heed the abundant advice: Don't go in the water, don't approach a river from the same place twice, and camp at least two hundred meters from the water.

First I had to get out of Darwin. I introduced my American computer to the Australian telephone, a one-day courtship ultimately consummated with the help of the male-to-female plugs supplied by Hobbs. The next morning I bought a bird guide whose pictures looked as if a child had gone nuts with a sixty-four-color box of crayons. Back in my room I wrote a letter to my wife, enthusing over the Hotel Darwin and signing off with a simple yet touching, "Don't get pregnant until I get home." I slipped my camping and computer equipment into my bike panniers and slapped on greasy sunscreen from head to toe, working around my sandals. Outside, under a sun like a glowing gong, the palms drooped and cicadas shrieked. There was nothing left to do but wheel out in the direction of Lake Eyre.

CHAPTER 2

Darwin to Lake Eyre

Bloody Big Stretch of Salt

WITH THE FIRST TURN of the pedals I leave behind more than Darwin. Two months of preparations, of maps and letters, are now past. I ride in the present, and the first fifteen miles of Australia leave me feeling as if swaddled in wet laundry. "Tropical paradise" is a useful term only when sitting very still and clasping a chilled drink, so I stop for an iced coffee at the Palmerston Tavern.

After a review of the cryptic notices on a community bulletin board ("My Jenny wants a Jack. Any about?"), I take a seat beside a sociable motorcycle gang. Bikers spend a good deal of time roaring through the great outdoors, catching insects in their teeth, and swimming naked whenever possible—a solid background for any naturalist. I introduce myself and my plan.

"Heading towards Fogg Dam?" asks Craig, pulling a cigarette from the biggest box of smokes I've ever seen: Horizon 50's. "Better watch out for them mossies. Come dark they'll find you fast."

Mosquitoes. "And there's not just your regular mossie, but the Kamikaze, too. It doesn't bother to land before it bites—she flies in nose first and hits you straight away."

"You mean the Zero, not Kamikaze," says Wayne.

"Ain't no difference but the name," says Dood. The words whistle around the slobbery stub of a cigar. "Like Yank and Rebel. That's you, a Yank or a Rebel, same thing. Zero and Kamikaze are the same, and they's all bad mossies."

What's more, Dood says I'll have to keep an eye out for the native Australians. "Abos—they's primitive people."

After Dood shows me his immense tattoo of a Harley-Davidson engine, covering most of his back, I pedal another fifteen miles, feeling better as the sun sinks lower. At the last "bottleshop" and pub before Fogg Dam I buy some fried chicken for dinner and a beer to go with it. The beer I stuff into my sleeping bag, so it will still be cold two hours later.

"Fogg Dam," says the clerk, "has the highest percentage of something in the world. Maybe it's snakes. Take your torch out on the dam and you'll see it crawling with snakes. But they're just water pythons and no problem, mate."

This I remember: avoid the dam.

"And if a croc chases you, try to zigzag, because they can move out right well but don't turn the corners too good."

The last ten miles are gorgeous and ominous: sun blurring behind the limp eucalyptus, backlighting the big termite mounds that, as Alan Moorehead wrote, "give the land the appearance of a graveyard." I pass a disturbing roadkill—a goanna lizard as long as my bike—and reach the Fogg Dam turnoff at dusk.

The sun near the equator heads pretty much straight down for the horizon, and dusk is a brief affair. After only a few miles I realize I must find a camp soon. The first spot I try looks dandy, and I'm ready to scout out any nearby crocodile waters when I see a beehive nearby. I'm allergic to bees, swelling up like the Michelin Man within minutes, so I quickly move along to another potential camp. Before I can unpack I am attacked by ants. I press on in the muddy light to a fine open patch beneath the canopy of an immense tree. Suddenly the mossies and the kamikazes are on me, like blood bullets, and I fling up my tent and collapse inside.

Dark now, with spangles of moonlight on the mesh roof, but still hot. I read the *Northern Territory News* ("ROGUE CROW CHASES WOMEN!") while I eat dinner, with sweat dripping from my forehead onto the pages. Something crackles through the leaves outside, but its silhouette looks to be only that of a dingo, the Australian wild dog. I return to my chicken. While listening, of course.

There. There again. I shine my headlight outside, and at the same time realize that I've just made perhaps my last mistake: I don't know if I'm camped near water. The bees, the ants, and the mossies have all conspired to knock me off on my first night out. Worse, I realize with horror that I'm eating chicken—the croc's delight!

I'm sweating a wee bit more as I stuff the chicken into a plastic bag, that bag into another bag, then into another. Should I throw it outside, or will that just attract them? "The crocodile may have a very small brain," said the tour guide in Crocodylus Park, "but he uses 80 percent of that brain. That's a very high percentage." I hope the missing 20 percent is the sense of smell.

More sounds. I sweep the perimeter with my light. Nothing. Crocodiles are the biological and mythical equivalent of grizzly bears, but with this key difference: there's advice on how to deal with a bear. Play dead. Avoid eye contact. It may be bad advice, but you have a chance, however small, to fool them. There isn't a wisp of hope with the small-brained croc. They've been around since the dinosaurs, swallowing the unlucky. They are so good at it they've lazed away the last 200 million years without bothering to evolve hair or the ability to do crossword puzzles, and their smug ignorance makes them more terrible.

I debate the choices: stay and pray, or go outside and see if there's water nearby. The mosquitoes sound like an air raid siren; I'll be drilled within seconds. And what of the snakes? What if I'm near the dam? The poor dingo may already be just a tail sticking out of a knot of pythons.

A fruit drops off the tree above and pongs off the tent. More sweat. I listen closely, very closely, and realize how different the insects and birds and all the night sounds are from my Arizona home. I really am in Australia.

And when I notice that one sound is missing, I smile to myself and slump off into sleep. No frogs means no water.

IN THE MORNING the tent is dripping with dew, although the temperature never fell below 80 degrees. Early April is the end of the wet season, and the reservoir behind Fogg Dam—a failed rice farm taken over by the birds and the bees—is brimming with water lilies. Each leaf has collected the dew into a shining drop that rolls like a ball bearing when the wind blows. My *Bush Tucker* guidebook claims that the seeds of the water lily are good eating. After a croc search, I snatch a plant out of the water and pull its pod apart. The prize tastes like sweet peas.

There are plenty of wetlands on the ride into Kakadu National Park. Three wide slow rivers slide north to the sea. Bordering each river is an immensity of puddled floodplains, head-high grasses hiding carmine flowers shaped like bells, and silty channels leading to mud bogs and animals I don't want to meet. Not just crocodiles and mossies, but a predatory invader.

It came in 1935, when Aussie farmers in tropical Queensland believed they'd found a way to control a species of beetle that was munching their sugarcane. They hoped to take the cane beetle by surprise by importing a killer from South America, a wonder-toad that grew as big as a two-slice toaster. It seemed a terrific plan, and it's easy to imagine the farmers eagerly watching the first immigrant toads loosed in their fields. The cane toads spotted their quarry, their big trap-door mouths opened wide—and the cane beetles simply flew away.

Cane toads can't fly, but they have the can-do spirit of successful pioneers. That first batch of 101 toads gulped everything from frogs to dog food, from bees to still-glowing cigarette butts (they think they're fireflies). They reproduced with pope-pleasing speed, because a four-pound female can lay thousands of very special eggs. Poison eggs. They grow into poison tadpoles and poison toads.

Crows and college students are among the few animals that dare to mess with a cane toad and occasionally survive to pass on their genes to the next generation. The brilliant crows have learned to flip the toads over and eviscerate them, avoiding the poison glands and eating only the guts. Less brilliant college students in search of a buzz have tossed back an egg or two. Back at the Australian Museum in Sydney, Michael Harvey had told me the tale of "a fellow a year below me at university. He didn't believe me, ate two or three eggs. His heart stopped three or four times that night. He survived, but most other animals don't. Usually you find the dead with the toad halfway down its throat." Every year the cane toad brigade marches another dozen miles west into the tropical savannah, and now Kakadu is in their sights. Nothing but aridity can stop them, and I see nothing but water around these parts.

All that water makes a desert man wonder, keeping my mind off a miserable head wind. I churn along in a low gear, legs pumping fast and bike moving slow. Little lemon butterflies flutter by, into the same wind, like tissue paper defying the laws of aerodynamics. The lucky bastards. Alone on my bike, every two bits seems a marvel. The butterflies go where they please, and when they catch the sunlight just so, they shine with iridescence.

I gleam with sweat. Toward the late afternoon the eastern horizon dulls to gray. The wind quits. Thankful for the shade, I pedal on blithely. A half hour later the gray deepens to black and the low-flying cumulus look like they're sending down roots, long tendrils of mist that come down at odd angles. It will be the second storm of the day, and although I found cover during the first, this time there is no place to hide. When the wind suddenly returns I stop and cover my bike panniers with plastic shopping bags, discovering my hidden crocodile chicken. I toss it aside and ride on under the bowling-alley rumble of thunder. The temperature drops as if a refrigerator door has been opened, and hysterical flocks of parrots and cockatoos fly in a panic from tree to tree.

The sodden heat and wrong-way wind—it was all worth it to be here when the storm hits. Dead ahead it comes barreling down the road, a white whirlwind flecked with leaves. I ride off the shoulder, take off my shirt, and hunker down, pleasantly terrified as the leading edge bullies over me with the glitter-bang of lightning. When it lets up, twenty minutes later, the big stems of spear grass are busted and flattened, and I see why the Aborigines call this season Banggereng. It means "Knock 'em down."

KAKADU NATIONAL PARK isn't very popular with tourists during the wet season, for at least a thousand good reasons. That's how many species of fly call Kakadu home, and over the next three days of riding it seems most species form a buzzing banner in my slipstream. Whenever I stop to rest, the flies take their cue and creep into my nose and ears. I blink and swat and remember that the flies have nothing against me personally—they probably just feel an urge to lay eggs in somebody's brain, and here I am.

Kakadu, like most wet and warm places that have yet to be transformed by people, seethes with life. Anyone fond of diversity can sit in the shade of a beach hibiscus and take in the scent of their enormous yellow blossoms while keeping one eye open for rocket frogs and the fish with the unhappy name of Black-Blotched Anal-Fin Grunter.

Not that I tried to. A few days on the floodplain taught me that sniffing flowers meant snorting flies. I hurt my shoulder throwing a rock at an appealing bird that wouldn't turn for a picture. The blue kingfisher ignored the rock; it wouldn't even give me a cackle. Crocodiles either don't move at all, in which case they're as lively as stones, or they move very quickly out of sight. The one I passed today—it was basking within ten feet of the road—swapped ends in a flash and was gone in a splash.

Kakadu is mostly woodlands of languid eucalyptus with drowsy leaves and streamside galleries of paperbark melaleucas. To the east is the sandstone escarpment of Arnhem Land, but much of the park is too flat for a visitor to be able to see more than a few hundred feet.

But it's what I can't see that makes Kakadu alluring. Most of the park's 7,700 square miles are inaccessible to vehicles, a raw and hectic stronghold of the nonhuman world. From the road's edge you can merely look in and wonder, or you can stop for an hour or a night and poke around. At least until the flies and the crocodiles show up and the sensible action is to run away. Try to zigzag.

A few hours after the last fly attack, a bit of a climb brings me out of the floodplain glop, up to the foot of the escarpment. Runoff from the day's storm is sheeting down an alcove in the rock, collecting in a clear pool too small for crocodiles but big enough for me to palm up some water and splash off the sweat. The trees have sent a spaghetti bowl of roots spreading over the stone walls. A sound like a whimpering baby comes from a colony of flying foxes hanging upside down in the branches. They look like oversized bats but lack echolocation and rely instead on big saucer eyes that reflect redly in my light. Some biologists think they're not bats, but primates. Nobody's sure, and the flying foxes don't care. They drop out of the trees and beat wings into the night with the heavy flap of somebody shaking out a rug.

The rain resumes, but it's just a sneeze, not another great bawling blowout. I find a broad and spacious shelter under the brow of the cliff. Wetlands are for the birds. I'll take a rock camp, perfumed by flowers I have no name for, serenaded by a bird I do recognize, the "poor-will" call of a nightjar.

I'm not the first to be drawn to this open-air room with walls varnished by water-lain strips of manganese and iron. It's a fine surface for painting, and everywhere are figures of muscular kangaroos and fish and see-through humans with skeletons revealed, X-ray style. Kakadu is home to about five hundred of the original Australians. Some call themselves Bininj, others Mungguy. The rock is called Nourlangie, and one of the paintings features a man with a fish for a head and a serpent for a penis. A sign says it was done by a man, in 1964, painting over a similar, older piece that was, in turn, painted over the same work.

Why the paintings? More signs explain the mythical significance of each work in clinical language, but the interpretation comes off like Freud explaining the virgin birth of Christ. I find a better explanation of the paintings the next day, in an oral history exhibit down the road at the War-radjan Aboriginal Culture Center.

Why the paintings? A quote from Bill Neidjie:

> *Look see*
> *this good one, that painting.*
> *Give you all that feeling of life,*
> *all that big story.*

That sounds about right. And it is a big story, reaching back 50,000 years. The oldest paintings show arid-adapted trees and animals, because an ice-age Kakadu wasn't a coastal wetland but nearly two hundred miles inland. That's how far the sea level dropped with so much water captured in the ice caps. I try to imagine Gramps telling me a story that his grandfather told him, and so forth, a story that extends back in time to when Australia was connected by land to New Guinea. I can't imagine it. In my town you're an old-timer if you've been around for more than twenty years.

But what better way to learn how it might feel to be someone else than to go where they would go? Because no sensible Aborigine would be hanging out during the Wet at Fogg Dam, I aim my bike to the sort of place they might favor: Gubarra Pools.

The way there is six miles of corrugated dirt road plus a two-mile walk, but the reward is the perfect croc-proof pool, guarded top and bottom by waterfalls. The water is stained by leaf tannins to the color of bourbon. One swim changes my mind: Kakadu *is* fit for humans. Gubarra is the sort of place that extravagant hotels try to emulate, but always fall short. Tree frogs and rose-crowned fruit doves don't thrive in the atrium of the Grand Posh Lodge.

I keep my eyes peeled for the archerfish. It's been thirty years since I first found its picture in the *World Book Encyclopedia* (see *Fish, Unusual*) but there's no forgetting its method of capturing dinner. The archerfish spies an unsuspecting insect perched on overhanging greenery, takes aim, and drops it into the drink with a jet of water from its perfectly formed mouth. Anything within five feet is fair game. As a boy I was delighted by the discovery of a fish born to spit, and as a man I'm content to sit and wait for a single squirt.

The canyon funnels in a breeze that keeps the flies down and carries away the blue curl of smoke from my pipe. I dig my toes into the sand and wish most of the world was like Gubarra and Kakadu—say, 90 percent wilderness, 10 percent people and roads. My eco-fascist urges are excited by the setting, but ultimately silenced by no archerfish and the prospect of hunger unless I head to the park hotel. Besides, I must attach my computer to the World Wide Web.

If I lived here, really lived here, I might follow the animal tracks that lead away from the pool and into the palms. With luck I'd find the beast. Kill it and cook it and eat it. But I never was a hunter. With the sun fading and the mossies waking, I flip through my notebook and find the words of someone who might have lasted a while longer at the pools: Sarah Flora of the Girrimbitjba.

> *Walk up (South Alligator) River to Eva Valley,*
> *then down bush track to Nitmiluk.*
> *Good place to walk,*
> *long grass,*
> *you and buffalo might meet up.*
> *Oh shit.*
> *Make really hard spear,*
> *through the heart,*
> *cut him off at the heart . . .*

That's what it takes.

Later, I bag dinner with my credit card at the Barra Bar and Bistro. I feel like celebrating after my phone plug collection allowed me to slip my data into the mysterious network that links the computers of the world. If I had a "Sober Driver Card," I could show it to the barkeep for a free soda pop.

On the jukebox is Van Morrison, and on the bar is a copy of the *Northern Territory News* ("PYTHON POPS OUT OF PRINTER!"). A quick read of the paper and I know my Kakadu honeymoon is over. Cyclone Olivia is coming. The eye of the storm is stuck out at sea, so it's not lethal. Just wet.

Not so long ago I was very fond of clouds, but now they remind me of only one thing: tomorrow, I've got to get out of the tropics.

As I LEAVE KAKADU, the woodland opens and the polished trunks of the eucalyptus are salmon against the black-bellied clouds. The view spreads as the road climbs, and there's that feeling, that good one, of beginning to know a place. At the Jim-Jim bridge a pair of Aborigine kids with faultless teeth want me to join their stone tossing. I make sure to hit the river and miss Mom and Dad squatting on the shore, stoking a fire. Lunch will be two short-necked turtles, big ones, the size of turkeys. Each is a meal that comes in its own bowl.

The only traffic is an occasional four-wheel-drive Toyota outfitted like a submarine, with a snorkel for the engine to ford streams. Invisible lizards rustle the tall grasses. Gangs of big pink-and-white parrots called galahs yuk it up while hopping indecisively from branch to branch. Some swing upside down, probably just for kicks.

It rains in brief fits all day, then gives up with the dusk. Lucky me finds the perfect camp, overlooking flat-topped hills and the indefinite floodplain beyond. I set up the tent and lie outside on my belly with a book on extinct marsupials and a beer, a Melbourne Bitter, extracted from my sleeping bag. There's lightning, far away I think, then the storm breaks so fast I scarcely have time to grab my bike bags and throw them into the tent. By the time I follow, cursing and stumbling under the stroboscopic bolts, I'm slicked with rain. The storm's a thrasher, but I'm comfortable on my inflatable air pad. Too comfortable, perhaps—almost as if I were floating.

My waterbed rises as a pool forms under the tent. I tear through my gear, pull out the electronics, and heap the stuff in the tent vestibule. Higher and drier there, but when I unzip the screen a tree frog jumps in and adheres to my arm. Its black eyes are lidded with gold and the wings of an insect protrude from its thin lips. I fling it out and search for my spare garbage bags to spread out as an extra floor. Another frog leaps in, translucent green with bones visible under my headlamp. Then another frog, or perhaps the return of frog number one. While you're floating in your tent and reeling under the flash-crash of a storm, they're not easy to catch. I give up and spend the night on my artificial lily pad.

In the morning I'm pleased to find a roadhouse for breakfast just five miles down the road. I say, G'day, I'd like a steak sandwich, but before I eat I would like to hang my tent out to dry. Caught in last night's storm.

"I'll ask the boss lady."

The boss lady: head flattened laterally, like an archerfish, ready to spit. "Don't hang nothing up on the tables or the picnic area. Use a gum tree."

She doesn't seem pleased to see me. Come to think of it, I wouldn't be pleased to see me. My glasses are spattered with bugs and my wet bike seat has left a suspicious pervert stain on my shorts. Maybe that's why real cycle enthusiasts wear black tights. I stay seated, and ask if perhaps there's a line I could use.

"That's for the people who stay here. You didn't stay. Use a gum."

I hang the dripping tent in a gum tree—a eucalyptus—and return to a piece of cow flesh on soggy white bread, wrapped in plastic wrap. A napkin would be nice. "None to be had."

The ugly tourist versus the fish lady. Two children scamper out of the kitchen to sit at my side and watch the man who came on a bike. One is voraciously gnawing the ears off her chocolate Easter bunny, and the other is playing with a toy jet fighter, incessantly pushing the button that makes it roar. Sniffing my foot is a four-pound rat-dog with a fogged-over eye.

By the time I pull my tent out of the tree, the clouds are cutting loose with gray whippets of rain. They come and go, but come often enough that it's not easy getting out my little binoculars and spying on the birds. At least I can hear them. The kingfishers speak with voices variously described by field guides as "loud chuckling" or "extended maniac laughter" or a "harsh, cackling scream." When it comes to parrots, the ubiquitous and sassy galah sounds like a bird in need of lubrication, and the bulky corella almost purrs before it squawks.

Not far from the roadhouse, one of my favorite birds is smacked by a speeding tour truck, right before my eyes. The red-winged parrot pinwheels through the air and makes his last landing only ten feet in front of me. I stop and pick him up, amazed he's still alive, blinking slowly, moving his tongue in and out of a thick red bill tipped with orange. It's the most beautiful bird I've ever seen, and its head lolls to a dead stop.

This road, I'm told, was paved only this month. The old road was gravel, and slow going. Now people can get to Kakadu as fast at they want.

That night I lie in my tent naked, with arms and legs splayed apart to maximize heat radiation. The night insects are going *cha-cha-cha*, like maracas in a hot salsa band. Come dawn, it's 78 degrees. Dew slides down the tent poles, hidden birds purr like cats, and Typhoon Olivia is moving in for the kill. I get up and ride like a maniac, determined to race ahead of the weather. Olivia moves faster, platoons of cumulus with cauliflower tops and bottoms planed flat by the wind. The clouds run in packs, dumping on me, then fleeing so quickly that the sun's out before the rain spatters my glasses. When I reach the town of Katherine I'm soaked from ten such cloudbursts, and I'm not surprised that today's headline for the *Northern Territory News* is "I AM GOING TO KILL YOU."

"Don't take it personal, mate," says a grocery clerk. "The paper will print anything to get you to open it up. Last month the headline was 'Family of five run over in hit-and-run,' but when I reads the story, it's not people that got run over, but a family of ducks."

It's another sixty-five miles to Mataranka. If I'm desperate enough I can ride long and fast, and every time I look over my shoulder I see them coming: clouds like wet socks. They catch me, of course. I just ride faster, lashed on by the wind on my tail, all the way to town.

Salvation is a friendly hotel and a little watertight room. But I've only one spare change of clothes, and they're wet from the previous day's ride. Everyone has their private horrors, and for me the prospect of slipping into soggy underwear in the morning ranks right up there with putting my hands in dirty dishwater and encountering a mangle of mystery food.

I hang my clothes from the blades of the ceiling fan and hit the switch. It wobbles dramatically, but spins on. Sitting naked on the bed, I record my misery on the folding computer. After a photo of my clothes spinning overhead, I'm ready to send off a dispatch.

A search for a plug on the phone or the wall reveals only a single seamless line. Lacking a wire cutter and soldering iron, I go to Plan B: the acoustic crumpler. Or sonic scrambler. Something. It's a device that converts silent data to audible sounds. It straps on the phone's mouthpiece and talks to another computer. It takes hours to send photographs that have been transformed to hisses and squeals. The only other sound is the groaning ceiling fan.

Rain again in the morning, and only three miles out of Mataranka it turns from a sprinkle to a shower to a tree-bending blur. That makes up my mind: I'm hitching a ride south until I reach the land of dry underwear.

Three hours and twenty miles later I'm still pedaling in the rain, acutely aware of a flaw in my hitching plan. Although this is the only paved road across central Australia, there's only one car or truck every half hour. The Northern Territory is twice the size of Texas, as big as France, Spain, and Italy combined, but with a more reasonable population—only 160,000. Most live in or near Darwin and Katherine, long behind me. I neatly button my shirt, but who will stop for a fanatic on a bicycle festooned with garbage bags?

Dave Hawcroft. He's only going to the next town, Larrimah, but I'm confident we'll make it in his rotting yellow Datsun with a hole where the radio should be. He's returning from a hundred-mile grocery run to his bachelor hut, and I can hardly do better than a friendly man with a car full of food. "Computers used to be my business. That's what I did in the Solomon Islands before I came back to Australia." I tell him what I'm doing, and then he tells me what I'm doing, literally, since I didn't understand how I was sending my stories and pictures on something called FTP.

"File transfer protocol," says Dave. "Allows you to hook up your computer directly with another. We can do it at my place."

Dave's place in Larrimah, population 7, is a trailer set a comfortable distance from the charred ruins of his former neighbor's trailer. Dave's "caravan" escaped the fire, but the inside appears to have been struck by a miniature cyclone that scattered books and mustard jars and two clarinets.

I connect on his fiber-optic hookup, wow him with my 24 megachomps of rambunctious memory, and show him my story on the Aborigines at Kakadu. He kindly feeds me Polish sausage and tells me a thing or two about the natives.

"We've got to face up to the fact that the Aborigines are not a museum exhibit that should be kept on lands they really don't own. They're twentieth-century Australians who've been psychologically baffled and buggered by our prevailing social attitudes and systems. Would you like some mustard on that sausage? There's more orange juice. Watch their children some-time, listen to them, see what they paint—it's just like kids all round the world, and they want and need the same things as other kids. But we want the blackfellas to stay in their old ways, to paint snakes and dots—a million snakes and dots, over and over."

On other matters Dave is an optimist. "It's either hot and wet and miserable or hot and dry and miserable. So things can only get better in Larrimah."

Still raining at 4:30 when a bus pulls into Larrimah and takes me two hours down the road to Elliot. It's hell on wheels. Twelve inches from my head is a speaker carrying the sound track to the video *True Lies*. The racket of Schwarzenegger dispatching bad guys drills into my brain like a jungle parasite, and I vow not to ride a bus again.

And I don't. After a night in a "demountable"—a roadhouse hotel whose rooms are steel boxes with bed, light, shelf, and air-conditioning—I hitch a ride with Carl and Tess in a doorless Jeep. I must share space with bedrolls, five fuel cans, sheepskins, soot-blackened camp pots, a 12-gauge pump shotgun, a 30-30 rifle, and Sonny the border collie. Carl, with his fantastic beard and dreadlocks, looks as safe as a cannibal, so I strap my bike on the front and wiggle into the back. Once we get moving, Sonny drools on my leg, but he's better looking than Schwarzenegger.

More worrisome is a large bloodstained towel down by my feet, wrapped around something bigger than Sonny. Part of my brain alerts me to the possibility of a *Northern Territory News* headline reading "BLOODY BICYCLIST IN BITE-SIZED BITS!" But the rest of me is happy to be delivered from the tropics and Olivia. Already the land is sandier and the trees sparser.

"We work on the Aboriginal lands in western Australia," Carl yells over the rush of wind. "Helping them get grants and such. Tess and I are moving from Cotton Creek to a place near the Giles Meteorological Station, so we took the long way around to make a little holiday of it. A shame it's rained every day—but look, there's a bit of blue ahead."

Tess shows me photos from their last job. "And here's Carl cutting up a camel we shot for meat."

Is that a chainsaw he's using?

"Camel's a big animal, but a chainsaw makes quick work of it."

Carl and Tess are into natural foods. "Whenever we're on the road, whatever we hit, we eat."

Happiness is the discovery that I'm sitting next to a dead kangaroo. My benefactors peeled the roo off the road just yesterday, and what a waste it would be to let it rot. "Tea time!" announces Carl as we swerve into a roadside picnic area. Australians call lunch "tea time," and I know what's cooking. I collect the firewood while Carl hacks away at the kangaroo.

Roo tail is elegantly simple to prepare. Cut off the tail and toss it on the fire to burn off the hair. Remove it and with a large dangerous knife scrape off the charred bits. Throw it back on the coals for ten or fifteen minutes. Voilà! Carl gags with his first bite, but he claims it's only because he swallowed one of the bush flies that orbit our heads in plasmatic swarms. I have trouble eating around the tendons, but Carl points out that they're useful for sewing up leather goods.

They're generous folk, not only sharing their roadkill but taking me to Tennant Creek. Three hundred miles of Jeep and bus have had the desired effect: the lip of the storm is directly overhead, with muddled gray behind me and unfettered blue ahead. Wonderful. Balanced between the wet and the dry, I choose the dry and ride off into the desert.

TWO WEEKS AGO in Darwin a man recommended that I carry at least forty liters of water when traveling in the desert. "But that's forty kilos!" I said. Eighty-eight pounds. "I'll die not of thirst, but exhaustion." He leaned close and said, "Look, mate—there's nothing in the center—nothing at all."

The wetlander's throat-clutching dread of deserts isn't so different from my claustrophobia when hemmed in by trees. It's a matter of what feels like home, and for me home is where the bulb of the sun pops up and the fine yellow dawn slides over the world and, without even getting out of my sleeping bag, I can see the true horizon, land's end.

That's what it's like my first morning in the desert, a cool and dry morning camped near a heap of granite boulders called the Devil's Marbles. Between the rocks are sandy watercourses with an occasional ghost gum—a eucalyptus that appears to have not bark but skin as white as a Nordic princess's. Out on the flats beyond the rocks are the narrow-leaf mulgas, each as forlorn as Charlie Brown's Christmas tree.

They suit me and the birds fine. This isn't a he-man death desert, like the truly waterless Atacama of Chile, but a relatively sissy desert getting some ten inches of rain yearly, similar to my Tucson home. One difference from home, however, is *Musca vetustissima*, the bush fly. It's just a wee thing that doesn't bite, which is more than you can say for some human toddlers. On the other hand, a child doesn't walk across your eyeballs.

The female bush fly is merely in search of protein, says Jim Heath in his delightful little book *The Fly in Your Eye*. She needs proper nutrition from your mucus, tears, sweat, or saliva. Only then can she muster the energy to lay a clutch of eggs in her favored nursery, a fresh piece of dung. The bigger the dung, the better. Sadly for the bush fly, Australia's largest animals vanished during the last ice age, perhaps on the menu of the Aborigines. Without gold-medal dung producers like the one-ton *Diprotodon optatum*, which looked like the offspring of a rhino and a grizzly bear, the bush flies of arid Australia eked out a living on teeny kangaroo turds.

If those long-ago bush flies could dream, it would surely be of a thousand-pound slobbering herbivore with big moist eyes and bigger moister dung. The dream came ashore in 1788 with the British First Fleet. Half of the 1,500 passengers were convicts, most simple thieves like cheese snatchers and laundry grabbers, and the others were seamen and penal colony administrators hoping to survive beyond the fringe of the known world. Sensibly, they brought livestock, including two bulls and three cows.

As Heath puts it, "The bush flies watching the scene must have felt a dawning sense of unbelievable good luck." Within twenty years there were over a thousand cows, and "there was *plenty* of dung. Huge, splashy cow pads." Today there are over 20 million cows in Australia, and about twelve times a day each cow lets loose a dung heap capable of supporting two thousand baby flies. Don't bother with the math, unless you wish to be truly frightened.

Top-notch Australian entomologists have imported dung beetles to compete with bush flies. Things are getting better wherever the beetles can win the thrilling race to the fresh dung. The Devil's Marbles doesn't seem to be one of those places. I try my repellent, but they eagerly lap it up. I've been told that a powerful spray called Rid is the only thing that works, but it's like Agent Orange in a can, and difficult to apply to eyeballs.

So I ride off toward Alice Springs. The flies chase me, but mostly they ride on the back of my shirt. Keep moving and all is well. I find I can scribble, on the roll, shaky notes of whatever catches my eye. Big gourds on vines crawling across the sands. Zebra finches opening their orange bills to lick the leaky spigot on a cattle tank. The purple blooms of a deadly nightshade, seducing pollinators with sexy yellow stigmas.

The spaces between tourist stops are not empty—they just seem that way if you're in a car. Although we can move between points quicker than ever, the places between still exist, so the world is not shrinking after all.

It's a hot day, silencing the birds, everything waiting. The road is hypnotically straight for twenty miles, then doglegs though a pass in a long, low ridge of shattered rock. Late in the day I cross an actual creek and strip to wash in water that looks as though it came from a very rusty radiator. It's better than sweat.

Evening is the sweetest time in a hot place, because although dawn is the coolest moment of the day you know it's just going to get hotter. With dusk comes the promise of the night. The wind quits, the leaves relax, and I keep riding. With the road to myself I ride as the stars blink on and Venus becomes queen of the sky. Birds in the dark whistle laconically, and I ride, all alone, approaching the center of Australia.

WITH EVERY DAY CLOSER to Alice Springs the trees shrink and my skin dries and the sun's lower on the northern horizon. But the roadhouses stay much the same: pit stops for most folk, but oases for a cyclist with sixty miles to the next café/motel/pub/gas station. Like Pavlov's dog, I start salivating when I hear the growl of a power generator or see a crude sign painted on the hood of a wrecked car. I know that inside the screen door awaits a relatively fly-free dining room, a bathroom with a sliver of soap, and a counter where I'll order my road coffee and meal.

"Do you want that steak sandwich with the lot?" the counter woman will ask. Her name might be Bronwyn. The coffee will be instant. "The lot" is a processed cheese slice, carrot curls, fried egg and onions, and a slice each of pineapple and sugar beet heaped atop the slab of meat, all on white bread that soon regresses into dough. One bite and the sugar beet oozes what any biologist would recognize as "warning coloration," the sort of hue that animals and plants use to say: Eat me and you're in for a potentially unpleasant surprise.

It's no longer a surprise and it's no worse than the usual alternatives: toast with a can of baked beans poured on top, or toast with a can of spaghetti poured on top, or toast with Vegemite, a spread served in the ubiquitous little plastic cup with a tear-off lid. I've tried them all, even the Vegemite, smearing a dark blob across my toast and immediately recognizing its smell and texture. It's really nothing new, being widely available in the United States. It's marketed under the name Form-a-Gasket, an adhesive I once used to install a fuel pump in my car.

The Vegemite package claims it's "concentrated yeast extract." That's odd. In Vegemite-less societies I'd never heard the complaint, "I'd love to eat more yeast, if only it were concentrated into something a bit smaller." So it was no shock when a waitress told me that Vegemite wasn't invented by intelligent life—*Vegemite just happened.*

"I believe it was discovered by accident. They found it while making beer, the stuff that had settled to the bottom of the vat."

When was that?

"Huh—long, long ago. I can't remember when there wasn't Vegemite. It's a part of regular life."

Timeless food, reminding me of the truth in Cervantes's words: The road is always better than the inn. He wrote that four hundred years ago, and it doesn't appear that roadhouse food will be changing soon. The people in charge are generally too busy trying to attract more than the usual truck drivers. The signs out front proclaim a Wildlife Sanctuary, but it's just a big cage with a pair of emus or a talking cockatoo. Anything is better than nothing, including mildlife like a goat or a burro. Inside, above the cash register, the parade of animals continues with a display of pickled death adders and scorpions in murky jars. Yesterday's newspaper is for sale, as is this month's issue of *People* magazine, which apparently enjoys different ownership in Australia, with the current cover promising "Rudest Nude Wives."

Any newspaper article mentioning that particular roadhouse joins the yellowed archives tacked on the wall. One roadhouse also enshrines every newspaper account of UFOs reported over the desert. I ask a waitress about my chances of seeing one. "The owner sees them all the time," she says while taking a break and a smoke beside a stuffed lizard. She adds wistfully, "But I wish I'd see something more than little lights in the night sky. Lots of pretty stars, but . . . "

Later that evening I'm lying on my back, smoking my pipe under the pretty stars before the moon rises. Of course they see things out here, I'm thinking—it's the Vegemite and the glow-in-the-dark sugar beets. But when I take off my glasses and look up at the blaze of constellations I see for the first time in my life what appears to be a fried egg sizzling in the Milky Way.

NEAR THE TOWN OF ALICE SPRINGS, I stop to pick up a little road-killed lizard and place it in my handlebar bag alongside pipe and sunglasses. Collecting dead reptiles isn't a hobby, but I can't resist a better look at what appears to be a knot of barbed wire. It's called a thorny devil, and its armored skin of deep reds and russets—precisely the colors of central Australia—make it even more handsome than America's horned lizard. Otherwise, the two look so similar that it's reasonable to guess that they're related.

They're not. Separated by an ocean and millions of years, the thorny devil and the horned lizard *look* the same because they *do* the same thing for a living. You would not be surprised to find that steelworkers in Australia and Arizona wear hardhats and gloves. Thorny devils and horned lizards wear spikes and camouflage. The outfit is a lovely example of convergent evolution, the power of time and natural selection to find the right tool for the job—a job that, in the case of the lizards, consists of crouching by an ant trail and flicking their tongues out to snag, one at a time, over a thousand ants a day. They must take their meals wherever they find them, which is often in the open and exposed to whatever predator happens by. That's why the thorny devil and the horned lizard are disguised as dirt and rock (call it Plan A) and are as pleasant to swallow as a pincushion (Plan B).

Even in death the thorny devil is bizarrely beautiful. At least until decomposition forces me to place him back in the desert, just as I reach Alice Springs.

Only sixteen days since Darwin, and I'm dazzled by the superabundance of material goods in a town of only 25,000, over nine hundred miles from the nearest city. There's everything an intercontinental athlete could desire. After a heady splurge at a donut shop, I huff over to the SmokeMart to buy real pipe tobacco, then join the other tourists at the Midland Hotel.

Two young Swiss men are lounging at the pool in swimsuits and earphones, grimacing in primal satisfaction to the music. Mark politely removes his earphones to say hello, and I ask what he's listening to.

"Slayer."

Sounds like metal, I say, thinking of a piston engine critically low on oil.

"It *is* metal," says friend Christopher.

"But it's no good saying that Slayer is just a metal band," says Mark, "because there is speed metal and doom metal, thrash metal and slow metal."

"And white metal and heavy metal," adds Christopher, "and death metal and black metal."

So . . . what's Slayer?

"Black metal," says Mark.

"Doom metal," says Christopher, beginning some deep introspection on the role of Satan in Slayer's music. It's too bad I can't pull out the dead lizard and entertain them. Look, boys: Thorny Devil. Death Metal. Roadkill.

I waltz around my hotel room, inspecting the mini-bar and marveling at the ingenious Aussie two-button toilet. One button delivers a petite flush and the other lets loose a heroic flush. It's entirely up to the user to decide which is appropriate. I sit in the shower for thirty minutes, paralyzed by pleasure. As for the rest of Alice Springs, it's a very nice town in which to sleep, to wake, and to leave on a April morning.

I've got sixty miles to the next water, but that should be no problem with a light and fresh wind on my tail. The flies are sluggish in the morning cool, and the road is extra-lovely—no power lines or poles, just a strip of pavement through a land that dries with every mile closer to Lake Eyre. Passing motorists pulling Kamperoo trailers are giving me the thumbs up. The drivers can tell: that bicyclist is happy. A simple rolling happiness, so light it leaves scarcely a memory.

By my own reckoning, I am now a man of the Australian highway. Only occasionally will I be reaching down for my water bottle and then look up to see a car hurtling at me with its driver apparently reading the newspaper. My eyes will bug out, then I'll remember: Australian steering wheels are on the right side of the car, so that's the passenger with the paper, not the driver.

The car is often not really a car but an Australian hybrid, much like the now-extinct Chevy El Camino. In America, pickup trucks are evolving into something akin to a car; in Australia the cars are mutating into pickup trucks. The front half is a car, but the back is a truck bed to hold the spare, fuel cans, and a four-foot-tall jack known as a Hi-Lift. Up front there's a roo-bar to protect the headlights and grill and a pair of auxiliary lights, so you know what you're running over.

The bigger the vehicle, the bigger the roo-bar, and the biggest of all are on the road trains, the triple-trailer tractor rigs up to 174 feet long and 230,000 pounds—roughly the bulk and volume of eight hundred pasta-fed Italian baritones. Since there's no speed limit outside of the towns in the Northern Territory, they drive as fast as they can manage. So do the cars. I hear them coming several miles off—like a jet they sound, shrieking through the desert at 100 mph. I've never seen cars driven so fast, and nobody at these speeds considers swerving for a mere kangaroo. Hence, the roo-bars and a road littered with roadkill. I've seen more species of mammal and reptile dead than I have alive.

If they're not too badly mutilated I pull their bodies off the road and lay them in the brush, as I do today with a fifty-pound kangaroo. It's still warm, and I find the little fur pouch where they nurse their joeys. A female. I move her for my sake; she no longer cares. She reminds me that this road is like a tunnel for our stoic machines, boring through a nonhuman landscape. The road is paved with asphalt and broken kangaroos, with decapitated skinks and puffs of feathers. Ten feet from the pavement, among the drifts of red sand, are skittering lizard tracks and the excited mumblings of quail. Late in the day I hear the seismic whomp of a kangaroo in flight—I've seen six so far, and scared every one.

The bicyclist pedals along the margin between these two worlds, trying to make the best of both. I like the smooth pavement and the oiled whir of my machine, and I like the green flash of mulga parrots and the slashing stride of sand goannas. Come dusk, when the dunes turn to cinnamon, I find a dirt track leading into the desert and spend my night with the survivors.

"THE COMMUNITY KNOWS NOT TO MESS WITH ME," says the manager of the Mount Ebenezer Roadhouse. The community is the roadhouse and the scatter of Aborigines idling outside in the final light of day.

What's your method? A firm hand?

"Hard. It's a hard place." He's thin and anxious and getting thinner. He glances outside. "There's sniffers out there, right in front, watching your bike."

Sniffers?

"Petrol sniffers. Dangerous folk, I'm telling you. They's camped out all along the next ten or fifteen kilometers."

I think: *Oh shit-a-roo.* And I ask: Maybe I should camp out in the other direction? Back towards Erldunda?

"Maybe you should camp out in back."

I do, and I'm so beat that I sleep through the racket of the roadhouse generator. In the morning the manager is still in something of a panic, which appears to be his resting state; it just gets worse from there. "You should see his wife, mate," says a man sweeping the grounds. "She keeps giving him letters of resignation."

Resigning from what?

"From the lot—everything."

It's hard not to be sympathetic. The ingredients for insanity vary from person to person, but one recipe might include an interminable stretch of time at Mount Ebenezer in the company of the manager, the sniffers, and the flies.

My personal psychosis currently involves telephones and the computer. At Mount Ebenezer I cannot send my story without resorting to Plan C: dictating the piece into my editor's answering machine. While he sleeps on the other side of the international date line, I leave a two-minute message before the machine cuts out. Then I dial the twenty-four-digit number and start where I left off. Until I, too, want to flee Mount Ebenezer and the lot.

It's a brilliant day, and the Aborigines have either vanished or linger unseen in the thick shade of the desert oaks (whose leaves and cones more resemble a desert pine). A glorious tailwind pushes me down the road, a free ride until lunchtime, when I find a picnic ground and an amiable utility worker.

While we share lunch with each other and the zebra finches hopping across the bloody sands, he tells me of the efforts to civilize this desert with power and water. His is a good job, he confides. Yet something nags him.

"If you think along the lines of big time scales, it's easy to get worrying about things. I mean, the Romans—they didn't last."

He squints out into the desert, at the things that last. "Just look at calculators—what if the people who make them were all stricken by some disease and they died? And then where would we be?"

I'd never thought of it quite that way, I say. He leaves before I can decide if he's a sage or simply addled by the sun.

Out here in the heart of the continent, without a Roman or calculator in sight, the desert seems ferociously resistant to all forms of civilization that involve staying in one place. There simply isn't water enough. No rivers pierce the drylands, because there are no interior mountains big enough to push up and cool the air and wring out the moisture. In contrast, every state in the arid American West holds mountains over 11,000 feet. They are islands of wet in a sea of aridity, and from them flow the Colorado and the Snake, the Missouri and the Rio Grande.

Australia has no big mountains. For 200 million years during the tectonic dance of the continents it has been the wallflower, sitting out the bump-and-grind routine that shoves mountains up from the plains. Australia instead drifted away from its neighbors—first Africa, then India, and finally Antarctica and New Zealand. The continental plate Australia sits on did eventually ram Asia, but New Guinea took the blow and ended up with all the mountains. Australia got nothing but wind and rain and sun, wearing down the land into its present topographic stupor.

This is the flattest continent on the planet. Forget the brilliant parrots and cockatoos; for Australians, they're like very loud pigeons. A truly big rock is what they hunger for. Moby Rock. Something that lasts.

AT DAWN THEY COME by the thousands, in tour buses and little airplanes, in concussive waves of helicopters and Harley-Davidsons. Nobody appears to notice the blue sleeping bag tucked between the sand hills; nobody sees me swatting the first fly of the day and spilling my coffee. All eyes, mine included, are on Uluru, also known as Ayers Rock, or simply The Rock.

They're mad about this lonesome block of arkosic sandstone rising clean and smooth above the desert. Twelve hundred feet high and five miles around, its solitary mass generates its own gravity. It's just a petrified lump that could easily be lost in the Grand Canyon. But it's not in the Grand Canyon. It swells from the plain, a ribbed dome of rock the height of the Empire State Building and the size of Central Park.

Thirty miles to the west are the Olgas, a huddle of domes even higher than Uluru. But because the Olgas are too steep to climb unaided, the action is here. With my binoculars I see a line of dawn-patrol tourists inching up the rock's flank, the midget forms of what the Aborigines call the "ants." They're aiming for the top, shuffling up a stripe others have worn into the rock, a route made possible by a safety chain running along posts drilled into the stone.

Not every tourist is game for the climb. Some sit beside folding tables draped in linen and set with champagne flutes. Others simply gaze at the monolith from their suite in the Sails in the Desert Hotel, where the bush-hatted staff is forever cleaning the expanse of windows or tallying up your bill on the touch pad of the Micros Hospitality Management System. But for the young or the ambitious, the climb's the magnet, and I pack up early to join the flock.

A stop at the "culture center" crimps my plans. The ranger woman tells me that the local landowners, the Anangu, don't want anyone to climb the rock. "They let the tourists climb it only because of a compromise between the Anangu and the government. The Anangu got title to the land, but only if they agreed to lease back Uluru for ninety-nine years. The government's not keen on limiting such a big tourist draw as climbing the rock. But the Anangu . . . Here, read this."

It's a pamphlet explaining why "we never climb." For the Anangu the rock isn't a morning scoot and hoot. It's a "sacred site."

Like most white guys, I like diversity—until it gets in my way. I pedal on to the rock, which by now is faintly quivering in the heat, looking like a successful experiment with the world's largest Jell-O mold. With the arc of the sun, the rock changes flavor throughout the day and has already turned from predawn plum to tangerine. The closer I get, the farther my head tilts back to take it all in, until I reach the parking lot at the base of the climb. People pour from an Ayers Rock Plus tour bus and head straight for the climb. Others are descending in a mincing, hesitant step, safety chain in one hand, disposable camera in the other.

Here, as I feared, there's a small sign asking you not to climb the rock. I corral a few exhilarated folk who have just finished the climb and ask them about the view ("Tremendous!") and then about the native taboo on the climb. "Stuff that!" says an Aussie man in a burgundy polo shirt. "This is a tourist attraction, and the Aborigines are making a fortune off of it. They get their ten dollars a head; we get to climb it." His climbing friend adds, "If we did everything the Aborigines asked, we would all have to pack up and leave Australia, wouldn't we?"

He's right. But after a cloud of diesel fumes drifts over from the Down Under Tours bus, I'm thinking that leaving may not be such a bad idea. I'm not a sacred sort of guy, yet the idea is easy enough. For the Anangu the rock means water, the currency of life. With a single storm every runnel and gully of Uluru carries the runoff into plunge pools. For most tourists money is the currency of life. I wouldn't want my bank account PIN passed around. The Anangu don't want the rock's secrets casually thrown to the masses.

I suppose that includes me, so I reluctantly turn from the climb. It's true that this is a national park, so the rock belongs to all Australians longing for the big view. Let them climb it. I go for a walk around the base of Uluru instead, and am glad for it.

The rock is skirted with fig and gum trees that deepen the shade of the alcoves. Up in the branches sit kingfishers, thuggish birds with bills like chisels. A lady is watching them, a lady wearing a remarkable anti-fly hat, with a curtain round its brim of wine corks hanging on strings. A tourist from New Jersey, she too elected not to climb. "I know the Australians do it, but they don't like the blacks telling them what to do. It's a racial divide, just like the States."

It's as good a time as any to ponder the racial divide, the flies, and the sandstone arching into the light. The Rock is a model of geologic complacency. Even the Aborigines seem a pin-drop in time. The lady with the anti-fly hat heads back to the parking lot, leaving me with the enduring words, "My husband's in the car. He says you've seen one rock, you've seen them all."

MY TRICK OF packing a beer in my sleeping bag—so I'll have a cold one for the sunset—finally backfires at my Uluru camp. The bag I pull from my stuff sack reeks of Victoria Bitter. A down sleeping bag doesn't dry quickly, and my clammy night is made worse by a damp wind. I've been camping for five days straight, and the beer bag, night wind, and sweat have me dangerously close to decomposing into human mulch.

In the morning I peel off the bag, skip coffee, and immediately set off in pursuit of a hot shower. I find one at the home of Scott Medhurst, a friend of a friend of a friend. Scott works for the Ayers Rock Resort, where, among other things, he's the official reptile remover. "People freak out when a goanna gets in their house," he says while serving up some Weetabix and a cup of Moccona instant coffee. "That's a physical animal, mate. They scratch and bite and shit on you. It stinks."

I'm grateful for his hospitality and his fully plumbed staff home, and don't mention my aversion to scaled creatures. The truth is that I'd rather spend time with most any bird—say, a gray-crowned babbler or a gibber chat—than with a death adder.

Thanks to my training as a professional biologist, I knew that life lasts longer when you don't die, and that birds are unlikely to kill me. The silent reptiles I've left alone—until, after breakfast, Scott brings me out to the desert to release a yellow-faced whip snake he captured yesterday. Scott wears his "hard yakka" shorts, government-issue King Gee brand, whereas I would feel safer in Kevlar waders. No need to worry, he soothes. "The whip snake is dangerous, very painful, but it's not nearly as bad as a king brown snake. That's a snake with enough venom to put away about 300,000 rats. I caught a five-footer in someone's backyard. It's a very muscular animal—all muscle, and it wants out of the bag."

How does the whip snake rate in rat power?

"I'm not sure—maybe three thousand rats."

Yesterday, the whip snake cruised past someone working under his car. Scott caught it with the snake tongs, bagged it, then left it outside last night so the cold would slow it down. Now, as I stand by with my camera and notebook, he unties the noose around the black bag. He seems relaxed enough, and I ask him how long he's been a snake expert.

"I'm not. It's an adrenaline rush, and they pay me $10 a day for being on call and $30 per call."

I take two steps back.

"Also, it's interesting and a challenge. I'm learning as I go along."

The whip snake drops out of the bag and onto the sand, as lively as a noodle and not much fatter than my thumb. "Now is your chance for a photo, because when the sun hits him he'll be moving." I'm ready to jump like a roo, but don't have to. The whip snake is dazed by the circumstances. Like most wild things, it shows no urge to tangle with people. It warms in the light and elegantly slides off in the direction of Uluru. It moves towards freedom as well as tour buses, and for the first time I am faintly glad it is poisonous and will be left alone.

THE OODNADATTA TRACK looks like a good place to be left alone. Nobody else is turning off the highway onto the 280 miles of unpaved road to Lake Eyre. It's nicely graded, for the quarter mile I can see; beyond that, who knows? The prudent explorer, I carefully examine the Landsmap Tourist Guide before setting off. A bit of text in four-point font had earlier escaped my eye, but now I see the "Tips for Tactful Travellers."

1) Take your time—*you are on holiday*
2) Plan ahead—Don't forget drinking water, hat, sunscreen

It appears I'm set. Onward, and downward. Nobody passes all morning, leaving me free to weave from side to side in search of smoother riding. The road changes color as it dips and climbs through different strata, from eye-squinting white clays to crumbling green shales to sands the thick red of spaghetti sauce. There are no roadkills, but instead the clawed tracks of sand goannas dragging their tails. The trees manage a living only along the dry creek beds, and the plains are free and open. I see my first emus, big birds with little wings that are as useful for flight as the tail fins of a 1958 Cadillac. They tear off in a cloud of dust, jinking and dodging like soccer players.

The emu's relative, the ostrich, lives in Australia, too, but Africa is its native home. It was introduced to Australia, as were rabbits, cats, and foxes. Like the cane toads, all have proved more successful than anyone imagined. The carnivorous cats and foxes are busy dismembering the increasingly rare native marsupials. The rabbits came from England in 1859, a couple of dozen hopping targets for sportsmen. The lucky survivors encountered few natural enemies. Like college students on spring break, there was nobody to control them. They bred like mad, and by 1940, 600 million rabbits were nibbling the landscape down to the dirt.

People tried gassing the underground warrens and blasting at them with guns, but Australians could not slow the European bunnies until 1950, when they unleashed a rabbit virus from Uruguay. The number of rabbits plummeted, then bounced back to a diminished but still very hungry population of a hundred million or so.

Aussie biologists found hope in the sudden deaths of 64 million European rabbits in Italy in 1986, and immediately went to work on achieving the same results. The killer—or savior, depending on your viewpoint—was a rabbit hemorrhagic virus from China. The pathogen was brought to an isolated island off South Australia for testing, yet in 1996 managed to escape the supposedly bio-secure laboratory. It's heading for the Oodnadatta Track.

Trouble is, rabbits are considerably cuter than many of their victims— the voiceless plants and the myriad animals that depend on those plants for food and home. Ranchers and ecologists might agree that the rabbit is the devil with floppy ears, but rabbit lovers smell a conspiracy in the "escape" of the virus. It's no accident, they say—it is cruel bunny-cide condoned by the same government whose PR campaign insists that the "benign virus" is painless, and the infected rabbits "go quietly" in the privacy of their warrens.

Meanwhile, there is a push to eliminate the traditional Easter Bunny and replace it with the Easter Bilby—a long-eared critter otherwise known as the bandicoot. It's neither ugly nor poisonous, but its long nose gives it the look of an Easter Rat, so the Easter Bunny and the Euro-rabbits will probably win.

Repeated invasion seems to be Australia's fate, from the Aborigines to the British, the dingoes to the sheep. I'm part of the tourist invasion, and I'm glad someone got here before me—I need to fill my water bottles just as I pass the Copper Hills homestead.

Hugh Fran is a rancher, hobby painter, and hospitable geezer who seems to have been expecting me all along. He gives me a slow tour of his little bungalow, pausing to hitch up his pants now and then. He gladly lets me try out his remarkable solar-powered telephone. When I succeed in connecting the computer, he hoots to his wife, "Honey, look, we're on the Internet!" Laurel ambles over from the living room and says, "I'm not sure what that means." I explain that it's all the information you need, and more, before you even knew you needed it. Laurel listens politely, then says, "I'm going back to my ironing. Tell me if something interesting happens."

The Oodnadatta Track is not a happening place. At dusk, the only vehicle of the day passes me. I could camp in the road if I like, but prefer the clean sand of a dry creek bed. The land smells vaguely of broccoli. Night comes without a sound, without a puff of wind. Sixty miles of dirt road and I collapse into sleep.

Sixty more miles of dirt to the town of Oodnadatta. The next day I bleed air from my tires, to soften the ride and help float through the sands. It works, but it also allows an unnoticed rock in the road to pinch my tube and give me the first flat of the trip. I pull out my pump and find it perhaps fatally bent. I get thirsty just looking at it and, beginning my descent into lunacy, give my pump a pep talk. "You better work, buddy."

It does. The road curves north into the sun, and the glare off the rocks has me searching for my sunscreen. The goop makes a nice base for the dust. Late in the day, my skin and everything else turns rosy, including the town of Oodnadatta. There's a pink phone booth. And a pink canoe—no, two pink canoes—parked in the dirt outside the Pink Roadhouse. I roll to a stop and a kid sitting in a pink canoe greets me with, "I say, old chap." Tilly is her name. She says I can get a shower at this, the best roadhouse yet. It's 120 miles from the pavement, yet there's real coffee, not instant. Oodnaburgers, too, which a sign claims are "The choice of the discerning palate—and they taste good, too."

Owner Lynnie Plate, a mother lode of brains and charm, leaves the office open for my exclusive use. I try to get the phone to connect, working into the night. I can't get a line out of the country. Failure, and there's nothing to do but yawn and rub my eyes and see taped to the wall a poem whose final stanza reads:

> *The best place is in a bloody bed,*
> *with bloody ice upon your bloody head.*
> *You might as well be bloody dead,*
> *in Oodna-bloody-datta.*

Then Lynnie comes by and offers me a bloody bed for the night.

MORE ROCKS, MORE SAND. Ten miles out of Oodnadatta and the headwind is drying my eyeballs. Ten miles and two hours farther, I bog down in the sand. When I stop pushing there is only the sound of the wind and the possibility that I may not make it to Lake Eyre. I'm not going to die out here, a picturesque sprawl of bones. But if by midday no vehicle has passed and I'm not halfway to the water cache arranged by the Pink Roadhouse, I'll have to turn back.

No trees, no clouds. This is the gibber desert, a pavement of varnished wind-sculpted stones. When the sun is low and behind me, the gibbers glow like burnished copper, but now they're black as charcoal briquettes. Poking up through the gibbers are skeletons of saltbush, quivering in the wind. I push on, chattering across the rocks, plowing through the sand, crossing a basin of dried mud aglitter with half-buried gypsum crystals.

It's the sand that kills me. When I'm stuck again I lay the bike down and take a quick and furious inventory of my stores. The harmonica I deem essential, but I sincerely want to fling the blasted computer onto the gibbers. That I wouldn't have a job without it makes no difference at the moment. I can't eat it, wear it, drink it. An appropriate term comes to mind: *dead weight*.

Dead weight cursed the earliest effort to cross this desert, the 1860 Burke and Wills Expedition. They aimed to be the first non-Aborigines to cross the arid heart of the continent. Alan Moorehead tells the story, in *Cooper's Creek*, of how they set out from Melbourne with a "fatal luxury of supplies." Twenty-one tons of equipment for fifteen men, distributed over twenty-three horses and twenty-five camels. Thirty-seven firearms and, inexplicably, twenty camp beds. And, in event of flood, life preservers for the camels. They fretted over the camels, but an expert from India promised that "all would be well if a certain amount of rum was added to their rations." They brought sixty gallons.

The rum proved popular. Soon the male camels were fighting over the females. The camp cook was hitting the bottle. When others joined in, Burke ordered the rum abandoned.

Sobriety didn't help. The creaking wagons fell apart. Overloaded, addled by bad weather and worse organization, they trudged into the desert east of Lake Eyre and set up a base camp on Cooper's Creek.

Four men, now traveling light, pushed on to the northern coast. When they shambled back into base camp four months later, having eaten every morsel of food including their horses, they discovered that the others had given up hope and left that very morning. The explorers couldn't follow— they were little more than a tatter of clothes hung over skin like parchment. The sole survivor, John King, had wits enough to realize that only the Aborigines could save him, for they knew what to eat.

Yes, things could be far worse. My fig bars are still edible, and I have an emergency box of Coco-Pops. I mount my bike and creep ahead in low gear. The wind ebbs and I'm able to shift up a gear or two. Landforms that seemed impossibly far ahead—long low dunes and the dead glare of salt pans—eventually fall behind. Fifty miles out of Oodnadatta I reach my water cache, arranged by Lynnie and kindly put out by the Williams family, of the nearby Nilpinna Cattle Station. At the same time a truck rumbles up and a federal range ecologist gets out for a chat. Awful nice of the Williamses, he says—let's return the water jug. I hop in for a little detour off the track.

Before I see it, I imagine the Williamses' place—a dust bowl shack with whip snakes in the outhouse and a pedal radio for communications. The pedal radio was another clever Australian invention born of the fantastic isolation of the outback, a shortwave that generated its own electricity so long as you were willing to crank away.

But that was in the 1930s, and it seems things have changed. Within minutes of my arrival at the Williamses', their eleven-year old, Nick, is checking out my laptop computer. He stops singing "Waltzing Matilda" long enough to express his amazement: "What sort of computer doesn't have games?" He drags me over to their home computer and shows me how to play Star Trek.

Paul and Krystal Williams immediately adopt me. Here's the shower, here's the phone, and here's dinner: pan-fried steak ("schnitzel"), heaps of veggies, mashed potatoes, and strawberries. After dinner the young girls, Katrina and Renee, show me their outstanding at-home school, then play a kind of tug-of-war with a large and apparently boneless tabby cat. Nick confesses to me: "We drove our last governess *mad*!"

Mum and Dad offer me a bed. Tempting, but I had one last night and now prefer the comfortable sand of a dry creek. I haven't used a tent since the tropics. Under stars like sequins, I sleep the sleep of a man whose fortunes seem to have changed for the better.

But the road hasn't improved. The next day it's still a mess of pointed rocks and sand traps. At least the wind is sleeping, and by midafternoon I arrive in William Creek, population 9. No creek, naturally. The William Creek Hotel is the sole business, a sun-warped, wind-stripped hovel with flies zipping through the holes in the lopsided screen door. It looks like paradise to me; I wobble in, find a chair, and order an orange juice. It costs the same as water in a place where it hasn't rained in thirteen months.

Meanwhile, the local ranchers with blood-spattered hands ("Been branding, mate") drop in for a bottle of "VB." After my juice is gone I figure I might as well have a Victoria Bitter myself so long as the men are dropping coins into the jukebox. The 45-rpm record sticks until somebody whomps the machine on its side. Then the music gets scratching and the joint is grooving to Rolf Harris's hiccupping, accordion-based, acid-outback version of "Stairway to Heaven." Nothing else like it, I'm thinking as my gaze is drawn upwards to a frighteningly large bra hanging from the rafters. It's big enough to carry twin bowling balls, but is loaded with coins. I don't ask why. Might be something tragically personal.

The men drink and ramble in a cheerful crude lingo. It's plenty entertaining, but can complicate otherwise simple tasks like finding the bathroom.

"That way, up a chain."

Thanks . . . but how far is "up a chain"?

"Length of a cricket pitch."

I'm the only tourist in town until a gang of Japanese motorcyclists roar in and clear out the local cola supplies. They're sweating madly in head-to-toe articulated plastic body armor, looking like lobsters with video cameras instead of claws. They film the coin bra, my bicycle, and the Operation Anti-Rabbit bumper stickers on the trucks ("Eradication through Co-operation") featuring a devious slit-eyed bunny with killer incisors.

After they tear off, with a vicious blat of exhaust, a mail delivery brings a just-in-time General Delivery letter from my wife, Sonya. It's full of glowing reveries of spring in Arizona, of mourning doves and sweet acacias and baby tomatoes. I'm mortally homesick, and the man at the bar wants to know where I'm heading "with that push bike."

Lake Eyre, I say—and now I feel stupid as well as melancholy. He doesn't want to know why, and instead asks, "Then what?" That's it, I say. After Lake Eyre I'll ride another day to the next town down the track, Roxby Downs, and catch a little plane out of the desert.

"Lake Eyre," he says, "is a bloody big stretch of salt. Salt far as you see. There's only one reason to go out there." He pauses, for dramatic purposes, and to lick the paper on his hand-rolled smoke. "It's the only place where it takes the flies five minutes to find you."

I'm easily pleased, and this is blessed news for me. Winds willing, sixty miles and one more day to Lake Eyre.

CROWS WAKE ME in the predawn cool. They're taunting each other, or me, but it's still a nice alarm clock. I open my eyes and watch color seep back into the world. Small clouds above the warming horizon are lined up like pink commas. The usual splendid workings of earth and sky—but I worry over the wind-swept curve of the clouds.

Last night the dingoes moaned and cried. When the explorer Charles Sturt came this way in 1845–46, he wrote that the dingoes' "emaciated bodies standing between us and the full moon were the most wretched objects in creation." Sturt was one of the first to systematically explore the center of the continent, prodded by his dream of an inland sea. He even brought a boat into the desert, "for it will be a joyous day for us to launch on an unknown sea and run away towards the tropics."

Sturt wasn't crazy. About 500,000 square miles of Australia—a sixth of the continent—slopes not to the sea but instead into the closed basin that is Lake Eyre. The Volga River, Europe's largest, drains a similar expanse, and also flows to a closed basin—the Caspian Sea, watery proof that Europe is wetter than present-day Australia.

Sturt was ten thousand years too late to discover Australia's equivalent of the Caspian, Lake Dieri. After the Pleistocene it literally evaporated, and its ghost is Lake Eyre. Blurts of runoff from rains up to five hundred miles away can flood one corner or another of Eyre. Once every twenty or thirty years the lake can be sixty miles wide and fifteen feet deep.

This isn't one of those years. Like the man at William Creek said: lots of salt out there. Fortunately, that's all I'm expecting. A little bird they call Willie wagtail keeps me company, snapping up flies as I pack my bags. Feathered in formal black-over-white, Willie inspires me to jazz myself up for the special occasion. A fine-looking shrub with cotton puff flowers, ready for the craft fair, supplies a nice boutonniere for my shirt.

When the sun appears and only the solitary can hear the daybreak angels sing and toot their long horns, I set off like a bloodhound, hot on the scent of Lake Eyre. It's a fine start, wheeling along with my shadow in pursuit, the desert air as clear and intoxicating as gin, everything reminding me of why I ride: to be outside. The bicycle amplifies life, making good times better.

And bad times worse. After one hour the headwind revs up and my spirit cracks like the skin on my hands.

To the cyclist, and the sailor, there is never simply a "wind." It's either a headwind, crosswind, or tailwind. A headwind is worse than any mountain. The mountain delivers tangible rewards: a view at the summit and a downhill on the other side. A stiff headwind drains you out of spite, simply to show you who's boss.

A truck pulls alongside. After the dust blows back, the driver cranks down the window and asks how I'm doing. Miserable, I say—ten kilometers per hour, max.

"Need a lift to Coward Springs?"

I'm not sure where Coward Springs is, but I remember the lesson of the sole survivor of the Burke and Wills expedition: never refuse help from the natives. My rescuers are a wheat farmer and a nurse on holiday. At the spring they're meeting the nurse's son, a herpetologist. When we arrive twenty minutes later, I'm treated to some freshly captured reptiles, including a barking gecko with blinking shining eyes and skin as soft as a peach. With a single croak it wrecks my notion that Australian reptiles are deadly silent.

From Coward Springs it's twenty-five miles to Lake Eyre, which I figure will be a good four-hour battle into the wind. I'm no longer cursing the elements, because nothing is going to stop me now. My knees are aching, but I pedal on and without stopping reach into my shirt pocket for the aspirin bottle and toss back three tablets.

Five miles from Lake Eyre is Curdimurka, an abandoned railroad siding on an abandoned railway. The well still functions, and I stop to fill my water bottles and to snoop inside the stone building. The wind is gusting and the door slams shut behind me.

No more wind. I sit in a chair and rub my thighs and realize how living outside for a month has made me appreciate being inside, out of the sun, sheltered from the blowing dust. One lick of comfort is all it takes to make me consider spending the night inside, but I'm not quite where I want to be.

A half hour before sundown I crest a rise and there's Lake Eyre. It extends beyond the horizon, just like the sea, if the sea were white and silent and you could ride your bike on it. I push and drag my machine through the dunes fringing the shore, bump over a scatter of gibbers to reach the salt crust, then pedal onto the lake. There are a few snags of driftwood to avoid, locked in the salt as if frozen in ice. Beyond, it's clear sailing. I could pop open my tent, strap it to the bike, and in this wind set a land speed record.

Turning back into the wind, my speed drops and I break through the salt and sink two inches into a damp black clay. No matter: I stop and take a picture before pushing the bike back to shore. Like a sand creature, I find a hollow between the dunes and hunker down out of the wind. I dig through my panniers and find my meager reserve of brandy, just in time for a bloody sunset over Lake Eyre.

The problem with Mount Everest is that you can't spend the night on top. Tonight my noodle dinner is ready extra-fast because water boils hotter at forty-nine feet below sea level. Tonight the wind fades and the quiet settles in and comforts me. I fall asleep, all alone at the edge of a salt lake in the desert. In the night I wake to find the moon down and the stars zinging bright, and although I'm at the very bottom of Australia, I'm feeling pretty high.

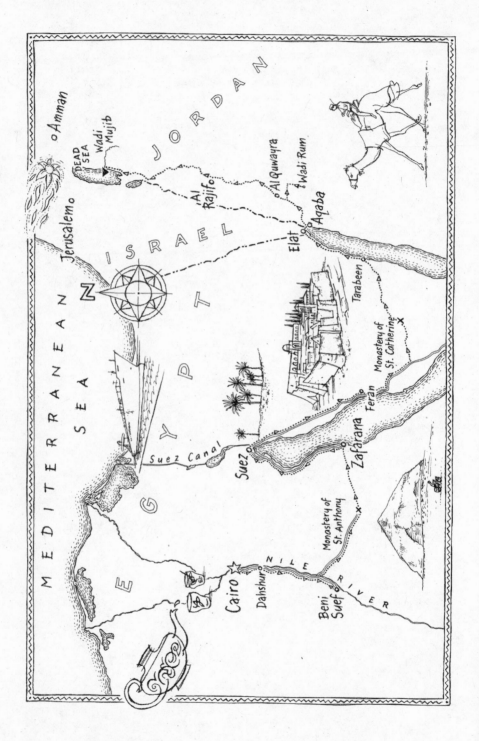

ASIA

*I remember the maps of the Holy
Land. Colored they were. Very pretty.
The Dead Sea was pale blue. The
very look of it made me thirsty.*
—Estragon, in Samuel Beckett's
Waiting for Godot

CHAPTER 3

Tucson to Cairo
We Cannot Guarantee Your Safety

DEPRESSIONS BECAME my destiny. Shortly after my return from Australia, Discovery Online sent a gift basket of fruit to my door. Nobody had ever sent me a fruit basket. It seemed that Lake Eyre was a test pit, and the results were positive. The editors gleefully reported a high number of hits on their internet site and advised that an encore was on the horizon.

I munched my gift fruit and marveled at my accidental career. It wasn't much of a career—I'd been asked for one more continent, not the remaining five—but this did not stop me from reveling in my success. Once my Royal Pear was reduced to a core, I turned on my computer to read e-mails from those who'd followed me to Lake Eyre.

> JOHN HERE FROM SCOTLAND HOPE TO FIND YOU
> IN GOOD SPIRITS AND NOT DEPRESSED. JOKE.

I pictured that Scot, spilling a wee bit of whisky on his kilt and keyboard. A crude message, but I liked it and read the next.

> I just want to know what chain lube you are using?
> chris from toronto Canada

I used something called oil, but wasn't about to disclose my secret to a gear-head with a lubricant fetish. Worse, he neglected to include a bit of flattery—the key to my heart and a reply.

> Subject: Will there be others?
>
> Mr. Malusa, Thank you for doing these stories. Are you going to follow through with your plans to tour other continent's low spots?
>
> Jon

Of course I replied: Yes. But then I thought: really? The blurt of mail made me realize that somebody besides my editors expected me to carry on, to pedal to every depression. And, to my surprise, this wasn't an entirely happy feeling.

Australia had been a pleasant lead-off. Not that I'd forgotten the crocs and the cyclone and the flies. But it was remarkable how the passage of time burnished my memory. Plus, in Australia I could drink the water straight out of the tap. The people spoke a kind of English. I could whip out the computer in a roadhouse and nobody blinked.

But what of the remaining destinations in my bottom-of-the-world scheme? They were no longer simply a list on my desk and dots in my beautiful atlas, a book that made every country inviting. I pored over the maps, considered my chances, and submitted my proposal to Discovery Online. I would go to Djibouti, Africa.

I was not brave. I knew nothing of Djibouti, and my imagination filled the void with fierce folk and slobbering carnivores. I was afraid, and in my mind it was best to get the African pit out of the way, finished, forever. The powers-that-be didn't agree, however. A month later, the Queen Editor rang me and said: Africa, no. It's not safe. We're thinking a better choice is the Dead Sea.

I grumbled but gave in after realizing that nobody else had offered to pay me to ride my bike. My fate decided, I pulled out the atlas and flopped it open to Plate 35, Israel-Jordan. It was not remotely similar to the map of Australia. Lake Eyre is a broad splash of salt on a desert plain. The valley of the Dead Sea cleaves a high plateau with a gash as deep as the Grand Canyon. The little Jordan River twists and turns along the valley bottom, not much as rivers go, but enough to form the thirty-mile-long Dead Sea. The seashore is pegged by surveyors at minus 1,350 feet. That makes it the lowest point in Asia and the grand prize winner for the deepest depression on the surface of the globe.

East of the sea is Jordan. To the west, the map reads, "Israel Military Administration"—the Palestinian West Bank. It took me all of ten seconds to imagine a soldier, sweating under the moonlight, his finger on the trigger of an Uzi as he crept toward my camp.

That settled it: I would finish my ride on the Jordanian side. But where to begin? Jordan is only a third the size of Arizona, and I hankered to ride farther. To the north is Syria, and to the west, Iraq—more guns, more soldiers. To the southwest is Egypt, and there I found my route.

I would begin in Cairo and take the most topographically interesting route, which happened to be the same path blazed by Moses and crew during the Exodus 3,200 years ago. The convergence of our ways was a coincidence, but it made me suspect that Moses had more in mind than eluding Pharaoh's army.

Some Exodus scholars have objected to the popularly accepted route of Moses on the grounds that it seems unnecessarily scenic. But making a beeline from the Nile to the Dead Sea would have been the biblical equivalent of taking the interstate, a straight shot across the most tedious landscape. Why not swing south to dip a toe in the Red Sea's Gulf of Suez? Once there, Moses likely caught sight of the mountains of the Sinai Peninsula and headed east for the stupendous heap of granite 8,000 feet above the desert—surely there would be water and palms in the canyons, and a chance to consult with Yahweh at the top. From the summit of Mount Sinai, the remainder of the route was obvious: down to the eastern shore of the Sinai, the Gulf of Aqaba, then north to the great scarp rimming the Dead Sea. The Promised Land.

Moses had a little help with the parting of the Red Sea, but the best evidence that he was truly blessed is this: he pulled off the trip without a single permit from the Egyptian authorities. "The first documents that attest the existence of bureaucracy," wrote Lewis Mumford, "belong to the Pyramid Age." Mumford puts it at 2375 BC.

Nearly 4,400 years later, while I worked the phone in an effort to get official permission for my trip, an Egyptian minister of information explained to me, "When you go by bike, they cannot say where you go. There is rules in Egypt. No nudity. The officials are concerned—they cannot give their approval."

They were concerned because they didn't want me wandering the country unescorted on a bicycle loaded with spy equipment—a digital camera, a computer, and a Nera satellite telephone. The sat phone was a consequence of problems I'd had trying to get an internet connection in Australia. I assumed it would be impossible in Egypt without a satellite phone.

I called the journalists in the Egyptian Foreign Press Center in Washington, D.C. They gave me their gung ho support and forwarded my scheme to the proper state officials. Weeks later, the Foreign Press Center called me back to gloomily recite from the fax they'd received.

"*'To ensure that,'* blah, blah, blah, OK, here it is: *'Because your equipment is worth $10,000 and the road is dangerous, we cannot guarantee your safety.'*"

Who, I asked, cannot guarantee my safety? And I didn't ask for a guarantee, just permission.

"The letterhead and signature are blacked out. Top secret stuff. It is possible that they just want to keep an eye on you. In Egypt, a non-Egyptian with a camera needs to meet all the requirements."

I wasn't granted permission, but neither was I denied. The Foreign Press Center recommended I bring as many official forms and letters as possible. "Everything must be original, not a copy. Better if it is stamped. Much better."

I accumulated a fat portfolio for Egypt, then sought permission from Jordan. A pleasant man from the Ministry of Information said: "No problem. You do not need a permit for a telephone." Disbelieving, I asked for a letter repeating these words in official form, but was told there is no such form. "Just bring your visa."

I didn't want to beg. Besides, I had to move on to Israel, a slender piece of which lies between Egypt and Jordan. An Israeli official first made clear that they were not a bunch of hayseeds living in the past. "Such telephones are common in Israel." That's wonderful, I said—can I bring one in? "Of course. But there can be new security concerns at any time."

Meaning, it was a crap shoot. Forms were necessary but made no difference in the end. All that mattered was the moment I crossed the border.

I turned my energies to Arabic lessons. Sadly, I have trouble enough with English (I struggle to understand song lyrics on the radio), and Arabic has sonic nuances like the "voiceless pharyngeal fricative." I learned little more than hello and good-bye, yes and no, how to give thanks to God, plead for water, and declare "I am lost." My Egyptian-born tutor, stressing the primacy of the family in Arab lands, also taught me "Your children are very nice" and "My wife is pregnant." In theory this was a form of life insurance, because it was not honorable to kill a defenseless family man. The theory was my own, invented to soothe my friends and family who worried about my safety whenever the news carried another story of an Arab who blew up himself and several Israelis.

Such desperate acts were hard to reconcile with the legendary hospitality of Arabs. The World Trade Center still stood, and I wasn't venturing into a war zone, so it was more likely I'd be killed by a taxi than a terrorist. I assumed that although Arabs might despise the American government's support of Israel, they would recognize that I was not the government. I was just a man who wanted to ride his bike to the Dead Sea.

Exactly one year after Lake Eyre, I was roused from bed by the spring chortle of a backyard mockingbird. Laid out on the dresser were my travel pants with the secret money pocket, proof that I was leaving. I paced the cool concrete floor and checked essentials: bike box securely taped, stapled sheaf of plane tickets, passport in a slender wallet that hung from my neck. Driving to the Tucson airport with Sonya, down Speedway Boulevard and past a billboard for Tuff-Sheds, I was glumly aware that we would have separate beds for the next forty days.

I felt better with a window at 30,000 feet, with free peanuts to boot. A flight attendant leaned over row 34 and confessed, "I was almost crying watching you two say good-bye." It's love and hormones, I said: my wife is pregnant with our first child.

This father-to-be looked out onto the slumping gravel heaps, frozen lava spills, and jump-off-and-die mesas of the American Southwest. It was certainly possible that the Dead Sea desert looked like this, but I'd scrupulously avoided photographs. Travel without surprise was merely an agenda.

THE MOMENT FLIGHT 346, Zurich to Cairo, lifted off the runway, every man in my row lit a cigarette. And they were all men, Arab men, sipping Cokes and enjoying our unveiled stewardesses. The fundamentalists were right: hair *is* sexy.

My neighbor, Ahmed, sucked on a Marlboro and offered me a stick of gum. He was from Alexandria. "Cairo, big people," he said. "Alexandria, little people." Smoke leaked from his honest smile, and I realized that Ahmed and I shared the same gift for foreign language.

Another Egyptian explained, "He means Cairo has many people. Fifteen million. Why do you come to Egypt?"

Journalist, I said.

"I think you find it a very strange country. Very rich people, and very poor, with not many between."

The very strange country was across a Mediterranean only an hour wide. The rim of Africa was wind-smoothed desert, and the delta of the Nile dense green and spotted with tight villages of white homes stacked like boxes. The desert was blank. There was no intermediate zone. It was the Nile or nothing. A hundred miles inland, the enormous triangle of river distributaries and farms came to an apex, and at that point was the city of Cairo.

The notarized forms for my gear emitted a glow of authority that impressed the customs men at the airport. The camera wasn't a problem. Nobody asked if I was going to bicycle in the nude. But the satellite telephone caused a minor sensation. It looked like an office phone in a folding box the size of a laptop computer; the lid was the antenna. The device had power enough to talk to a satellite floating 24,000 miles above the equator. Warning stickers with lightning-bolt graphics suggested that the user shouldn't point the antenna at children or reproductive organs or anything you hoped would last a long time.

There ensued much hand-waving and pleading on my behalf by Abraham, my special "expediter" from the airport Press Office. The customs men, crowded around the telephone, paid no attention. They opened the lid and uncoiled the antenna cable. I didn't know what would happen if they hit the ON button while their faces were inches from the antenna, but I guessed singed eyebrows and the end of my assignment.

A customs man ejected the battery from the phone and gave it to Abraham. He kept the phone. We had lost. Abraham said, "I am sorry, Mr. James, but you must leave your satellite phone. You must go to the downtown Press Office tomorrow and get the papers for the phone. Then return to the airport to get the phone." He rolled his eyes to the bank of fluorescent lights and the heavens beyond and added in Arabic, "God willing."

God willing, I would at least reach my hotel, despite being unable to find the words to tell my taxi driver that he'd forgotten to turn on his headlights. This wouldn't have worried me as much if the taxi were not painted, like all Cairo taxis, black with white fenders, distressingly similar to the checkered pattern on crash-test dummies.

I tried some English on Mohammed: No lights?

He smiled and patted the seat of the Peugeot wagon, which looked to be upholstered in tinsel and wool. "This Egypt. No problem." He pointed to the streetlights. "Light."

Because Mohammed's horn was frequently in use, he reserved the headlights as a sort of second horn for running red lights. At first this was deeply alarming. But nobody in Cairo expected anybody to stop at a signal, a mutual understanding shared by the farting buses and the silent Mercedes, the blue-smoke motorbikes and the diesel tractors. Like blood cells jostling to fit into a capillary, this honking, headlight-blinking mass of steel, rubber, and flesh pushed into the clot of downtown Cairo.

IN THE MORNING I set off to retrieve the phone. Only a mile to the Press Office, so I walked, smiling at the teenage police toting Kalashnikovs. They grinned back. I resisted the lure of cafés hazed with the smoke of water pipes and slipped between the cars parked on the sidewalk. It was OK to double park so long as you left your car unlocked; the driver of the blocked car simply pushed yours out of the way.

The Press Office was sharp, with TV monitors and potted plants trembling in the blast of Power USA air conditioners. The brawl of traffic on the Corniche along the Nile was reduced to a subsonic rumble tweaked with horns and an occasional motorcycle buzz. The staff was appalled at the loss of my phone. Within an hour, the Press Office whipped up some handsomely stamped letters for me to bring to the Telephone Office, maybe one mile away.

With a neat man named Masoud from the Press Office as my guide, I was led into the maw of Egyptian bureaucracy. Behind the massive Corinthian columns of the telephone building was a warren of halls, crowded with government workers and fire extinguishers, with the latter just in case the former ignite with a cigarette the towering stacks of receipts.

Masoud was good-natured as we searched for the proper office through the main building and the first annex, but his smile waned in the second annex, and vanished when we were told to return to the first annex.

"I am angry!" He was sweating in his camel-hair sport coat. "These foolish people do not know anything!"

But they knew how to cheerfully give directions that led to more directions. The Telephone Building had offices with missing windows, offices with crank telephones, offices with people scribbling in tremendous ledgers, and one office with a man asleep with his head atop his phone. We did not disturb him, and after two hours we shambled into an office with an Immarsat satellite map and a man behind an impressive four-telephone desk. I thought: *This is it.*

It was. While we waited, Masoud explained why fans were superior to air-conditioning. "I like things natural. The fan moves air, and the air is from God."

The air in Cairo was an eye-stinging blur of God's dust and the unholy by-products of internal combustion. In search of something more divine, I asked Masoud to translate the ornate wall hanging.

"It is from the Koran. Only one God."

But, I said, it looks like there's more written.

"Only one God," he repeated. Before disappearing behind a glass door, he snuck in the last word. "God not pregnant, have son you call Jesus. One God." A minute later he returned with the news. "I think maybe you do this story without your phone. They say you must pay 220 pounds ($70), then wait for permission. Could be one week, two weeks, two months. Nobody knows such things."

I had the money but not the time. Without the satellite phone I'd have to rely on Egyptian phones, a system presumably run by the people in this building. I cruelly concluded I'd have better luck using carrier pigeons.

Back at the Press Center, I was offered coffee and consolations and promises: the phone will be released. God willing. It's my fault, I said—I should have declared on the customs form that it was a phone, not a *satellite* phone. Then they would have never known.

"Oh, give me a break," said the big chief with the big desk, Mr. Agamy. "We're not that naïve. They would know." He glanced up at a row of six clocks, each set to a different world time zone. "What we must try is to go quickly to the end of the process. How long will you stay in Cairo?"

As long as it takes to get the phone, I said.

Outside the Press Office I was swallowed by the stunning clamor of the city. I had a deadline for reaching the Dead Sea, but I could always hitch a ride if I fell behind. The problem was surviving Cairo. It was an easy city to hate. Bawling boulevards trimmed with trash! Fifteen million people! Lawless drivers invading the sidewalks!

I headed out into the lunge of traffic, in the general direction of my hotel and the stupendously frank sign for Flit Insect Killer. But I was soon diverted by sidewalk booksellers hawking racy Egyptian romance novels and Victoria's Secret lingerie catalogs wrapped in no-peek plastic and dog-eared English paperbacks ranging from *The Catcher in the Rye* to *Body Armor 2000*.

The sound of work drew me into a dim alley. It was blacksmiths and brass-smashers and metal-cutters. The alley was too narrow to allow even the midget trucks favored in the inner city. The afternoon sun, too, was excluded, and men pedaled cargo tricycles through shadows that still held the cool of the spring morning.

A peek into a tea shop led to a quiet seat among quiet men, a cup of tea and a water pipe of my own. Very sweet, the tea and the smoke, with honey-soaked tobacco kept burning by glowing coals atop the bowl. I was the only tourist, and I quickly exhausted my store of Arabic. When asked a question I might understand but didn't know how to answer, I reflexively spoke the only foreign language I knew. "Si." Nobody minded.

I left the tea shop and stuck to the little streets, wandering until the day faded and the lights came on over the meat market. Spastic chickens in wooden cages awaited the whack of cleavers. Most stands were simply a table of bloody meat dripping onto the sawdust floor, but from the ceiling of the Modern Flower Butcher Shop hung crystal chandeliers and sides of beef. From some hidden place came the strings of Vivaldi's *Four Seasons*.

Women with scarves hiding their hair loaded up on liver and brains, taking care not to spill blood onto their surprisingly sleek pumps and fancy black ankle stockings. Children roamed freely into the evening. They were unescorted, but not unwatched. The sidewalk chatter was completely unintelligible, but unmistakably gossip among friends and relations. I'd been reading about such a place in Naguib Mahfouz's novel, *Midaq Alley*, but it was set during World War II in a Cairo I'd assumed had vanished with television.

Midaq Alley was at my bedside in the Cosmopolitan Hotel, a relic with fifteen-foot ceilings and gothic armoires. In the morning I woke to bird-song and the clanging of metal. I rose from a mattress that felt as if stuffed with rags, and threw open the shutters to look down four floors to an alley. From a bicycle fitted with enormous cargo racks, a man unloaded propane cylinders the size of basset hounds. Blue and green parakeets sang from a wicker cage on a balcony opposite, where a woman stuffed grape leaves. A street sweeper whished past, and in his dusty wake men and women in gowns emerged and took their places in the alley, washing tea glasses in pails and dragging out display cases of sweets.

Breakfast at the Cosmopolitan was arid toast and a very hard-boiled egg. I read my complimentary copy of *Egypt Today* magazine, perplexed by the advertisement for the Smart Car: *When we have no one to compete with, we keep our slogan alive.*

The front desk receptionist called my name. Telephone. It was Hala from the Press Center.

"Good morning, Mr. James. We are working on your problem. We need to know the frequency used by the satellite telephone."

That anyone cared seemed like a good sign. I explained—1.5 gigahertz, transmit and receive—and my day's work was done.

But sometimes the best travel agenda is none. I returned to the alleys and shops of Old Cairo. Ball bearings in one shop, light switches in another. Men pressing pants with irons hauled from a glowing oven. Digital micrometers for machinists.

In an alley devoted to wedding dresses, I was tailed by Mohammed, an unshakable fifteen-year-old. "I take you to most famous mosques. I learn English in school."

I don't want a guide, I said, but you're welcome to come along.

"I am your friend. Come."

Mohammed didn't pester me for a tip because he operated on a commission: he took me to see his uncle's store, Ramses II Papyrus, Factory Price. I wasn't interested.

"Why you no want to visit papyrus store?"

"I don't like papyrus. I like that bicycle." I had spotted another cargo carrier outfitted with special racks.

"But this bike is common. It brings the milk."

"I've never seen a bicycle like this. Such things do not exist in America."

In this way I became Mohammed's guide to America, expanding on what he had learned from Westerns featuring cowboys and cactus. In return he stuck by my side through the day and into the night, through the city new and old, from the spic-and-span subway run by the "National Authority for Tunnels" to the southern gate of Old Cairo, the nine-hundred-year-old Bab Zuwayla—a pair of stone towers and massive wooden doors sheeted with iron and studs.

The gates were built to repel the Christian Crusaders. They never came. Cairo grew beyond the Bab Zuwayla, and the gates were useless by the time Napoleon Bonaparte invaded the city and the country. Bonaparte claimed that his ambition was not to control the Gulf of Suez trade route. No—he was freeing the Egyptians from their nasty leaders, the Mamluks. The earnest Bonaparte donned a turban, mounted a camel, and announced his plans for hospitals and dams and liberty.

But the baffled Egyptians preferred to suffer under the thumb of a local fink rather than listen to an infidel tell them right and wrong. Meanwhile, the ousted Mamluks reconstituted themselves as guerrillas. The British preferred that the French not hold the key to Suez, and Admiral Nelson obliterated the French fleet off the Egyptian coast. After three years, the French went looking for other nations to civilize in their image. The civil war they left behind did not end until the rise of Mohamed Ali. In 1811, he took care of the Mamluk opposition by inviting their leaders—somewhere between sixty and five hundred, depending on the account—to a plush affair at the fortress just up the hill from the Bab Zuwayla, the Citadel. After coffee, they were slaughtered. Their heads were displayed on spikes here at the lovely Bab Zuwayla.

Some said it was barbaric, and others said you had to kill the barbarians if you wanted to improve matters. It makes no difference today. Egyptians have a soft spot for deep history, and the Bab Zuwayla is the perfect place for a wedding.

Just around the corner from the gates was a tethered and illuminated hot-air balloon, the grunt of the power generators, and a band playing at jet-engine decibels. At least three hundred people were seated beneath a gallery of lights strung over the street. People urged me into the party.

The bride and groom, in yellow silk and black suit, sat atop enormous chairs—thrones, actually—before a backdrop of drawn blue velvet. The bride's father interrupted the music to ramble into the microphone. Mohammed said, "He is thanking the friends of the family." The accordion and finger cymbals revved back up, while a twelve-year-old Lolita performed a remarkably erotic dance. Dad returned to the mike.

Mohammed said, "He is thanking the friends of the family."

The band began thumping again, and a more matronly woman shook her booty. There was some jostling for a view of her generous figure, blocking my vantage, leaving me to watch the event as simulcast on color video monitors. Dad returned to the mike.

"He is thanking the friends of the family."

Again?

"Those people come and give gifts."

The band roared back to life, the cymbals slapping while another woman, in a zebra-stripe dress, danced alongside Lolita. A smoke machine wrapped the stage in garlands of fog.

While Dad thanked all three hundred guests by name, a few English speakers in the audience were drawn to the American. A man asked for my address. I gave it to him. "Is Egyptian dream to go to America. But visa not easy. And airplane costs . . . how much?"

Somebody else answered obliquely, "You must have money to make money in America. I know because I stay two months in New Jersey."

Another young man wanted to know, "Are you a Muslim?"

No, I said. I have no religion.

"No religion? But why not Muslim?"

I am a scientist. God is nature—the sun, the earth, the Nile.

Amazed looks from all, yet they pardoned me and offered another cigarette. Profession of no faith was apparently better than a competing theology.

They excused themselves: the feast had begun. It was 12:30 AM. I cut out for the hotel, leaving Mohammed with a postcard of a giant saguaro cactus. I believed I was heading in the right direction when I stopped for a shave at a dinky barbershop, a meticulous shave with a straight razor under framed pictures of Presidents Nasser, Sadat, and Mubarak—a double-shave, in fact, finished off by the barber combing my unruly eyebrows and clipping my nose hairs. But upon leaving I forgot which way was north. The shops were shuttered. I stepped lightly over puddles of donkey piss, scared a cat and myself, until I was stopped by a pile of rubble in a dead-end alley. I looked up for the moon and found nothing but the feeling that I was truly lost.

I wouldn't have tried my luck if I didn't suspect that the alleys of Old Cairo are something extraordinary among huge cities. The people do not kill you for your wallet. They don't even take it. As in *Midaq Alley*, which "overflowed with sharp tongues and roving eyes," bad people face social castigation in Old Cairo, a punishment worse than jail. What happened to me was this: A man walked up and led me out of the maze.

The next morning I described my wedding adventure to a woman at the Press Center. "And where was this wedding?" she asked.

I told her, Butneya, at Bab Zuwayla.

"Butneya! This is not such a good place. It is where drugs are sold. Hashish. It could be dangerous."

It had the look of a drug wedding, very ostentatious. But not dangerous.

"These people have money and like to show it. Nice houses, but they are dirty. The women have expensive dresses but bad makeup."

In the United States, I said, such a thing is sometimes called "new money."

"It is the same in Egypt, except here we call it, 'Recently Having Good.'"

I WAS RECENTLY HAVING GOOD. Summoned to the telephone building to pay for a phone license, I cheerfully trotted out into traffic, positioning myself behind the fattest woman pedestrian, figuring she'd take the blow. At the telephone building I flashed my authentic Egyptian press pass to enter, found the correct office in a mere fifteen minutes, and presented myself to Mr. Ali Samir.

A gentleman in a gray suit and baby-blue vest, Ali reviewed my papers and said, "Good. Now go the fifth floor, room 30."

At room 30 they shook their heads at my form. "No, sixth floor, room 32."

Room 32 sent me back to Ali, who was genuinely sorry and equipped me with a helper. We marched off down the hall to an office with a calendar picturing two happy Egyptians yakking on cell phones. My form was scrutinized. We were sent to the cashier. The cashier was out to lunch. My helper picked up a helper, and the three of us walked to the annex. They rapped on a door, which opened to reveal women counting immense wads of cash. They took my money and asked me to wait outside. Security, please!

With two tissue-paper receipts in hand, decorated with multicolored arabesques, I returned to Ali. He nodded sagely. "I think we can get your permit in one or two days." Thank God, I said in Arabic. The office personnel cracked up. Perhaps I should have said "God willing," so I threw that in for good measure.

I returned to the alleys, where every random venture led to a comfortable seat, a cup of tea, and a water pipe. The smaller the alley, the better, and in the evening I was drawn to a big wooden bench next to a spice shop. I sniffed the half-barrels of saffron and hibiscus and unknown herbs while a man swept the alley. He stopped to ask, *Would you like some hibiscus tea?* After I figured out the Arabic for *hibiscus*, I accepted. Three hours later I was still sitting on the bench.

A parade of visitors: yelping infants, slick teens, ancient creepers, and a Nubian from southern Egypt—a giant even without the superstructure of his white turban. A whirling dervish of a man popped in and to my surprise was immediately tackled by the others, who pummeled him with blows. "Don't worry," said the man next to me, Abd Al Hady, "because it is joke. The man comes always and make disturbance because there is no business at his shop. Why not make disturbance for fun?"

I agreed: Why not? Besides, Mr. Al Hady seemed a wise creature for his fifty years, and because he was a communications engineer at the airport he knew more about my satellite phone than I did. Slightly disheveled, bad teeth askew, he peered through thick, dusty lenses with magnified eyes and wished me luck in getting the phone out of customs. When the conversation veered off into religion, Mr. Al Hady clutched his prayer beads and told me of his devotion to God. "Every day I thank God for my life. Thank God for my ears, my mouth, my eyes."

But your eyes, I pointed out, aren't so good.

"God can fix."

Mr. Al Hady was devout in the most appealing way, head slightly cocked while he explained the amplified prayer of the muezzin I heard five times daily from the minarets above the mosques. "Allah Akbar—God is Great." And when the crazy man appeared for another wacky beating by his buddies, Mr. Al Hady held my hand gently and said, "Do not worry."

I told him, I like this place, this little alley I happened upon. Did it have a name?

"Yes, it has a name. Have you read books of Naguib Mahfouz?"

Only one, I said. *Midaq Alley.*

"Well, you are in Midaq Alley. Of course it is bigger in the book. But here you are, in Midaq Alley. Thank God for your good luck."

THE GOOD LUCK that brought me to Midaq Alley didn't last. I had to return to Cairo Airport Customs—the basement of Dante's Inferno.

I arrived at the airport confident I had every paper in order, having secured the final permit from Mr. Ali Samir at the telephone building. A helpful man from KLM Airlines guided me to a precustoms hurdle, a window where I exchange money for paper with pretty stamps on it. Then to the customs storeroom, where my phone sat on a shelf with fax machines and other illegal entries. I showed a man my stamped form. He pointed to the phone. I picked it up, kissed it, and said "Thank God" three times. The man laughed and then directed me to Mr. X, who guided me to Ms. Y. She glanced at my form and said with the finality of a judge, "This is permit for phone, not letter for customs. You must bring us correct letter."

This was a test, of course—of my self-control. If I grabbed the phone and made a run for it, the machine-gun soldiers would perforate me. Ms. Y gave me a look that said she was ready to pull out her devil's pitchfork and jab me in the behind if I didn't comply.

Abraham, the airport representative of the Press Office, stepped in and began a three-hour appeal to progressively higher ranks in customs, until we had the attention of a four-star customs man. Eureka: the phone was in my mitts.

Back at the hotel, I unboxed the bicycle and screwed on the racks, pedals, handlebars, and seat. Into the handlebar bag went the precious map, showing my route south along the Nile, east to Suez and the Sinai, north to the Dead Sea. I fortified myself with a meat-stuffed pizza-pastry called a *fitir* under a sign, "Egyptian pancakes at your service." Bought two oranges and an apple, and hailed a taxi to drive me and the bike through the tussle of traffic along the Corniche, under the deep shade of riverside fig trees and past the rowboats propelled by clumsy, hand-hewn oars, past women demurely riding sidesaddle on motorcycles, all the way to the city's edge.

Then I was off, at first a little wobbly under the load, then smoother, leaving Cairo behind for the farms of the Nile Valley.

CHAPTER 4

Cairo to the Dead Sea

Do Not Forget That You Are in a Holy Place

So CROWDED IS THE FARMLAND south of Cairo that it is impossible to look around and not see a woman lugging a water pail, or a man chopping a furrow with a short-handled hoe, or a kid on a donkey buried under a bundle of palm fronds. When I stop to rest in the shade of a eucalyptus, within a minute a thin man with a thin mustache rolls up on a bicycle. He cordially offers greetings, good health, and a smoke from a pack of Cleopatras. But what he really wants is to squeeze my brake levers and get a closer look at my machine.

The feeling is mutual. I ride a battleship-gray bike, with handlebar-end shifters working triple chainrings up front and seven gears behind. It rides like a dream, but it's simply a snooze compared to a one-speed, made-in-China Flying Pigeon that's been Egyptianized. The spokes are laced with bunting in colors not found in nature. Pinwheels are spring-mounted to the handlebars. Spangled with reflectors and wound with barber-pole spirals of electrical tape, his bike looks as if it were yanked off a carnival ride.

Yet it's wholesome proletarian transportation. Clamped or welded to the frame are cantilevered platforms that fulfill personal needs such as mobile chopping block or mother-in-law seat. I flip through my Arabic notes, hoping for small talk, but it doesn't seem the right time to announce that my wife is pregnant. He wants to know how much my bike costs, then he bids me safe passage and pedals off with a heartening yet ominous "God willing." I figure he knows the score on Egyptian roads. I'm happy to share with the buckboards and donkey carts, but fear the taxis with prayer beads swinging from their rearview mirrors.

The trucks move slower, though the drivers say hello with their terrifying musical horns. And no matter how big the truck, its load is bigger. Men in flapping robes cling to bales of cotton, in accordance with an unwritten Egyptian law: There Is Always Room for One More.

All space in the Nile Valley serves a purpose. Crops are planted between the date palms. Dates dry atop a mud home. Only the muck of the canal bank is useless. It's spiked with pincushion grasses or thick with castor bean, plants either too vicious or too toxic to serve even as donkey fodder.

After a week of puffing water pipes in the dust bowl of Cairo, I'm feeling vaguely poisoned myself. Searching for a camp at dusk, I veer west onto progressively smaller roads, then paths, until I ride out of the cultivated lands and into the Sahara.

Alone, just like that. I drop the bike behind a low dune and set out my pad and sleeping bag. I lie back, faintly wheezing, then recover in time to climb, in the final light, a bigger dune. The view across the valley is over palms and the silent Nile and a startling string of smoking industries and sodium-vapor lights.

Dinner is ramen noodles. From the nearest village the muezzin's call to prayer fades and is replaced with the bleat of irrigation-ditch frogs. The view overhead is familiar and comforting. My camp is at nearly the same latitude as my Tucson home, so the night sky is unchanged, complete with the effervescent spume of the Hale-Bopp Comet.

I wake in the dark with fever chills, and shiver to the accompaniment of barking dogs. In the morning my fever is still there, and so are three men standing atop the big dune. They're pointing and shrugging their shoulders to say: What's up? One skips down the face of the dune to greet me with God's blessings and to explain that they are pyramid guards. Would I like to have some bread and tea?

First I need a little more sleep, because (I pantomime, with hand to forehead) I'm sick. He reaches into the folds of his ankle-length shirt and pulls out some foil-wrapped pills. Apparently they are good for any malady, but I decline. He counters with an offer to let me rest at the guard station. I accept, despite needing to carry the loaded bike up the sand hill.

To both south and north are pyramids I'd missed yesterday while keeping an eye on the taxis and lusting after the bicycles. Some are proto-pyramids, proof that the Egyptians didn't build Cairo's stupendous pyramids of Giza without practice. To the north is what appears to be a six-slab wedding cake, the Step Pyramid, each layer smaller than the one below. It's a big cake, two hundred feet high.

Of course architecture critics existed well before the pyramids, prob-ably dating back to the Early Hut Era. The Step Pyramid apparently got a mixed review: *Nice work—but let's try it again and fill in the steps this time, so it has smooth sides.*

To my south is the curious result, a 340-foot-tall pyramid unlike any other. The Bent Pyramid slopes up steeply on the bottom half, and not so steeply on the top half. It still comes to a point, but appears shorter than intended. People who study such things wonder why. Some say there weren't materials and nonunion labor enough to stick with the steeper slope that would have made the pyramid a good deal taller. Others claim that the simple fear of collapse forced the reduction in height. Finally, the most elegant theory of all: the Bent Pyramid is *supposed* to be bent.

King Sneferu saw room for improvement, and soon the utterly sym-metrical and perfectly boring Red Pyramid reached for the heavens. I'm lucky to be ill within sight of this durable tomb. It's possible the guards know the basics of embalming the dead.

The three men, Mohammed, Abd, and Abdullah, prepare mint tea on a single-burner kerosene stove, then break out some pita bread and falafel wrapped in a greasy cone of newspaper. Very good, I say, and it's the truth. After Mohammed and Abdullah split for other duties, Abd unrolls a sleep-ing mat for me.

An hour later I wake to the stirrings of a sandstorm. The Red Pyramid softens and vanishes, as if seen through a camera while twisting the lens out of focus. The nearby military radar installation vanishes. Out of swelling murk comes Abd's twelve-year-old daughter, Hebey, and the three of us hustle into the single room of the guard shelter, ducking under blankets and clothes hung from wires.

A ten-foot-square room, three humans, one bike, and $10,000 worth of electronics that I'd like to remain hidden for reasons of modesty. Abd and Hebey listen to a tiny radio while they work. They're turning palm trees into sleeping mats. Working with only a sliver of light from a window on the lee side of the shelter, they loop palm-leaf fibers around a toe, then twist them into one strand by deftly rolling them between their palms. Each cord is woven into a mat. Every hour they brew up some tea to share, and together we peek outside and agree: big wind.

The sandstorm won't quit. And, glancing at my watch, I realize that my editor in Washington can't wait—I've got to finish my Cairo dispatch. With a sheepish grin I pull out the computer. It elicits little more than raised eyebrows, and I get the feeling they'd expected an expensive toy in my bags all along.

When the sandstorm ebbs and the valley emerges from the gloom, I give Hebey a postcard of Tucson and a pencil, slip Abd a few bucks, and trundle down the dune back into the valley palms. In the village of Dahshur there are oranges and bananas at fruit stands where old vendors whisper their thanks, bow slightly, and bring their hand to their breast. I ask for bread, and a man volunteers to guide me to the bakery.

My tour of main street is along an irrigation canal that looks like a trench through a landfill, then down an alley of homes collapsing into rubble and mud. They aren't abandoned—not in a place where even a sheet of corrugated steel tilted up against a palm is inhabited. Egypt is 94 percent hard desert, leaving 6 percent for everyone and their crops. In 1900, "everyone" meant 10 million people; in 1960, 26 million; at the time of my visit it is approaching 70 million.

Most are kids, it seems; by the time we reach the bakery there are forty children crowded around me. My guide shoos them off while I buy a pita, then takes me clear back across town so I can buy boiled eggs and visit a tea shop. I provide a pleasant diversion from dominoes. When the sun sinks weakly into a veil of dust, I'm directed to a hotel ten miles out of town.

Waving good-bye forever, I bump off along a dirt road. Very white egrets take flight from the canals and bank sharply into the wind, dangling absurdly skinny legs. Everywhere, people are toiling in the fields. I spring for a hotel room with a marble bathroom. Out in the courtyard, a pair of six-foot-tall Ninja Turtles are teaching the dance craze La Macarena to some lucky birthday kids.

TWELVE SEAMLESS HOURS of sleep, then it's my birthday, too. I'm forty, but feel only thirty-nine. My fever's ebbed, my lungs work, and the road to recovery leads past villages a cut above the misery of yesterday's landfill. The slender, vigorous farmers no longer seem to be toiling amid rows of corn and carrots, but merely working, and occasionally chanting. When school's out the kids still swarm around me, and now I see why they scream *Hello!*—it's the title of their English primer.

The cultivated valley is only ten miles across, yet I never see the Nile, only the canals. Herons spear frogs in the slow water. A kingfisher with a Zorro black mask and a stiletto bill hovers like an enormous humming-bird, waiting for the moment to dive. I watch, pedaling slowly and feeling sneaky on my noiseless bicycle.

There are beggars, too. It's usually a broken old man, head wound with turban, waiting, waiting. If I stop he'll say, *Peace upon you,* then extend his hand for alms. Such people do not pursue you and spin tales of sudden bad fortune. It is simply a matter of your paths crossing, as God willed, and the wealthier are expected to help the less fortunate.

When the sun is setting I'm still short of my destination, the city of Beni Suef. Honking, crumpled taxis whiz by in the failing light, prompting me to figure the odds. Better, I decide, to be inside a taxi than to be creamed by one.

My ride is a Peugeot wagon with a free-and-natural sandblasted finish. The desert preserves a taxi just as it does a mummy, for nothing rusts or rots where the yearly rainfall is less than half an inch. From my guest-of-honor front seat position I've a pop-eyed view of the rear bumper of another taxi we tailgate and of the donkey that dumbly steps from a field of beans into the highway. There's just time enough to straight-arm brace myself against the dash for the squeal and smack and blossom of glass and steam. Nobody's hurt beyond some scrapes and bruises. The donkey escaped injury, but our taxi is hissing its final breath.

An instant audience materializes. People gesture and babble and by consensus deliver the verdict: the accident is the fault of our taxi. Because nobody is actually dead, there will be neither police nor lawyers.

Our driver pries up the hood and mutters what should be the last rites but proves to be closer to *I've got a pulse.* A cry goes out for a chain, a crowbar, and a bar of soap. Two hours later the radiator is mostly plugged, the doors work, and the fender is pulled back from the tire. Defying the scrap heap, the taxi heroically wobbles into town.

The kings left no monumental tombs in Beni Suef, but it's just as well. "As for the pyramids," grumbled Henry David Thoreau, "there is nothing to wonder at in them so much as the fact that so many men could be found degraded enough to spend their lives constructing a tomb for some ambitious booby." Thoreau could be a sourpuss (he heartily endorsed celibacy), but he'd be happy to discover that it wouldn't take a lifetime to build a pyramid in Beni Suef. There's a gigantic cement factory churning out over 8 million pounds a day.

Yet most of the homes are brick and mortar, clumsy dwellings that fairly shout *We built it ourselves.* The dirt streets are home to shy dogs shaped by natural selection. No toy schnauzers or lanky wolfhounds—all dogs are just large enough to tip over a garbage can, but not so big as to require buckets of food.

Beni Suef isn't pretty, but it's a beautiful place to get a glass of just-squeezed sugarcane juice on a downtown corner and watch the old bald men in barbershops get their heads buffed and ear hair clipped. I imagine they do it for the comfort of ritual. That would also explain the horse-drawn carriages, each with pinstriped wheels and a canopy hung with snazzy dingleballs and tin stencils of very small hands.

Downtown Beni Suef is middle-class dads in cardigan sweaters and moms with billowing black gowns and tattooed chins out for a evening stroll. This city of several hundred thousand is undoubtedly safe, definitely polite, and probably dull. Teen boys, hungry for action, do the same thing in Beni Suef that teens do in Des Moines, Iowa: they pilot their fantastic bicycles to the video store and rent *Snake Eater III* and *Attack of the Fifty-Foot Woman*.

I have friends here, or rather friends of a second cousin of my telephone-friend Amina, who works in Egypt's Washington embassy. In the morning, after "God Is Great" blasts from a klaxon outside my hotel window, Emad comes by my room. With his wire-rim glasses and button-down shirt, he looks like the budding librarian he is.

Emad checks out my bike and expresses mild amazement that I, no spring chicken, hope to ride to the Dead Sea.

"I'm twenty-four and I don't know if I would try that."

As of yesterday, I brag, I'm forty.

He fans the air and gasps, "Whoa!" Outside awaits a red Fiat and his friends Hilal and Milad; we all scoot through the city to visit Saint Mary's Church. Together with Father Stephanos, whose cheerful beard and locks make him look like Mr. Natural, they take me to the nursery school. I've no idea why, until the waist-high students are lined up and sweetly singing "Happy Birthday."

Milad is the painting teacher for the school, specializing in Walt Disney and primary colors. Hilal is an accountant for a taxi company. Only later will I notice the crosses tattooed on their right wrists, the mark given to Egypt's Christians when they are five or six years old. One in eleven Egyptians is Christian, and the figure is closer to 50 percent in Beni Suef.

The Vatican has no authority in Egypt. This is the Coptic Church, and they've been on their own since AD 451. The official breakup was theological—something about the "true" nature of Jesus—but mainly they wished to be left alone. Saint Mary's Church, says Father Stephanos, was built with timbers from Jerusalem—proof of its authenticity. He gladly gives me a tour of the church icons.

"Is Saint Paul. Is Saint George."

And this one, I inject, is Gabriel.

"Oh, you read Arabic?"

No, I say, I just saw the angel wings.

Like all tours, it ends at a gift shop, where Father Stephanos slips some inspirational music into a cassette deck. There are weighty Christian tomes for the serious, toy cellular phones for the children, and Jesus wristwatches for all. Except for Father Stephanos, who wears a swank Seiko under his robe.

But Saint Mary's Church is only a farm operation, literally, for the Monastery of Saint Anthony. It's a hundred miles east of the Nile, smack in the desert, on my route to the Gulf of Suez. Saint Anthony, says Father Stephanos, "is beginning of monk system, is number one monk."

Why, I ask, did Saint Anthony go to this place? "To be alone."

Seventeen hundred years ago there were considerably fewer people in the Nile Valley, but apparently it wasn't lonesome enough for the Number One Monk. Anthony escaped the throb of humanity by trekking into the wilderness until he found an old fort with a reliable spring. He spent the next two decades alone.

It's safe to say that Anthony was on the fringe, but I can relate. The next morning, the minaret outside the hotel window comes alive with a hundred-watt call to prayer, reminding me that a quieter place is just beyond the Nile. I pack and leave for the desert.

At Beni Suef the river runs hard up against the eastern edge of the valley, and from the bridge I can see plainly the desert ahead. The river below is fat and slow. Rowboats pull across the current to reach little islands; these, too, are cultivated and grazed.

My tires are bulging under the weight of my stores and two gallons of water. I stop to give them a shot of air at an Olympic gas station at the road fork to the monastery and the Red Sea. The two attendants are full of advice on my route. Number one is leery but confident of success—if God wills it. Number two says it's not a matter of God—it's the wrong road.

There's no sign at the junction. The Arabic road map I prudently purchased for just this occasion is beautiful, but the men ignore it. With a hundred miles of desert before the next town, I wait for a third opinion to show up. It comes with a family on a pilgrimage to Saudi Arabia, in a car with four official Mecca flags snapping in the wind. I lean over the driver's window while he straightens his alligator-skin Kleenex box holder on the dash and ask where yonder road goes.

"To Minya. Where do you want to go?"

Zafarana.

"It go Zafarana."

Not Minya?

"Go two. Minya, Zafarana."

This neither jives with the map nor makes Cartesian sense: Minya is in the Nile Valley and Zafarana is on the Red Sea coast. Eventually everyone agrees that the road goes to Minya and Zafarana, but it is not the road to Zafarana. "This road dangerous road," says attendant number two. Why? I ask. He draws his finger across his throat. "Bad people. Look! Here come truck that take you to good Zafarana road. You go?"

Absolutely. I hop on a truck carrying sixty tons of cement bags, and they soon drop me off on the real Zafarana road.

My timing is perfect: hardly any traffic, the wind and sun at my back, pale desert and the faint rise of a plateau many miles ahead. I'm so pleased I hardly notice that there are no pretty dunes, no wind-polished stones, no fantastic towers of rock. Back home in Arizona, the mesquite trees should be unfurling their April leaves, creating something called shade. Here there are only knee-high spheres of patient salt bush, rising from the cracks of dried mud in the watercourses.

Panting as much from excitement as from effort, I crest a rise and look back. The Nile Valley is gone. "Why," asked Melville in *Moby Dick*, "upon your first voyage as a passenger, did you yourself feel such a mystical vibration, when first told that you and your ship were now out of sight of land?" There's nothing mystical about the vibes: it's the thrill of leaving civilization behind. Desert or sea, it's the same feeling when you cross the threshold.

But then I see, in the distance, a few camels rocking along with a peculiar side-to-side gait. With my binoculars I can make out the robed Bedouin not far behind the big beasts. I don't wait. I ride on, gliding actually, shoved along by the wind until Hale-Bopp turns on and I turn in, hiding from the road behind a low ridge of gravels. Out here, fifty miles from the nearest lightbulb, the comet's tail looks like the spray from an un-corked champagne bottle. Perhaps the Star of Bethlehem looked like this.

AFTER TWENTY YEARS of gazing at heaven, Saint Anthony could no longer ignore humanity. A colony of ascetics had formed outside the fort, and they begged Anthony to come out.

He came out. To everyone's surprise, twenty years behind the wall hadn't touched him. He looked the same, the story goes, as when he went in.

When I appear at the wall, I look like I've just pedaled up a thousand feet into a damp headwind.

"Sorry!" says the gate boy. "Monastery is closed."

Please, I say while I struggle to read the name scribbled down by Father Stephanos back in Beni Suef. Please let me talk with . . . Father Deoscoros.

I hate to be turned away from the only habitation between the Nile and the Gulf of Suez. Fortunately a group of wealthy Lebanese tourists drives up and wheedles its way in. Father Deoscoros calls down to the gate boy to let us all in, but "only for five-minute tour of church, no more. This is special time for us."

I'm grateful. If they wished, the monks could keep everyone out by sim-ply closing the gate on the mile-long, thirty-foot-high wall that surrounds the monastery. A fortress it is, at the foot of the tremendous limestone scarp of the Galala Plateau, 5,000 feet high. For centuries there wasn't even a gate, so exclusive were the monks—everyone had to be winched up in a basket over the wall.

Inside are palm and olive groves, grape arbors, and dozens of stuc-coed buildings scrawled with gothic graffiti. Black-robed, piously hirsute men shuffle in and out of the dormitory. It's a hot day, but cool inside the thirteenth-century church filled with glittering icons of saints on horse-back, murals of seraphs, and a painting of Saint Anthony by Velázquez. The Lebanese drop to their knees and make the sign of the cross before a lighted display case with mother-of-pearl inlays. "Is remains of Bishop Joseph," says Father Deoscoros, gesturing to a linen sack with bulges sug-gesting knees and shoulders. "*Complete* remains. He died in 1826."

Collecting the remains of the holy is serious business for monks and really brings out their competitive spirit. Back in the seventh century a troop of Saint Anthony's monks disguised as Bedouin sneaked into another Egyptian monastery (there are thirteen) and stole the bones of John the Short. They claimed that the remains were rightfully theirs. The other monks later stole them back.

There's no shortage of bones at Saint Anthony's now: all monks stay until they die. The first three years they wear white and study the Copt language of ancient Egyptians. King Tut is dead, but the words he spoke survive in the liturgy of the church. After the white-robed years the monks switch to black and expand their universe to include the more prosaic. Says Father Deoscoros, "Some are accountants, some study engineering."

Someone has to run the place, but in truth I'd expected more monkish vocations. Say, advanced crypt chiseling. I want to learn more, but Father Deoscoros is already herding us to the tour's end at the rather excellent gift shop, the only religious outlet I've seen that stocks geologic maps. I tell the father that I'm an internet journalist, and I'd like to put Saint Anthony's in my story.

"I did not think you could send these things from bicycle. Father Bishoy will be very interested in your project. He is our computer expert. I will call him—if you can stay a little longer?"

Certainly.

A couple of hours later, after both fathers have posed for pictures, and I've finished off my guest lunch of sautéed vegetables and rice and a demi-tasse of espresso, Father Bishoy is still curious. "Do you send your files on e-mail?"

I remember my computer lesson in the Australian outback, and tell Father Bishoy, No, it is something called File Transfer Protocol, or FTP, sent directly to another computer.

"Hmmm. Very interesting. But why do you do this on a bicycle?"

I see more, I tell him. And I like to sleep outside.

"You could sleep aside your car."

He's got me there. I say, maybe it is like your fasting—a little sacrifice, but good for thinking.

Father Deoscoros understands. "We fast during the day for two hundred days each year. It is good for the soul, not your body."

For the technological finale, I open my wonder phone and aim it at the satellite over the equator. Nothing. The enormous cliffs to the south block the signal. The monks aren't surprised. Perhaps they know something that I won't discover until I review my notes from the gift shop geologic map. The wall of Upper Cretaceous limestone shielding the monastery from the satellite is the Saint Anthony Formation.

SOMETIMES THE DESERT is a bust. I came for the silence, the space, the solitude—all that *sublime* jazz—but come morning it's obvious why this stretch of desert is mine, all mine. I'd hoped for crisp light over clean rocks, or at least wind-scalloped sand. I get dust and a milky dawn, a sunrise without the sun. It's midmorning before the thermonuclear ball rises above the scum.

Looking back at the Galala Plateau, I see that the monks have a comparatively sweet piece of real estate. With its spring feeding over a thousand gallons of water an hour into the monastery, they'll probably open a spa. Call it The Hoopoe, after the big bird that whistled *Yoo-hoo!* to me at the monastery wall yesterday, the bird dressed in black-and-white below and cinnamon above.

This happy bird doesn't come out today. The rocks, buried in dust, barely come out today. The highway is pushed through the dullest terrain by economic and engineering logic. Worse, there's a gas line to one side of the road, and an unfinished water line on the other. The desert does not hide its wounds, and the view from my bike is of endless heaps of dirt. They do serve, however, as a minor windbreak, and every five or ten miles there is a person hunkered down at the edge of the road.

Perhaps they are beggars. I'm nagged by the knowledge that charity is one of the five pillars of Islam, right up there with Only One God, prayer five times a day, the Ramadan fast, and, if God grants you the means, the pilgrimage to Mecca. Feeling uncharitable, I don't stop. The road has me in a mood. The sun is hot but a surprisingly chill headwind has come up. It feels like cold water on a burn.

I'm ten miles from the Red Sea's Gulf of Suez when I first see the mirages—the pooled reflections of sky on the desert floor—turning to black as I draw closer, then rising like a balloon and vanishing. This shouldn't happen with such a wind—it upsets the lenses of warm and cool air that create the refractive illusion—but now there are ships on the desert, too, phantom freighters making visible headway. Only when I reach the true blue of the sea will I see that the ships are oil tankers.

It looks like this is the road to Zafarana after all. The crossroads town is a bright new café/hotel/pizzeria plunked down in a forest of communications antennae on the shore. "Zafarana is most wind in Egypt," says my waiter. "Egypt have plan for wind generator, to make electricity here."

What are they waiting for? In the time it takes me to finish a cappuccino and a mushroom pizza, the wrong-way wind has decided my fate. My late start from Cairo wrecked my schedule for completing the trip. It's time to catch a ride north along the coast to Suez.

Every driver knows that psycho killers don't pedal. I wait no more than thirty seconds before a pickup stops and I'm heading towards Suez with Mohammed and Gamal. Their little truck is a regular Allah-mobile, with a "God is Great" sticker on the glove box, a "Mohammed is the Prophet" brass stencil hanging from the mirror, and a ridiculously long verse from the Koran covering the rest of the dash. It's a good thing Arabic is a lovely script; it all looks like poetry to me.

After the usual exchange of names and marital status, Mohammed asks in pretty-good English, "Tell me please, what do you think of the Egyptians, both good and bad?"

Well, they are very friendly people. More friendly, I admit, than typical Americans.

"American do not have time to be friendly like Egyptian," Mohammed explains. "He too busy."

That's exactly right, I say, but how did you know?

"I work with Americans, for Gulf of Suez Petroleum Company. Tell me, what about Egypt make you sad?"

Too many people in the Nile Valley. Not enough space, not enough hope for the children.

"President Mubarak tell us this. Should have less children. Every Egypt boy want to go to America."

I hope they don't get in until they learn to drive like Gamal, who actually stays in his lane on a road wedged between sudden mountains and the wind-frothed Bay of Suez. Wherever there's a bit more room, pick-and-shovel crews are working on the half-built shells of "holiday villages." Judging from the tea shops with names like Pussy Sleep, the developers hope to lure the freewheeling Europeans from their damp and drippy continent. The only problem with the plan is the beaches. They're cordoned off with barbed wire.

"There go BOOM!" says Mohammed.

Land mines?

"Yes. War with Israel."

Every antenna and depot and oil tank we pass in Mohammed's truck is surrounded by a wall and numerous guard towers, apparently empty. The soldiers are piled into jeeps with bent wheels, or digging inexplicable trenches, or learning to chain-smoke while sitting outside a flapping tent.

The gentlemen drop me off fifteen miles short of Suez. It's a grim ride into a glum city. Every ten minutes a junkyard dog tears after me. A squirt from my water bottle and they skid to a stunned stop. Some resume the chase, leaping over the flattened bodies of their comrades that fared poorly in earlier conflicts with cars. It's a fitting entrance to a city obliterated during the Suez wars.

The world's most contentious ditch is a shortcut that slices 5,000 miles off the voyage from Europe to the Persian Gulf and India. Egyptian muscle built the hundred-mile sea-level cut in 1869, but they never truly ran the thing until their first president, Gamal Nasser, showed the British and French the exit in 1956. The flabbergasted Europeans, who'd provided the engineering and money to build Suez, immediately found sympathy in Israel. Heaven forbid that the transport of Arabian oil through Suez be entrusted to actual Arabs, who seemed awfully likely to erect a big sign reading *No Jews Allowed.*

The British, French, and Israelis invaded and held the canal until a gale-force international scolding shamed them into leaving. Suez was an Egyptian canal again, but only a decade later the Israelis squashed the Arabs during the 1967 Six Day War. The Egyptians, sore losers, scuttled enough ships to block passage through the two-hundred-foot-wide canal. Suez remained a battleground until the stirrings of a truce with Israel in 1974. The canal was cleared and the city rebuilt. The new buildings of concrete and rebar are instant slums, accented by the occasional toasted shell of a blasted Israeli tank (actually, a U.S. tank, since we supply both sides).

Forty miles on the bike today, and I, too, am blasted. The brighter side of Suez presents itself in a hotel, nicely equipped. There's the standard Egyptian toilet, outfitted with a copper tube water jet that works like a bidet, but due to the tube's sadly exposed position in the center of the bowl, it suffers a frightful aesthetic flaw that I leave to your imagination. I take a shower with my clothes heaped in the bottom of the stall, mashing them like grapes as I wash my hair. From my window there's a view of the flaming stack of a refinery across the bay. Ships appear to be running aground, but that's just the entrance to the canal.

It's also the end of Africa. On the other side is Asia and the Sinai Peninsula, home to the highest mountains in Egypt. Naturally, the monks got there first.

THE ONLY WAY to reach the Monastery of Saint Catherine at Mount Sinai, midway across the peninsula, is through Feran, possibly the world's skinniest town and certainly one of the meanest. Four miles long and one hundred feet wide, Feran is an oasis squeezed between canyon walls. Hundreds of palms curve up from a rocky streambed, and little houses are backed up against the granite. Much of the road is in the streambed, only a stone's throw, literally, from the den of maniac children who burst out to heave rocks at me.

Ideally, this is when their mother appears and scolds, *It's not nice to stone visitors*. But she's busy prodding with a long stick the branches of an acacia, to knock down what the goats can't reach. They've already chewed the tree into the shape of a parasol, and now the black mob waits for more, bleating in anticipation.

The kids obviously practice tossing stones at the goats, and one little girl has a big-league arm. I see my chance for escape at what appears to be church grounds. Mercy! I duck in, and immediately it's quiet enough to hear the town roosters crowing. A man appears, angelic in white tunic and turban, and takes me for a little tour of the church and the nunnery. His name sounds like Awesome, and he says, "Moses stay Feran forty days." He isn't the first to say so. Christian hermits have hidden out in Feran since the second century, when nearby Mount Serbal was believed to be the mount of Moses.

"Cafeteria?" asks Awesome. Thank you, and soon I'm drinking tea near a garden of almond and citrus trees in spring bloom. A nun brings me a plate of scrambled eggs with a crumble of goat cheese. Caged parakeets bob and sing near a sign that says, "Do Not Forget That You Are In A Holy Place." And it works: I no longer want to kill the stone-throwing children.

Refreshed by the tea and a tailwind, I pedal out from under the feathery shade of the date palms into the April sun. The canyon walls are slashed with veins of red and black, of rock once melted and squeezed like toothpaste. Nothing on earth stays still forever, but few places are so clearly a landscape in progress. Slabs have sheared off the walls and crashed onto the road, leaving a glimmer of quartz and feldspar crystals in the noon light.

The resulting slalom is no problem: I'm going up, slowly, for the next forty miles. Each bend in the canyon brings a new view of the 8,000-foot-high mountains. That's lofty enough to snatch a little rain, water that eventually percolates out at scattered oases. Not much, but enough for Moses and his flock en route to the Promised Land. Although there's no archaeological evidence, the story itself is so old that it has gained credence simply by persisting, just as Australia's Aborigines have faith in the songlines of their ancestors. Helena, mother of Emperor Constantine, dropped by the Sinai in AD 327 and was impressed by a big bramble zealously protected by a group of hermits. They claimed it was the burning bush of Moses. Helena had a chapel built for the Virgin Mary, and it was later named after Saint Catherine, the Egyptian martyr whose bones were transported by angels to nearby Mount Catherine.

That's the easy way to the top. I'll need eight hours and three quarts of water to climb the 4,000 feet to the Monastery of Saint Catherine. A fleet of HolyLand tour buses are parked outside the Morgenland Village Hotel, whose marquee reads "We Organize Bedouin Nights for Groups."

I imagine this means a friendly campout with the nomads and not the sort of "Bedouin Night" that for centuries had the monks saying their prayers extra fast. Well before the birth of Islam, the Bedouin took pleasure in an occasional raid on the monastery, wasting a monk or two and munching on holy wafers. By AD 530, when Christianity had become the official state religion of Byzantium, Emperor Justinian decided that this outpost deserved something better: a fortress of granite. The thirty-foot-high walls were finished, coincidentally, in time for the first wave of Muslims that followed in the next century. The monks survived with a mix of savvy, guts, and humbug. In an early effort at cultural diversity, they built a mosque and insisted that the Prophet Mohammed himself had visited the mount of Moses.

It seems to have worked. Surrounding the monastery today is a living wall of Bedouin, hawking camel rides. Inside the fortress, through a portal with a slit overhead for pouring boiling oil onto the unwelcome, are so many of us tourists that I can scarcely peek into the church. It's not Coptic but Greek Orthodox, and the ceiling is hung with dozens of brass incense burners.

These are serious monks, in black robes, caps, and cardigans, and I know that there are some holy remains around, a mummified saint or at least a desiccated part of a monk. My prayer is fulfilled at the ossuary, guarded by Father Joseph. In the cellar behind him and a screen of chicken wire are sixteen hundred years of monks reduced to thousands of bones stacked like firewood. To keep everything tidy, the skulls are piled like cantaloupes in a cavern of their own—enough hollow-eyed brain cases to fill thirty shopping carts.

"We call this the University of the Monastery," says Father Joseph. "They are the teachers, and we are the students."

Yes—but the teachers are dead, aren't they?

"Saints never die. We learn through their memory. Their flesh is dry, but gives off a nice scent. They are not subject to ordinary limitations of space and time. God gave them special qualities."

Who, I wonder aloud, is the cadaver in the box in the back?

"Father Stephanos. He kept the steps to the Mountain of Moses in the sixth century," says Father Joseph. "Some saints' bodies are still fresh. Before they die they stink of tumors and disease, but after they die they smell good."

Thank you for your time, I say (but thinking: *I wouldn't want to bunk with Father Joseph*). Now I'm going to hike up the mountain.

It's another 2,500 feet to the top of Mount Sinai. A stiff climb, but Father Stephanos did nice stonework on the three thousand steps. For the weary there are Bedouin offering, "Good camel, good price." Along the way I pass English children and Israeli pilgrims and German birders armed with camera lenses like bazookas. At the breezy, bald summit is a chapel and graffiti ("The Bull Climbed Mount Sinai") and more Bedouin selling tea and holy rocks and stab-and-sip orange drink.

I sneak off and find a ledge to myself. Alone, with a dusty but inspiring view, it's easy to see how Moses could find God atop Mount Sinai. Or that Mount Sinai is God. Or, embracing gravity as well as theology, to see that I have one hell of downhill ride tomorrow, to the Gulf of Aqaba.

ANOTHER MURKY EGYPTIAN SUNRISE, scarcely bright enough to roust me out of the sleeping bag to pump up my miniature stove. Flame on, and in a few minutes I can dip a bandanna in the roiling water for a face wash, then prepare my coffee. When I kill the stove, the world falls silent. There's only a hopping black bird with a white cap—a wheatear, says my bird book—and he or she has no interest in my breakfast orange and fig jam on a pita.

Camp is easy enough to pack up—a ground cloth and sleeping bag, journal and book, stove and cup. The big drop to the coast is fifty miles east. Meanwhile, the road, narrow and new and very black, leaves the crumbling Precambrian granites and crosses a maroon plain of little sharp stones, each as if shattered with a hammer.

An easy climb over a low pass drops into a valley bounded by cream-colored sandstone eroded into lonesome buttes. When I stop for a closer look on an exposed shelf of rock, I find the ripple marks from the waves of a long-ago shore. And see, not far from the road, a single black tent. There are people, too, squatting in the sand beside a little cook fire. They wave me over, and five minutes later I'm sipping tea.

Salem is fifteen and the man of the tent, a swaybacked shelter of flour sacks and goat hair. Dad is out, I don't know where. Mother Hamda wears a black veil and a deep blue robe fastened with buttons of silver and malachite. Her feet appear carved from driftwood. While tending the fire, she smokes a cigarette through her veil—a chic solution to modesty. A three-year-old girl, with a wristwatch inked onto her wrist, flicks pebbles at the goats. When she plinks one on the nose, the family smiles, revealing rotten teeth all around. A donkey chews on a paper wrapper, and the goats sneak back to nibble on the plastic water barrel, the dinged teapot, the tiny cassette deck. There's not much else to chew on.

They're Bedouin, nomadic Arabs loyal to family, tribe, and land—and, like nomads everywhere, dismissive of political boundaries and institutions. This attitude is necessary not only for the pursuit of feed for their animals, but also for helping or hindering the flow of people and goods across the Sinai. Some Bedouin smuggle hashish in boats along the Mediterranean coast. If pursued by the police, they dump the hash into the sea, but only after putting it in a waterproof skin within a larger burlap sack filled with salt. The sack will sink, but after the salt dissolves in the course of a day it comes bobbing back up to the surface for retrieval.

A clever and slippery folk—and hospitable, too. I entertain the kids with "Oh, Susannah" on my harmonica. In return, Hamda pulls out an aluminum flute for a breezy tune. When the goats bug her, she whacks them with the flute.

There's no telling what's inside the shabby tent, but outside there is an excellent view and a single acacia tree. I wonder if they are simply poor or deliberately free. To my surprise but not Hamda's, a four-wheel-drive truck with a Egyptian guide and a pair of French tourists pulls into camp. They, too, have tea, while Salem pulls out a bag of beaded key chains and necklaces for sale. So this is why they are camped only a hundred yards from the road.

The guide gives me a sidelong glance and says, "You are not first bicycle."

Yes, I didn't think so—I saw one just yesterday at the monastery, but could not find the rider among all the tourists.

The guide turns away without a word. Oddly cool, I think, for an Egyptian—but then I understand. He'd promised his clients a visit to the Authentic Nomads of the Desert, not an American with a harmonica. And although it means I won't get a chance to play the Stones' "Hey, Mona!" with Bedouin backup on flute, I leave my hosts with a bag of coffee and head for the sea.

Every half hour or so a vehicle passes—a Mercedes tour bus, or a Toyota pickup with a goat in the bed, or a Peugeot station wagon taxi with suitcases lashed to its roof rack. Otherwise the road is mine, through drifts of yellow sand strewn with gray boulders like giant pewter eggs.

Which is not to say I'm alone. Overhead are dozens of hawks and vultures tilting on invisible thermals, making the spring migration from Africa to Asia. Crossing a watercourse traced with mustard and verbena, I catch the stink of trampled vegetation, clamp on my brakes, and stop. Across the sand are footprints the size of pie pans. A camel, I suppose, but I hear only a chirp like the squeak of a hinge, from a teacup bird in a thorn tree. Then the call of a child, a girl tending a ravenous herd of black goats. A little snooping reveals the family tent propped up against a sandstone monolith pocked with hundreds of shallow caverns. It looks like a ten-story sponge.

The goats pour down a dune and turn toward a shady cleft in the sandstone. If there's water up there, they'll find it. Bedouin goats can drink like no other goat. A forty-five-pound billy can suck down two gallons of water. To equal this feat, a 155-pound Jim would have to chug seven gallons at a sitting. If I could hold it down, I would not merely be uncomfortably bloated—I would drop dead from diluted blood. The Bedouin goat carries on because its gut is a canteen, slowly metering out the water over the next two, three, or four days.

Near the coast the stand-alone buttes are replaced with bare black mountains skirted with tremendous fans of gravel. My favorite road sign appears: "Let the engine work." This means a big descent is ahead. If I were driving I would downshift and spare my brakes. On a bike I upshift and shoot down a long canyon at a glorious 30 to 40 mph. With fingers lightly poised on the brake levers, I bank as deep as I dare through the last sweeping curve to the Gulf of Aqaba.

First things first: push the bike onto the beach, take off my shoes, and wiggle toes in the sand. Across the slender bay are simple stone mountains with the violet blush of day's end. The peaks are only fifteen miles east, but it's a long fifteen miles to Saudi Arabia, home of the most intolerant zealots on the globe.

Or so I'm told. I've never set foot in Saudi Arabia. I'm wondering what it's really like over there, when over here a young couple saunters up. The bikini beach babe and her headbanger boyfriend size me up with a single look. They must consider me outside the law. Like Eve offering the apple, the woman holds up an unlit joint.

"Do you want to get high?"

FREEDOM BEACH is a huddle of reed huts, each with a lightbulb, a flimsy door, and a hasp. Bring your own padlock, or pick one up in the village of Tarabeen. Beach entertainment includes a big steel cage with four monkeys so skinny they appear assembled from strands of roadkill.

"There are only two reasons to come here," says a young man from Cairo. "Sex, and to get high." He's sitting under a palapa of palm fronds with a bare-chested Israeli.

You mean there are Egyptian women for . . . rent?

"Oh, no! Not Egyptian girls, but Israeli girls from the kibbutz. No Egyptian girl like this for long time, the sixties in Cairo. There, along Ali Baba . . . you should know these girls!" He whistles and waggles his hand. "With black eyes, like Cleopatra!"

Oren, the Israeli, finds no offense in the reference to Israeli women. He ignites a Marlboro and asks, "You come on that bike?"

Yep.

He's appalled. I tell him it's not just a workout—the big hill down to the coast was an eye-watering blast. He counters, "You wouldn't think so if you were in a taxi and the driver puts it in fifth gear and goes into a power death dive."

Oren, who wears the kind of broad headband once favored by kamikaze pilots, is currently digging Guns n' Roses' "Appetite for Destruction" on his boom box. Oren also has an appetite for females in halter tops; he guesses at their flavor as they pass. "Israeli. She, French. There, German." It's educational, and he plans on staying "till the money runs out."

The money goes to the Bedouin. Although legal title is tenuous, they own Freedom Beach as well as Goldenfish and Moonland—the "touristic camps." The Bedouin were quick to realize that tending to a certain species of tourist isn't so different from tending goats. You simply herd them to a place with water and food and they take care of themselves, kicking up their heels and foraging for sex.

Farther north along the coast is a camp called Basata. A placid sanctuary compared to the hormonal riptide of Freedom Beach, it's run by an ex-engineer from Cairo with a pharaoh's goatee and an elegant robe. His name is Sherif and he's installed an ethic as radical as Freedom Beach's, except here there are organic veggies and recycling bins and a folk guitarist strumming "Get Back."

Like most of the patrons, I've brought my own Heineken. A barefoot man with a pigtail smiles an invitation to sit and relax beside an absurdly low table. An artist from Tel Aviv, Gershom respectfully inquires of my journey. I confess that I'm a pedaling internet journalist. A German woman sitting cross-legged wants to know more, for pragmatic reasons: she wants to be a travel writer. "But what do you write about?"

Everything. Rocks, people, birds, history.

"For example? How about you show me one story on your computer?"

I dig the laptop out of my bike bag and let her read the story of stumbling upon Midaq Alley. She giggles a couple of times, then looks up to say, "That's it? It is amusing, but I like to read for information."

This *is* information—it's about Cairo.

"People want to read this? Why do you get paid to do this?"

And I can't help but think: An Egyptian wouldn't have said that. An Egyptian would have kindly lied—because they're sweethearts.

This simple sentiment rings true the next day when I pass a road sign near the international frontier. It's just a piece of sheet metal with hand-painted letters in Arabic and English. Yet that someone bothered to write "Good-bye" in flowery script . . . well, that makes this farewell sing. I forget Egypt's suicide taxis and hair-pulling bureaucracy. I won't miss the pyramids of the dead, but I am fond of the living tea-happy Egyptians.

Excluding the diabolical customs people. Which reminds me: Israel is dead ahead, and it's time to repack my bicycle bags.

THE ISRAELI CUSTOMS WOMAN wears a sharply creased blue uniform. Dark military eyes move between my passport photo and my face, once, twice.

I just cut my hair, I explain. It's me.

"Put everything through the machine."

The X-ray machine. I put everything through. "Those," she says, pointing to the water bottles on the bike. I put them through. When the bike bags go in she stares at the monitor and mutters something in Hebrew, then reverses the conveyor belt to take a second look.

"Open these bags." I open the most innocent of my four bags. "What's this?" A flashlight. "What's this?" A lantern. "What's this?" Kerosene for the lantern.

She does not smile. She calls over a security expert and the questions resume, except this woman wipes every piece of my gear with what look like cosmetic pads. Dozens of them. They must be the same pads used in airports for detecting explosives. Still, I can't resist asking what they are.

No answer.

Are they secret pads?

"Yes, they are secret pads."

The Israelis are very clever. They grow tomatoes in the desert on drip irrigation using minuscule amounts of water. They breed featherless chickens that put on tasty extra weight to avoid shivering. Surely they will find my satellite phone, toot on large whistles, and take me away.

In bag number three she finds the computer and wipes it with a pad.

Does not say a word. The only bag left holds the phone, which I've packed in a tangle of unhappy socks and underwear, hoping, hoping. She takes one look at the mess and says, "OK—You can go. Welcome to Elat."

I make a mental note: *Don't wash my socks before Jordan.*

Which is only ten miles away. Israel wedges down to its southernmost point at Elat. Important not only as a port on the Red Sea's Gulf of Aqaba, Elat is also Israel's playground, a resort city spiked with construction cranes. Passover is coming, and the place is already jammed. The people have come to tour the rustic stockade of the "Texas Ranch," to throw money at the floating twenty-four-hour casino, and to see what's billed as the "colorful laser show at the ostrich farm, telling you the story of the period between the creation of the world and the Ten Commandments. The public takes part in the festivities of the sons of Israel as the chosen people."

After my stint in crumbling Egypt, clean and bright Elat has me feeling like a kid in Disneyland. The buildings are the same concrete cubes as in Cairo, but in Elat they finish construction before they move in. The streets are swept and the traffic lights work and the image of a Visa credit card marks the storefronts of the chosen. But with everyone busy cleaning and working and thinking up extra-creative tourist attractions, there's not much loafing among the residents. I didn't realize how much I like being invited to sit for a puff on a water pipe until I traded Egypt for Elat.

I try my luck with the leisure crowd at the beach, but am driven back by monster loudspeakers sending out disco shock waves. Wandering the streets in search of something akin to Cairo's blacksmiths and tea shops, I find stores with stuff like gold electroplated eagles with fake diamond eyes—the very definition of "disposable income." After four hours Elat feels like the United States with a lot of falafel joints and Israeli flags. There's surely more to the city, but tomorrow begins a four-day Arab holiday. The borders will close. I've got to get out of Elat or I'll end up at the "Dancing with Dolphins" show.

The border is a bulldozed berm topped with barbed wire. The Israelis let me leave more easily than they let me enter, but just as I'm about to ride to the Jordanian side a young man in a suit jogs up and says, "Sir! Sorry, but you cannot bring a bicycle to Jordan."

Really?

"It is new law: No bicycles between Israel and Jordan."

Could this be true? But he's a friendly civilian, not the Jordanian customs official. I'll find the truth soon enough.

There's only one car at the Jordanian border, and its driver is yelling in English at the customs man, "What is it you want? Is it this?" He waves some money, and the Jordanian says, "This is not the problem. The problem is your car."

I roll up on my problem bike. The border agents say "Welcome to Jordan!" and enthusiastically shake my hand. "How far on bicycle?"

Cairo, I say.

"Ooo-wee! You have visa?"

I sure do. Look: from the Jordanian embassy in America. They're impressed. A quick stamp in the passport and a slap on the back and "No problem! Enjoy Jordan!"

I pedal away like a bicycle zombie. Can it be so easy? Of course. Come to think of it, I'm usually never searched at borders. The innocuous bicycle traveler. I'm afraid to look back, but I do. Nobody coming. I pedal faster. One mile, two, then three, uphill and into the wind. Almost to the city of Aqaba when a car comes up behind me, slows, then begins honking.

It's two soldiers. "Sorry. Problem. You must go back to border."

Back we go. The apologetic soldiers usher me into the office of the top dog, a trim mustachioed officer. "I am sorry," he says, "but there is problem. You cannot bring a bicycle into Jordan."

I smile and explain that I am a journalist with special permission not only from the Jordanian embassy but also from Mr. Salim Ayoub of the Jordanian Ministry of Information. I pull out my Discovery Channel Online press pass, my Egyptian press pass, and my bank guarantee addressed to Jordanian Customs, a document I never understood but sure looks good.

It seems like Cairo airport customs again, but I'm wrong. The head of customs doesn't like enforcing a law prohibiting bicyclists from crossing the border. He tries to call Mr. Salim Ayoub, but apparently he's left for the day.

Two hours pass. He keeps trying to reach Salim, and between calls we make small talk on family and home and my pregnant wife. He flips through my passport, which the Egyptians stamped with evidence of the still-unmentioned secret agent satellite phone. Something catches his eye, and I catch my breath as his finger comes down on a page.

"I see that our birthdays are almost the same, only six days apart."

It's true, and the coincidence binds us in a peculiar way. Forty years earlier we were squalling infants, separated by fate and 8,000 miles until this day on the border of Israel and Jordan.

He opens a window. The sun is going down, the granite mountains flaring orange. He paces a circle around his desk, sits and scribbles down a phone number. "I think tonight you go to Aqaba. Tomorrow you call Mr. Ayoub and tell him to please call me at this number with the permission for the bicycle. Please enjoy Jordan."

I pedal away, and an hour later I'm enjoying Jordan with a gigantic bottle of Amstel beer in the lounge of the Aqaba Hotel. For company there are jolly Russians on holiday and a feline Jordanian in black satin and glittering bangles crooning the Egyptian hit "Habibi, Habibi." The rhythm stirs nocturnal imaginings, but they don't last. Not tonight. One beer and I'm ready to tip into the sweetest dreams, because I've cleared the last border between me and the Dead Sea.

In the morning I fail to reach Mr. Ayoub of the Ministry of Information. Of course: it's the four-day holiday. After convincing myself that all I must do is avoid the border crossings, I ride north from Aqaba. The road leaves the sea behind as it climbs 3,000 feet through valleys of blond sands washed out of the granite mountains. The air lightens with every mile from the sea, and the sands darken as the granite knobs are replaced with sandstone the color of yellow and red potatoes.

Bedouin camps are tucked into canyons, but for fifty miles there are no towns until the valley of Wadi Rum. It's a perpendicular place. To either side of a mile-wide avenue of pink sand are buttes up to 2,000 feet high, crowned by pale domes of sandstone swirled like cinnamon buns. The valley is treeless. There are only stiff shrubs armed with anti-goat spines.

The village of Rum is a scatter of tents and concrete-block homes with fluttering laundry, cannibalized cars under sprays of purple bougainvillea, and parked camels with their snouts in feed bags. A stroll through the streets earns me the usual lemming-rush of children, dirty barefoot goobers with toy cap guns. When a shoot-out erupts, I take cover in the only store in town, among the cans of condensed milk and motor oil. There are tea glasses, too, made in Russia, and ChocoLazer cookies. All the essentials, including a television tuned to a fat lady making a disastrous run down a playground slide: *America's Funniest Home Videos*. I hope nobody asks where I'm from.

They do, of course. Wadi Rum reminds me of my home, I say. The clerk replies, "Yes, we know there place Arizona like Wadi Rum. We see on television, with cowboy."

They know. With televisions snatching unseen signals and turning them into music videos and Marlboro men, it's no wonder none of the locals at the rest house are surprised when I dig my mobile communications studio out of my bike panniers and prepare to send a dispatch with my phone. They were expecting it all along. The only person attracted to my gear is a friendly German with a lumpy rucksack.

"It is a good feeling, no, to have the satellite phone for emergencies?"

He imagines that I'm having a wonderful electronic time. I aim the phone antenna out the window, and the invisible data surges over the southern horizon, possibly bothering a vulture or two, and further stimulating the German.

"You will probably carry it on all trips now, no?"

No, I admit—it's not a good feeling. And, no, I won't bring it along unless it's my job.

If he hadn't been summoned to his tour bus, I would've explained. Travel is a kind of running away from home, and with a phone on my bike I never completely cut free. A lifeline is also a leash. Even when turned off, the presence of the phone blunts the tingle of self-reliance—the feeling that if I screw up badly enough, the show is over.

That night I camp just outside town at the toe of a cliff, a black wall whose height is impossible to gauge. I'm in my sack, tucked behind a boulder, hiding from the night wind whistling through my bicycle spokes. The flame of my little lantern flickers in the breeze, and the voice of a village dog echoes off the cliff—but the closer it gets, the less sure I am it's a dog. Maybe it *sounds* like a dog but is really a bone-crunching hyena, the slouching prince of poor posture and worse dental hygiene.

But the creature is also afraid of me. It keeps its distance, and I find bedtime solace in a passage from Burton Bernstein's book *Sinai* that I jotted in my notebook before leaving home.

> A traveler who slept in the desert asked a nomad if there were snakes he should worry about. The reply: Don't worry. If God sends snakes, he sends snakes. You can't go to sleep every night and worry about snakes. There are certainly snakes in the desert, but one must sleep. God willing.

The little anecdote is a nice sleeping pill. When the sun comes blazing over the cliffs in the morning, I sit up and can hardly believe that I fretted in the night. On my way over to the rest house, the only carnivore I see is a limping pint-sized goat-hound.

The faint strains of a string quartet drift from the rest house sound system. While I breakfast on eggs and flatbread, the tour-bus drivers gossip and toss back olives, stab at slabs of white cheese, and wipe yogurt from their thick mustaches. Across the valley is a butte the size of Australia's Big Red Rock, Uluru. I consult my photocopied pages from *Walks and Scrambles in Wadi Rum* and discover that it's possible to hike not over but through the butte via a flood-scoured passage to the other side. The canyon is not visible from my vantage, and that only enhances its allure.

The obvious way across the valley is by sand taxi: the camel. Outside the rest house a crew-cut kid in Streak tennies urges me to choose his mount. "Hello! Special price!" No thanks, I'll go with the respectable adult over there, the quiet one in the robe. He names a price. I accept, and mount a deflated sack of fur that suddenly groans and slobbers and rises like a zeppelin until it seems I'm forty feet off the ground. It's a big camel, with feet like a one-ton duck's. I figure the owner will climb aboard his personal ride and we'll set off together. Instead he hands the reins to the crew-cut kid and off we go. The kid walks while I ride.

I don't object. All I really want is to sit atop the chug-a-lug champion of the world. A single thirsty camel can shame an entire fraternity house, sucking down the equivalent of 120 twelve-ounce bottles in twelve minutes. Once topped off, the camel is a water miser. Within that long nose are damp and thankfully unseen baffles of tissue that keep its lungs humid, yet allow precious little moisture to escape through its nostrils.

As for the fur coat, the tireless physiologist Knut Schimdt-Nielsen once spent an entire day shaving a camel. After that, it lost 50 percent more water. The naked camel probably lost 100 percent of its friends as well, but Schmidt-Nielsen had proven his thesis: like a Bedouin's robe, the fur keeps the sun off the skin. And when the camel inevitably heats up in the land of little shade, it needn't break a sweat, because its body temperature fluctuates up to 10 degrees daily, a swing that would drop a human in his feverish tracks.

And they do it all on dates and hay, with no scheduled maintenance. It's no surprise that, judging from my impromptu census of Wadi Rum, the Bedouin like their jeeps but love their camels. So long as I don't look down, my ride is a pleasure cruise to the base of the butte.

The boy and camel leave. Left to my own two feet, I find the canyon, noodle through narrows, and climb notches chipped into the rock. The canyon walls are warm on one side and cool on the other, depending on whether the sun has found them. I like the shady side, where I find a mint and steal a few leaves to freshen my water. The foot-long agama lizards prefer the sun, lounging contentedly. Fearless swallows with rufous breasts lunch on the wing, snatching insects out of the stripe of blue above.

I stick to my date bars and a melted ChocoLazer. After I've finished my first quart of water, I emerge from a slot on the far side of the massif and climb atop a red dune for a view down Wadi Um Ishrin, the valley running south to Saudi Arabia. The panorama tugs at me, and I end up hiking the long way back, looping around the butte I'd slipped through. Unlike at Australia's Uluru, no tour helicopters thrash overhead. Just the crunch of gravel underfoot until I stop for a drink and hear somebody singing.

I slowly spin in search of its source, but there's no telling in this land of echoes.

I retrieve my bike from the rest house and find a camping spot. Nightfall drains the color from the sky, the stone, and finally the very blue sleeping bag that I plump with a snap and shake. I lie back in a monochrome world, with a reef of clouds edging over the rimrock, under the cool dazzle of the Milky Way. Just as I'd hoped, God doesn't send snakes or hyenas.

WHEN IT COMES TO FOOD, ignorance can be the traveler's best friend. Falafel is the mainstay of every café in Al Quwayra, a village of little shops selling big pillows for your floor and wrought-iron bars for your windows. It's the same story in Egypt, and after gobbling the little fried balls for weeks, I don't care to learn of their origin. If I learned that falafels were derived from some unsavory body part—say, if they really were fried balls—I wouldn't be ordering seconds.

"Hungry?" asks the cook. He works behind a tile counter stenciled with blue flowers, and his mustache is limp with steam and falafel oil. Fuel for the engine, I say—I rode from Egypt.

"I am from Egypt," he says with the mildly sardonic grin of a man proud of his heritage—and glad to have it behind him. He motions to the other customers. "And he is from Palestine. And he is from Palestine."

The Palestinians, with the blackened knuckles of truck drivers, look up from their falafels and say hello with their eyebrows. Nearly half of Jordan's 5 million are Palestinian refugees, and I ask the cook, where are the Jordanians? He points out the window in the direction of the Dead Sea, to a limestone plateau 3,000 feet above the sandstone desert.

I may be aiming for the lowest beach on earth, but the slow rip and shove of tectonics that excavated the pit also tilted the little country of Jordan until the rimrock of the Dead Sea valley rose a vertical mile above the shore. This shouldn't be a problem so long as I maintain my blood sugar level, and by that I mean 50 percent blood and 50 percent sugar. I wash down the falafels with tea so sweet it gives me a toothache—and then it's on the bike, legs churning, lungs burning, head turning to the south for one last look at the Mesozoic standing rocks of Wadi Rum.

It's a long farewell, and my feeling at the edge of the plateau is both panting success and a reluctance to leave behind the rusty dunes for this land littered with pale jagged rubble as friendly as eggshells. The winter rains have left thin patches of stiff grass for the goats. The Bedouin live in camps of patchwork tents and crowing roosters, where slow donkeys with white muzzles carry girls in rags and bundles of sticks of mysterious origin. There are no trees. The oak and juniper were hacked down by the Ottoman Turks for the railway to Aqaba—the same line that Lawrence of Arabia blew up when the Turks unwisely embraced the Germans as allies during the first world war. Today, any sapling not defended by a stone wall is fated to be kindling or goat chow.

The road turns into the afternoon sun and rolls past farms where the earth has been worked into thin furrows like gray corduroy reaching almost to the lip of the plateau. There, on the verge of the Dead Sea Valley, villages huddle on terraces alongside pocket orchards of figs, apricots, pomegranates, and olives. Quiet places, except for the clang of a tire iron in a repair shop and the dinky stores marked by signs for soda pop. When I stop in Al Rajif on the roadside near a meek house with a bold view into the gash between Israel and Jordan, a young man pops out of his home to invite me inside for a glass of tea.

His name is Qusem. His father, Mohammed, gladly takes a break from enlarging his backyard with a pick and sledgehammer. He wears a profound mustache, red checkered headdress, and ankle-length shirt. He gives me the standard Arab handshake, a give-me-five hand slap—a thick hard hand on a skinny arm, like a bucket on a backhoe. Qusem introduces me to the rest of the family. "He is Salem. She is Ahmna. She is Aisha." The girls all wear head scarves. Each time I think he's got them all, another brother or sister appears. "He is Khalil. And Khalid . . . "

I tally them up. Ten kids? Must be a town record, I say. Qusem translates and Mohammed flushes with reproductive success before setting me straight.

"No, Mr. Jim—there is a family with twenty-two children."

Here's my chance at last: "My wife is pregnant." I pull out my wallet photos of Sonya, and win handshakes and congratulations on my Arabic and my fertility. Qusem says, "We are honored to have you as guest in our home. It is your home, too."

The kids stare at the guest from America. Thank goodness I brought enough balloons for everyone. Qusem is equally easy to please: he's crazy for maps, and we spend an hour retracing my route over various charts. He works as a policeman but his degree is in geography; a photo of Qusem and his diploma is elaborately framed with black velvet, stained glass, and gold.

Fake gold. The family had money enough to send only Qusem to the university, and on the walls of this home his graduation photo shares top honors with Mohammed's six war medals, and two verses from the Koran. Mohammed gets a military pension nowadays, but Qusem says it's not enough, and his fourteen-year-old brother is looking for work. I ask, what sort? Qusem gives me an incredulous look that means: you think he has a choice? "Any work."

The sounds of rush hour draw us outside. The goats are coming home, each herd accompanied by either women or children who trill and hiss and toss stones to keep them on course. I catch a glimpse of the mother only when she's hanging laundry, and the tender bulge in her silhouette reveals that she's pregnant with number eleven. I don't know if she lacks the time or the permission to join us. Maybe both.

Qusem invites me back inside. Big pillows embroidered with the minarets of Mecca sit on a swept concrete floor. Qusem checks to ensure we're alone, then pulls from his wallet a well-fingered photograph of a young woman.

I shouldn't have been surprised. The brief intersection of our lives means that both host and guest know that we've only this day to tell our story. Balancing piety and honesty, Qusem explains, "I am sorry, but this is old way. I cannot speak of my fiancée. This photo is only for me; nobody in family know."

And only now do I recognize the consequences of showing off Sonya's photo. Some may see it as disrespect or bragging: here she is, boys, and please note that gorgeous head of hair. Others wish to share their pictures of loved ones to thank their good fortune, their lucky stars, or simply to thank God.

I tell Qusem, she's lovely—and thanks for telling me.

"It is Muslim custom the woman she stay in the house, or working near the house, and she seen only by her husband, or children, or brother." So when friends drop by in the evening, it's the women in one room and the men in another.

The ritual of showing me every photo in the house resumes.

"This is a hyena," says Qusem. "The Bedouin trap the hyena because the hyena kill the goat."

He moves on to the next photo—"Here is my uncle, on camel"—but I am stuck on the hyena. It's dead. It looks like a cat-dog with a fantastic tail that begins as a mane behind its ears and runs the full length of its back. It is folded in a pathetic pose, and I feel ashamed to have feared the beast.

Likewise, my host Mohammed looks strikingly similar to the men I'd seen on TV, heaving rocks at Israelis. Until he smiles, and his small black eyes give him all the menace of a sand elf. Tonight he isn't sure I recognize goat soup as food, so he demonstrates by bringing my bowl up to his lips and taking a big slurp, as if to say: See, it's fine.

After dinner the men break out a deck of cards and a pack of Kareem smokes. I can't figure out the game, and they quickly hit upon the reason why: I'm dressed all wrong. To play cards with Arabs, you should be dressed like one. Within ten minutes I'm a counterfeit Arab from head to ankle, complete with skullcap hidden beneath my headdress. They show me off, like a Ken doll, to the women and children.

Considering the crowd, bedtime is simple. Males in one room, females in another. The sleeping mats and quilts are tossed down and, bang, everyone is out as if they were gassed.

In the morning, after a breakfast of yogurt and bread, I make a gift of the maps I no longer need. The bike I pack up more carefully than usual, merely to linger. I used to think that traveling by bike made me one of the regular folk. Now I know it just helps me meet them. My hosts know that when I grow weary of falafels and sandstorms, I'll be heading back to the incomprehensibly rich United States of America, where people buy Big Macs without leaving their cars. Mohammed and clan are staying put with their goats.

All the kids get a shot at saying "Good-bye, Mr. Jim." I top off my water bottle and straddle the bike. "Please come back to Jordan," says Qusem, "and you will always have a place to rest in our home."

He asks nothing of me. With my foot I flip a pedal into position, slip into the toe clip and shove off. For a minute I imagine my return—the surprise, the handshakes, the stories into the night—then I round the corner and realize that I'm probably never coming back.

THE ROAD NORTH DIVES into and climbs out of every cleft in the plateau. The descents pass in a rush, and I spend most of the day pedaling uphill, very slowly. This has its advantages. The olive groves are shade and peace. The donkeys are even slower than me. And there are views westward from the rimrock, down to a stone wilderness of golden domes and black canyons, the sudden drop into the Dead Sea valley. The sea itself, however, is still a few days north. It's also the Israeli border—land of no foreign bikes.

The next morning, from my camp on the rim, I telephone Mr. Ayoub of the Ministry of Information. I explain my little incident. He speaks candidly about customs and the no-bicycle rule: "I've never heard of such a thing. There is no rule on bikes."

He assures me that because no permission is needed, none need be granted. My trip, he assures me, will be trouble-free. Probably. Enjoy Jordan!

I thank him, hang up, and finish my cup of coffee while I try to figure out if this is good news or bad. The absurdity of the no-bike rule makes it likely my experience was an isolated misunderstanding. On the other hand, it could happen again. With caffeine whizzing around my brain, it's easy to imagine a lieutenant in starched uniform searching my illegal bike, finding the spy telephone and triumphantly announcing, "THIS is why we must ban bicycles!"

This image amuses me until the valley below fades into an opalescent smear of heat and dust. The khamsin is blowing, the hot spring winds out of Africa. It's late April, season of the first big heat.

Back on the highway, traffic is light but confusing. The horns of Jordanian vehicles are all wrong. A matchbox taxi with a rhino-charge air horn, a cement truck with a shy buzzer, a bus that makes music like an ice-cream truck. Everyone honks and flashes their lights at me. They are so glad to see me. They are driving me nuts.

So it goes for the next two days: the friendly locals, the ungrateful visitor. In psycho-physiological terms, I'm pooping out. If I were a month into climbing Everest, somewhere between Camp III and the South Col, I could blame my mood on thin air. I've no such excuse—just the feeling of relief when I reach the road into the Dead Sea valley.

I cruise down to the first hairpin curve and stop to peer over the guardrail to see what's coming. Five minutes later I'm still there, bug-eyed and unbelieving. The highway dives off the limestone rim, slips between fins of sandstone, then vanishes. Far below are the vague outlines of what must be acacia trees.

A 4,300-foot descent in eight miles is a cyclist's thrill. I check my brakes and tighten the elastic cords cinching the tent and sleeping bag. Gravity does the rest. With the wind tearing at my eyes and my shirt flapping, I'm happy save for the knowledge it's going to be a million degrees down there. I don't want to sleep in the heat, not tonight, and I stop to make camp after dropping maybe a thousand feet. Meanwhile a damp dirt fog blows in from the south. It looks and feels awful, but my camp is serenaded by an owl and the songs of Bedouin bringing the goats home.

I have my soup and potatoes and sit on a rock under a juniper tree and wish for a beer. The Dead Sea, the sunken Everest of my desires, is lost in the desert equivalent of a blizzard. The sun squats into the murk and quits for the day. Coasting down to the Dead Sea may not be the joyride I'd hoped for.

It's 64 DEGREES when I wake to the songs of children from a passing school bus. I'm a lucky man, I think, to be given this cool and charming dawn. I change my mind when I sit up in my bag and look down into the valley. Although in the night the wind quit and hopeful stars blinked on, the morning sky is a viscid blur of dust. It's the blasted khamsin, hot out of Egypt.

Breakfast is an orange and a pita smeared with jam, a sticky meal I try to keep from transferring to the computer and phone as I beam off a story. I muse over my strange job and its paradoxical blend of the archaic and futuristic, while bands of yodeling Bedouin and their goats swarm over the slopes.

Then it's on the bike for the plummet into the big heat, past the wreck of mountains that look like sand castles mortally gouged by the first big wave. The road is so steep that a passing produce truck has lost some of its tomatoes. It seems a shame to let them rot, so I wash off the gravel and enjoy, particularly since the wind has now vanished as quickly as it came.

I imagine that I can feel the air pressure building as I pass below sea level and keep dropping. Nobody was sure of the valley's elevation until a pair of British explorers in 1837 noted an increase in the boiling point of water—proof they were "considerably lower than the ocean." My only clue is the change in vegetation. By the time the slope tapers off into the valley bottom, the junipers are long gone and I'm more than 1,000 feet below sea level, passing irrigated banana plantations in a stony desert. The water comes not from rain but from the canyons that drain the high plateau and spill out into the valley bottom in broad beds of flood-flattened reeds. There are mom-and-pop farms with stick houses and all-purpose donkeys. There are big industrial farms with Sudanese and Egyptian laborers— more evidence that the world's food is generally plucked by the world's poorest people.

From the shade of another immigrant, a Mexican palo verde tree, two young men pedal out on bicycles. It's a relief to see their super-wow Egyptian rides, with plastic scorpions clipped to their spokes and paper roses attached to the front forks.

My little thermometer says it's just over 100 degrees when I pass the southern edge of what used to be the Dead Sea. Now it's a grid of dikes enclosing the evaporation pans of the Arab Potash Company. Potash is, like wood ash, fertilizer. It's Jordan's number one export, four billion pounds a year, not including the stuff that blows off into my face when the trucks pass.

There are no towns along the Jordanian side of the Dead Sea. The

Israelis would not even let them build a road until last year, so sensitive is the border. Before I reach the true Dead Sea I must pass a military checkpoint. Nobody mentions the bike, but I am subjected to the usual grueling interrogation: How do you like Jordan? And won't you have some tea? Will I visit their wonderful capital city of Amman? Why yes, I say: tomorrow morning I'll pedal to the main highway and catch a bus up and out.

It's a tough life for a soldier on the Dead Sea. Not enough guests, they tell me, and they must clean and oil their Beretta machine guns every day, or they'll rust in the salty breeze.

I'm glad I stopped, because by the time I leave the wind has collapsed to nothing and the sun has emerged from the dust swirl, lending a hot but cheering clarity to my final miles. It's 94 degrees at 5:30 PM—no problem on a breezy bike. The mountains abruptly rising above the shore are fractured and leaking, with water dripping down walls colored like a kindergarten fresco. When the road drops closer to the water, I park the bike and trot down to the shore.

The beach is scattered with sandstone boulders with elegant curving strata, and the shore looks like an emergent reef of white coral. Nowhere in the world is water saltier than the Dead Sea, and everything is coated with a thick rime of nubbly crystals—the rocks, driftwood, even pieces of trash. A discarded yogurt container is like a cave formation, shining in its husk of salt. The sea is calm and absolutely empty, as boats are even more taboo than bikes along the border.

There's only one more thing I want to do. I ride on, passing one, two, three narrow canyons and thin creeks coming out of the mountains. Then the big one, Wadi Mujib, with what would be called a river in Arizona, twenty feet wide and gushing between sheer five-hundred-foot walls. Swallows are cutting through the shadows, and frogs are cranking up for the evening. There's just time enough for a swim in the Dead Sea, and a rinse in Wadi Mujib.

I ride, then push, then drag the bike to the shore, 1,300 feet below sea level. The water is lucid. There are bacteria and algae that can tolerate the Dead Sea, but I see nothing. Nobody around either, so I strip and tenuously enter. My toe says the water is balmy. I try skipping a couple of rocks, and they bounce easily across the hyperdense water, ten times saltier than the ocean. I wade in, and refractive shock waves radiate out from my thighs and fade in swirls of distortion. I've never seen anything like it, and push on, to my bellybutton and my chest. One more step . . .

And although my head and arms are still above the surface my feet leave the cobbles and swing up and out of the water.

I'm weightless. A cross-shore current grabs me and takes me away, past the illegal bike that took me here from Cairo, along the shore of the loveliest pit in the world. I'm floating in the Dead Sea, and my elation is unsinkable.

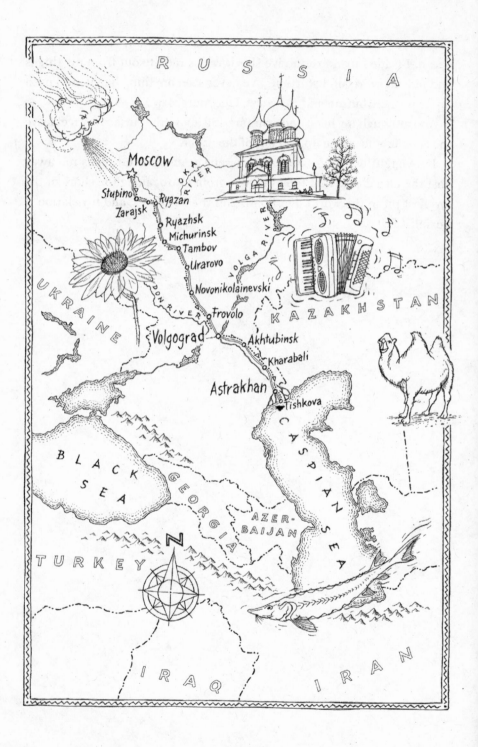

EUROPE

A bicycle was out—too difficult, too
dangerous; another stunt.
—Paul Theroux,
The Kingdom by the Sea

CHAPTER 5

Tucson to Moscow

Once in Russia There Was No Rich and No Poor

BY THE TIME another year had passed, our house looked as if a two-foot-high wave had swept through and removed everything chewable or breakable. Down the hall crawled my son, a midget engine of destruction with a busted rattle in hand, slapping it against the white tile floor, *clunk, clunk, clunk,* like Captain Ahab pacing the deck. His name was Rudy, and he wanted a ride in my over-the-shoulder baby holder. I slipped him in. He was a portable pleasure, with breath like cake frosting.

I had work to do, listed on a scrap of paper on which I'd scrawled RUSSIA. I took a scissors to my maps, eliminating Siberia to the west and the Ukraine to the east, leaving the lands between Moscow and the shore of the Caspian Sea, ninety-two feet below sea level. I unzipped my first-aid kit and checked my aspirin supply and the expiration date of my bee-sting epinephrine injector.

Medically satisfied, I left the now-dozing Rudy to my mother-in-law and pedaled off, through the warm puddles of an afternoon cloudburst to Ajo Bikes.

Tracy Cook threaded new gear and brake cables into my machine, greased the bearings, then gave the frame a once-over. He beckoned me over to the upside-down bike. There: a crack in the frame, a fissure thin as a Rudy hair.

"You need a new downtube."

"But I'm leaving the day after tomorrow."

"Then all I can do is take it to my place tonight and weld a big thick bead over the crack. It's going to burn off the paint and look like hell." He poked his glasses back up his nose and gave me a look of pity and envy. "But you don't seem the kind that would care about the paint job. The weld should hold for the trip, but keep an eye on it. Don't want the headtube and front fork to break away."

Pedaling a bike that could snap in two would have bothered me more if I were going somewhere other than Russia. It seemed a cross-your-fingers-and-pray kind of country. After all, the space station *Mir* had caught on fire and crashed into another spacecraft, and yet the Russians would not abandon it. Instead they would patch it and say, *Thank God it still flies.*

It was not my bike but the Russians that worried me. I spent my last day in America making Rudy smile and reviewing my Russian language notes. "Do not expect a Russian to reply to *How are you?* in the happy-go-lucky style of the Americans, who will say *Fine* even if their mother just died. The Russian might say *So-so*, or *Normal*, or *Could be better*."

This was from my first teacher, a Russian with fine skin that faintly glistened because she was doughy and squeezed herself into a tight sweater and slit skirt. My second teacher knew of my bicycle scheme, and concluded our lessons with, "I do not believe in God, but in Russia we make this thing for the good luck." She made the sign of the cross, and because she was teary-eyed it seemed especially sincere. "I asked my friends and they said that you are not brave. You are crazy."

Two weeks earlier the Russian currency had collapsed. This meant discount potatoes and vodka. On the other hand, a coup was not out of the question. *The Crisis*, cried the evening news, and proved the point with video of beet farmers with pitchforks. They were not happy-go-lucky. Their rubles were suddenly a joke, their banks locking their doors and taping up signs that said *Nyet Rubles! Nyet Dollars!*

Discovery Online decided the time was right to send, via overnight mail, an attachment to my contract, in which "The Undersigned acknowledges ... certain risks and dangers. ... " It was their lawyer's farewell: *Don't blame us if you don't come back in one piece.*

I signed it. I sorely wanted to pedal to the next pit. To any pit, actually. It was the moving I craved, away from the familiar. The money didn't hurt, either; I was certain I was a writer or a botanist only after the check came in the mail.

I crossed my fingers and did not pray and boarded the first of three planes to Moscow.

I HAD THREE SEATS TO MYSELF for the night passage over the Atlantic. My comfort and a bit of brandy gave me a warm feeling about Russia. The feeling lasted until I woke at dawn near the Arctic Circle. The entire planet appeared frozen, but it was only a blanket of clouds. The jet hurried into daybreak, accelerating the sunrise that tore the clouds into remarkably uniform strips of vapor. A coffee and juice cart rolled down the aisle while the sun continued its work, and over the next hour the strips of clouds humped like frying bacon, then broke into pearly bubbles.

Now I could see tin-roofed cabins and furrowed fields outside Moscow. The landing flaps curled out of the wings, and the plane dropped low enough to see Russians yanking cabbages from their gardens before the clanging finality of winter.

This worried me. My departure had been pushed back to mid-September by Discovery. The novelty of online bike touring to the pits had been surpassed by online whale sex off Madagascar. The humpbacks, I was made to understand, could only be aroused in August; I merely had to buy mittens.

Changing my route to something closer to the equator was appealing. The Caspian Sea is enormous—toss in Britain and it would glug out of sight—and there were a hundred thrilling routes to its shore. Sadly, many were potentially fatal for a cyclist with a spy telephone. The Caucasus Mountains were a crock pot of civil war, simmering in Dagestan and Georgia, blowing the lid off Azerbaijan and Chechnya. I didn't bother asking Iran, Turkmenistan, or Kazakhstan for permission to wander unattended.

It wasn't just phone worries or excitable fundamentalists. Those countries were in Asia, and I was riding to the lowest point in Europe, through Europe.

One look at a map and it's clear that the Asia/Europe divide is geologically bogus. The two have been one for around 400 million years. The boundary is cultural—us versus the barbarians—and dates back at least 2,500 years. The continental names have stuck, although the frontier itself has slowly crept eastward through time, from the Don River to its current location along the Ural Mountains and the Caspian.

Because my route was to go through Europe, Moscow was the place to begin. There would be no border interrogations—it was Russia all the way to the Caspian. Airport customs would not nab my phone—I would rent one in Moscow. And I knew Moscow from an earlier visit, less than two years after the fall of communism, when billboards had proclaimed "Glory to the Workers!"

Now, seven years after the fall, the billboards outside the airport bore ads for cell phones urging "Be Happy!" And along the drive into the old city were cheery banners festooning the light poles, and freshly painted wrought-iron fences around tidy parks.

"It is our mayor, Luzhkov, that make Moscow look good," said Sasha the taxi driver. "Nobody knows where he finds the money for this."

This seemed more than an observation; it was a warning, like the ones Australians gave of their crocodiles, of predators just over the horizon. Mysterious wealth meant Mafia and secret police. Sasha unzipped his genuine leather jacket and drove with one hand on the wheel while puffing on a slim Davidoff. I knew where he'd found the money for this: the fare was fifty bucks.

"Before the taxi I worked as a driver for the New Russians in the oil business. A good job, driving the German cars. It is also a dangerous job." Sasha ignored the lane markings, squeezing his Volkswagen into a promising slot between a mammoth Mercury Navigator and an armored Mercedes. "When my New Russian buys the bulletproof car, I think this is not a good thing. I have only one head."

Sasha knew the way to Stary Arbat, a pedestrian avenue awhirl with street musicians and tourists, where my satellite phone waited at the home of Mr. Laurent Barrion. He was a Frenchman from a French company, Geolink, but he was a kind of New Russian, too. There were buckets of money to be made in a country full of oil and gas and nickel, but to get the stuff out of the ground it helped to be able to swing a deal from Siberia on a telephone that cost $3,000 a month.

Mr. Barrion helped me find a bank willing to change money on a day when the exchange rate ricocheted between thirteen and twenty rubles to the dollar. He offered a spare room for my stay. The least I could do was show him my maps and my route to the lowest point in Europe: southeast from Moscow, out of the birch forests and across the farmlands. Then I'd slip into the valley of the Volga River and follow her to the Caspian Sea.

He approved, but added, "You must be careful where you bring such a phone. In the south the military is very sensitive about the Chechen problem."

I assured him I would stay at least two hundred miles from Chechnya.

Might not make a difference, said another man from Geolink. He was a local, a suave fellow named Dmitri, and he casually suggested that in all of Russia, "Things may stay the same. Or there may be a civil war."

Lacking an armored bicycle, I wouldn't be wise to ignore local advice. But Dmitri was only musing. Moscow did not seem to be on the brink of destruction, although there was no disputing that it was at least very flammable. Invading Mongols had torched the city in 1238. They liked the results, and repeated the show in 1382, 1547, and 1571. Moscow burned again in 1812, except this time it was lit by the Muscovites to spoil Napoleon's advance. During the mayhem of the 1900s Moscow was spared the flame but not the bloodshed. Who, I asked Dmitri, could possibly wish upon Russia another war?

"A war can be a profitable thing," Dmitri said. He wore a bomber jacket emblazoned *U.S. Air Force*. "You can break into buildings and steal things. Rob people. The poor see what they do not have."

The poor see many things, some of which were on television that evening. I stayed up with Mr. Barrion, flipping channels with the remote. I opened a Heineken and the window, and from the street came the chords of a guitarist singing "Jailhouse Rock." From the television came the image of two naked women. Although I was working overtime, I didn't waver when the women, apparently fond of each other, began squeezing the squeezables.

I presumed we were watching a cable channel. "Not cable," said my host, "just regular TV. This is democracy."

DEMOCRACY WAS THE BLATHER of car alarms, the sound of something worth stealing. It was kiosks selling *Playboy* magazine. And it was Moscow's Izmailovsky Market, an outdoor smorgasbord of goods from computers to carrots. Here the Muscovites had swiftly cobbled together a breezy mall, with faux log cabins stocked with Italian shoes, and fake yurts hung with Asian rugs. I was happily lost in the bazaar when a man asked me, "Excuse me, but would you like to buy some postage stamps?"

He looked like a Slavic leprechaun with small green eyes and bad teeth. From his Adidas gym bag he pulled a small album.

"Look, the history of the Soviet Union in stamps. This page is revolutionary stamps with Lenin, this page is space travel. This page is New Russia, with stamps of the three men that died defending our White House, in 1993."

But wasn't the White House in 1993 occupied by men who did not want a new Russia, Communists who wanted the old Soviet Union?

"Yes, maybe this is so, but these men were run over by the tanks and so became Russian heroes. Now nobody is sure. Here are the stamps. Ten dollars."

Sorry, I'm not a collector—but where did you learn to speak English so well?

"Buy my stamps and I will tell you."

I bought the stamps. He whispered, "I was supposed to be a spy. I was a candidate, but I turned down the KGB."

Was he making this up? But a liar would not have come up with this: "I was afraid."

I strolled the market with Vladimir, past steel sheds overflowing with CDs. He gripped my arm with surprising strength for someone born in

1943, and said, "Listen to me: the world is upside down. And it is your fault. Not yours personally, but I think you know what I mean. Once in Russia there was no rich and no poor. Everything was free. Education. Medicine."

He gestured to a meat stand. "Now look. This chicken is twenty-five rubles a kilo. American chicken. Last week it was ten. Everything is crazy."

He made a secret nod toward some rug dealers and said, "Look: they are Azeris. From Azerbaijan. They scare me. And there are Chechens. They have no mercy."

I tried to cheer him with a gift of American chicken. In return he gave me a small bottle of Istok vodka. We had a drink near the food stalls, beside the curls of dried fish and sacks of rice, and the liquor loosened us.

"Tell me," asked Vladimir, "where did you meet your wife?"

At the University of Arizona.

"That is enough. No more." He had another drink, a friendly swallow, and slipped the chicken into his gym bag. "I am alone in this world. I like women, but they do not like me. Nevertheless, I believe in God."

God and vodka preceded deeper introspection, which in Vladimir's case was family problems. His cousin's daughter, thirty years old and mother of two, was abruptly single after her husband had jumped eighteen floors to his death. "The family wants me to take his place. But I do not love her. She has a secret lover. What should I do?"

Don't marry her.

This pleased him—until he spotted foreigners.

"Listen to me! Those people are Vietnamese. And there are more men from the Caucusus. Moscow is flooded with non-Muscovites. They are taking over. The Russian is too . . . too . . . heart-minded. This word is my invention. It means they would not *make* you buy anything."

I was thinking of the stamps, but instead said that Moscow today looks like other big cities. Change is normal.

Vladimir was astonished. "What? You call this normal?" He turned to face the passing crowds. "You call this good?"

It was a fine day, glowing with the last touch of summer. Crew-cut dudes wearing headphones lugged shopping bags emblazoned with big-busted

babes in teeny bras. Teen girls in sheer blouses clomped past in giant platform shoes last seen on Elton John. I said nothing. Vladimir could only
fume. "They spoil the Russian character."

We parted, me leaving on the Metro. The subway cost twenty cents—
cheap for a ride and an art museum. The older stations were tributes to
the sturdy proletariat building and defending a new country. Glittering
mosaics and marble statues depicted Russian men working jackhammers,
Russian women loading howitzers, Kazakh steelworkers, and Chukchi
ice folk in sealskin parkas. I caught myself thinking, *Yes, let us praise the
miner, the farmer, the construction worker.*

But I was just a tourist; the others on the subway platform had borne
the full weight of the communist experiment, good and bad. During my
first visit to Moscow five years earlier, its citizens had seemed downtrodden,
and my host Boris Ivanov agreed. We were shopping for salami and beer,
waiting in line, when he said, "The Russian people do not look healthy to
me."

Foolishly, I suggested that maybe it's their diet.

"Forget diet," said Boris. "It is their soul."

Now, for an update on the Russian soul, I headed off to visit Boris and
his wife, Natasha. The Metro car was plastered with ads for Mr. Video,
Dallas cigarettes, and Vinorum Cognac, a glass of which was being savored
by former cosmonaut Alex Leonov, the first person to walk in space, now
sitting by a glowing hearth in his official jumpsuit. I got off at a station of
aluminum and glass, far from the center of Moscow and the triumphal art
of Stalin.

Boris was waiting. He wore comfortably baggy brown corduroy pants
and a smile that revealed a rakish gap between his incisors. Outside the
station I asked a flower vendor for four mums, please. For Natasha.

"You can have three or five, but not four," said Boris. "Even numbers of
flowers are for funerals and cemeteries; odd numbers are for the living."

Boris and Natasha live in a shoddy nine-story apartment block amid the
handsome dilapidation of autumn, both the building and the birch leaves
beginning to fall. Along the street were Russian garages, the semiportable
steel boxes that gave the neighborhood the appeal of a rail yard. Inside their

apartment, things were much rosier. Wooden parquet floor, big double-pane windows, and lots of books, from Pushkin to geomorphology.

Boris and Natasha, unlike their namesakes in the *Rocky and Bullwinkle* cartoons, are professors. She studies economics. He studies the impact craters of meteors, a vocation that I pointed out is uniquely suited to a Russian: their country is the biggest target, 6,000 miles wide. After a feast to fatten the bicycle tourist, Boris turned on the Sony to watch the "most acid political commentary."

It was Mikhail Leontiev, a young wit with a ten-day beard. Leontiev said Russia's military was very hungry, and if the generals drove their tanks and Red Army into Moscow, the soldiers would simply head for the stores and stand in line for food.

It was a good sign, this criticism, and on the walk back to the Metro I reminded Boris of his comment five years ago, about the Russian soul. Had he changed his mind?

"The soul of the Russian, I think, is related directly to the state of our country's economy. When we have stability in our lives, when we have regular prices and food like the rest of Europe, then we will not be so Russian. We will be like everyone else."

I rumbled away in the subway, back to my room and my bicycle in a box. I unpacked it and screwed it together, and I patched my sleeping pad where it had been punctured by the teeth of the chainring.

There was little point in asking further information of my host, Laurent. He had never been south. And the tourists did not go there. The thickest guidebook devoted only 8 of its 1,200 pages to the thousand miles between Moscow and the Caspian. The trusty *World Book* provided only a map with the symbols for pig and sugar beet.

The Russian heartland was the Europe that nobody knew. Or the Europe nobody wanted to visit. Even the Muscovites knew little of the rural folk, and that was pure gossip: they're exceedingly hospitable; they're crude barbarians; they're frankly dangerous.

The rumors made me wonder. I had a wallet full of questionable rubles and a bike that was priceless, and I aimed to reach the Caspian before the season of insulated underwear.

CHAPTER 6

Moscow to the Caspian Sea
Special Training for Survival

ONE CYCLIST, riding without grace under thirty pounds of gear, cannot challenge the fleet of Volga taxis that rule the main avenues of Moscow. I retreat to the back streets with good results, pedaling past just-raked parks of pointy spruce and broad linden, where grannies in black talk to the pigeons. My bicycle frame seems made of rubber, but does not crack anew. The weld is holding, and so is the weather, a scatter of innocent clouds.

On the walkway of a stone bridge over the Moscow River, kids eating cotton candy point with sticky fingers to the dome of Christ Our Savior Cathedral. Three hundred feet high, it's a just-completed replica of the cathedral that once stood on the same site: Tsar Alexander's gilded thanks to God for the 1812 defeat of Napoleon. The tsar desired the grandest church in Russia, and so it was sheathed with granite, marble, and bronze. The interior dazzled with nearly a half-ton of gold leaf. Like Notre Dame and St. Peter's Basilica, the cathedral was an extravagance and a masterpiece. For two centuries the Russian Orthodox Church had bestowed its blessings on the tsars, and in return the tsars had made the church a branch of the government.

This relationship the communists would not forget. In 1931, the general secretary of the Central Committee of the Communist Party of the Soviet Union, Joseph Stalin, had the cathedral obliterated. He had in mind his own temple, the Palace of the Soviets. It was never built, but the important thing was erasing the past.

Now Christ Our Savior stands again, its astonishing cupola high above the slow barges on the river a reminder of the enormous wealth of the tsars, the grip of the church, and the terrible energy of Stalin.

Two miles south of the river, at Paveletski Station, I hop a commuter train south out of Moscow. I've no particular destination, only the goal of escaping the traffic of Europe's largest city. The farther from the city center, the bigger the apartment blocks, until they are twenty-two stories of concrete and ceramic tiles that have absorbed the local color—mud, ash, smoke. The newer blocks have primary color cues—blue, green, red—so you can tell one building from the other.

With my bicycle held tight against the wooden bench, we roll away from the moneyed heart of the city. Hawkers jump on and announce, *Good afternoon, would you like to buy some batteries?* There are no takers. Thirty minutes out of downtown and we're clicking past the smokeless smokestacks of idled factories. Past the airport and it's the Moscow equivalent of suburbs, the summer gardens with attendant cabins called dachas. Not far beyond are deep stands of narrow birch and reedy glades and genuine farmers, full-timers toting gargantuan cabbages and tending goats.

I get off at the next station and head for the first town en route, Stupino. In need of food to camp out, I ask a geezer closing a crooked wooden gate, Sir, is there a store?

He kicks mud clods off his rubber boots and cocks his head. "Store?" he says incredulously, sagging against the gate. He begins rambling in Russian, and I believe he's saying that he's had no money for the last ten days or months or years, and so there is in fact *No Store*. But another man walks up and injects, *Yes, there is a store. That way.*

After more directions from a healthy lad on a bike, I find a store evocatively named "Store." There's bread, yogurt, candy, milk in a foil box, Baltic Beer, and Saint Springs Water blessed by the archbishop. I buy one of everything except the beer (two), then pedal out of town. Occasionally a blimpish bus grinds past, sounding urgently in need of gear oil. The wooden houses are edged with wedding-cake trim on the eaves and around the windows, and the picket-fence yards contain long-handled water pumps and fancy chickens. The birds can be any color, but the houses are mostly blue or green, the hopeful hues of sky and garden. The sun settles in the west, swelling gloriously in a haze of wood smoke. Satisfied with my escape from the city, I roll down to the Oka River valley, where I find not the river but the perfect footpath leading into a thick woods.

Somewhere dogs are yelping and a train is hooting, but they won't keep me up tonight. The tent isn't needed. I'd forgotten to get fuel for my stove, but the warm beer goes well with the heavy bread. I light my little lantern and read *Imperium*, Ryszard Kapuscinski's supremely unfunny account of the Soviet Empire. "In my imagination, the USSR constituted a uniform, monolithic creation, in which everything was equally gray and gloomy, monotonous, and clichéd."

With one puff the lantern is out and the stars are on. Gray and gloomy Russia was my cliché, too, and my first visit to Moscow had only reinforced the image. But I'd never left the city until today's little taste of the village. With a thousand miles to come, I'm certain of nothing but this: chickens are never gloomy.

I WAKE IN THE MORNING with leaves on my face—maple, oak, and birch. Hundreds are pinwheeling down in the slow dawn of the far north. It's a pretty sight and a bad sign. A big wind is blowing, the advent of a storm.

Out on the open road the wind is much worse, but this hasn't kept people inside. They're emerging from the little glassed-in porches that serve as a boot and coat room on most every house, and, depending on their age and occupation, heading for their tractor or car, for the pump or the well or the garden, or simply to sit on a bench and watch the leaves fall. When I stop to get a better look at the Oka River, a big man with rheumy eyes ambles out of his garden and intercepts me.

Boris Zvezdakov, with his grimy canvas coat and bashed thumbnail, looks like the other folk I've seen hunched over rutabagas—who would have guessed that he speaks English and was a representative in the Russian parliament? A member of the Our Home Is Russia party, Boris served in the Duma, the lower house of the parliament, which is much like the

U.S. House of Representatives. There's an upper house, too, similar to the Senate, giving voice to less populated states like Siberia.

How, I ask, Boris, is the new parliament working? Lousy. "There is not democracy in Russia—there are too many . . . too many bad people." He draws his hammy hands into fists and throws a fake jab. "Like Chuck Norris."

The current parliament is not the first trial for democracy in Russia. The Duma was permitted by Tsar Nicholas after the 1905 revolution, to quell the striking workers. It was a ruse—the tsar ignored its authority, and fifty days later the army ran the county again. Over the following decade the Duma was resurrected and throttled again and again, until Lenin and the Bolsheviks, helped immeasurably by the Germans and World War I and a mad monk named Rasputin, took the reins during the 1917 revolution. Since 1991, the Duma and the parliament have hardly been more stable— the 1993 coup meant to eliminate Yeltsin was stopped not by debate but by tanks.

Boris asks my ultimate destination, frowns, and asks for my diction-ary. He looks up "prudent" and "to fear." I explain that in the event of trouble I plan to run away. Boris lets me go with the Russian farewell, *All beautiful*.

Bucking the blasted wind, dodging potatoes that have fallen from the trucks, I ride to a town with a neat line of fir trees along main street. It's Ozery, and although it's home to seven thousand, there is only one café, and it doesn't open until 3 PM. Near a ten-story apartment block is a row of metals sheds, the ubiquitous kiosks filled with booze and snacks. The café is at least useful as a windbreak, and while I sit and watch the wind rip branches off the trees, the door swings open a half hour early, just for me, courtesy of Svetya.

She serves me hot, sweet tea, then gets to work slicing potatoes. I sit, thankfully, at one of six white plastic tables, listening to the rare disco version of the Monkees' "I'm Not Your Steppin' Stone," under a poster for Lucky Strike "Made in USA" cigarettes. I'm the only customer for over an hour, yet Svetya waves me away when it's time to pay. Leaving town, I ask a man for directions to a gas station, and he flags down a friend with a gas can in his trunk, tops off my fuel bottle, and won't take a single ruble. This stirs memories of Arab hospitality, but with a Russian bonus: an actual bike path out of town and down to an Oka River ruffled with whitecaps. The one-lane floating bridge creaks and tugs at its moorings.

Beyond lie open and rolling fields of potatoes in harvest. The farm equipment looks vaguely military, drab green, stenciled with numbers—just as Frederick Engels imagined, in 1847, in *The Principles of Communism*: "Formation of industrial armies, especially for agriculture." Bent ladies with headscarves—babushkas—trail the equipment and snatch up potatoes the machines have missed.

Twenty miles on, I reach the town of Zarajsk as a lid of clouds slides over and locks out the sun. Three fishermen on the banks of the Osetr River keep casting. Up the road are a pair of teens in Reeboks and Nikes, and I use my best Russian to ask *Where hotel?* They blurt out in tandem, "We speak English!"

That's great—where did you learn?

Sergei and Sasha don't understand my question, and exhaust their complete store of English in twenty seconds: Hello, Good-bye, Rap, Rave and Rock, Aerosmith, and Welcome to Hell. They can count to ten. And they know the way to a dreamy old hotel.

The little lobby holds a cushy divan, a still-living potted palm, and a three-foot-tall Sputnik-looking ashtray built of intersecting steel loops. Varnished wood floors shine in the weak light. The receptionist cooks dinner for me, a half-kilo of a hybrid between meatballs and ravioli. While spooning up the steaming morsels in my room, I accidentally drop one onto the crotch of my pants and leave a stain that is likely to cause future embarrassment unless attended to. So I am pantless when the night falls and the windows rattle in the black wind. For the first time I know it's true: it gets terribly cold in Russia.

THE RAIN COMES HARD in the morning, stripping leaves from the ranks of linden outside the Zarajsk Hotel and pummeling my mini-umbrella. I find breakfast in an old state-run café with walls upholstered in padded vinyl. The tall windows, taped against drafts, admit enough light so the electricity is turned on only when needed to run the cash register. The lady running the joint is a middle-aged lump, friendly and loud, and when I ask for an egg she yells *No!* then adds what may be *Too late* or *All gone* or *Never.* Then she bats away my dictionary, hauls me into the kitchen, and points to a rack of steaming poppy seed rolls.

Yes, I say. With tea, please.

Not until I leave do I realize that the cash register is being used only as a strongbox; the bill itself is worked up by zestfully slapping the beads on an abacus—an unbreakable technology without a plug, and the sort of minimalism that naturally appeals to a bicyclist.

I head out through the double-door airlock, a must-have here at roughly the latitude of Canada's Hudson Bay. Out into the gloom and then back inside at every little sign that says, in the grunting Soviet style, merely *Store* or *Products*. Former Soviet premier Mikhail Gorbachev lamented that "Our rockets can find Halley's comet and reach Venus. But our fridges don't work."

It's true. In every food store there are cans arranged in the defunct glassed-in meat coolers. Most everything is behind glass or behind the counter or on an unreachable shelf. I must first pay a woman in a cashier's box like a tiny jail; she gives me a receipt that I trade to another woman for a box of tear-and-slurp tomato juice and a can of mystery fish.

But the food is good, particularly the raisin scones I buy from a bakery where the women are outfitted in snazzy pink uniforms. Actually, it's a bakery-candy-liquor store. Almost every store in this town of 15,000 sells booze, apparently the key to consistent sales and staying afloat in the new Russia.

When the rain slackens the street vendors reappear, hawking newspaper cones of sunflower seeds. I take my scone to the town square. A dapper young man in a houndstooth sport coat tells me that a tourist in Zarajsk is a strange thing. He wonders, "Are you a capitalist?"

Yes, but not a very good one.

"There is a shoe factory in Zarajsk, but little else."

His name is Misha, and his polished loafers are beaded with raindrops. Born and raised in Zarajsk, he now works in Moscow for the "Russian equivalent of the FBI." It was not his intention. He studied laser optics in Moscow but says, "There are no prospects in my specialty."

We're standing in wet leaves outside the Kremlin—a church and its attending buildings behind a massive wall with pointy corner turrets. A Kremlin is any old ecclesiastical fortress built to withstand the Mongols or whoever happened to be invading that century—the French, the Germans, and even the Poles have all had a shot at Russia, a history that has left the country understandably skittish about foreigners. The hero of Zarajsk, says Misha, is the homegrown Dmitri Pozharsky, who rose to the rank of Russian general in the fight against the Poles in 1612.

Misha's history lesson skips over the last century. I ask instead of the future. He looks up to where the sun should be and says, "This is a difficult question. I cannot answer. In America you can say, 'This is what I want to do tomorrow.' In Russia you can no longer plan for tomorrow, because you have no idea what tomorrow will bring."

In the eyes of the Russians, there's no telling. The old people, too, are perplexed—particularly by the sight of me strolling the town and taking pictures. For decades there were no tourists, and now there's a foreigner with a camera and a goofy grin. One lady huffs outside with skirt flapping and shoos me away, yelling what I imagine is *Get lost, mister—you're scaring my chickens!* Another invites me closer, to appreciate the flowers she's carefully tended. When it comes to gardens, Russian have a very good idea of what tomorrow will bring.

RUSSIA SOMETIMES seems a thoughtful place. Along the cornfield road to the city of Ryazan, the bus stops are prettied up with ornate steelwork. And in the city itself, the traffic signals are equipped with little beepers to tell the blind when they can cross the street, and a four-way red light that allows just the pedestrians to cross while the cars and electric trolley buses wait. When I find a hotel room and turn on the TV news, there's a sign language interpreter for the deaf.

But I've no explanation for the mirrored ceiling above my bed. Unperturbed, I sleep and head out the next day to find the dot on my map labeled "Ivan Pavlov." Ryazan was the home of the Nobel Prize–winning physiologist Ivan Pavlov, and I figure there must be a museum honoring his experiments on behavior in the early 1900s. Pavlov conditioned dogs to drool when they heard a bell that meant chow time, and I hope to see one of the drool-meters Pavlov used to measure what he deliciously coined "psychic secretions."

On the streets of the old city center, mothers on park benches knit while their pink-faced babes sleep in prams of wicker and chiffon. I ask one mother about Pavlov, and she shakes her head no and asks, *Where are you from?* United States. She nods, "Ahh . . . California. Santa Barbara."

It's the same with the other ladies: nobody knows of the museum. I substitute another goal: a look at the Oka River, a nine-hundred-mile-long tributary of the Volga. Yet when I walk down to the river valley I find only a trio of thirteen-year-old boys throwing rocks at an abandoned floating hotel anchored in a slough. I show them my postcards of Arizona, and they become very excited, yelling in concert, "Cactus! Cactus!" (It's the same word in Russian.)

"I want Oka," I say to the boys in perfect Russian. Follow us, they motion. Down a path overgrown with thistles and pigweed, across gullies spanned by springy wood footbridges, and past the water-stained remains of dis-carded newspapers and magazines. Alexi, Slava, and Andrei are interested in everything, particularly a scrap of paper that looks suspiciously familiar to me. They're reading aloud, *One million rubles. . . .* I look closer and sure enough, it's a mailbox ad from *Reader's Digest* announcing that *You May Have Already Won One Million Rubles!* Russians, too, throw these things away.

My charming hosts march on, kicking dead birds. At a fence with a sign reading *The Port Territory Is Closed*, the boys sneak a look inside. The gate is open and they see nobody in a uniform, so they urge me inside and down a flight of mossy stairs. And there it is: a sunken dredge in a swamp.

This is the Oka? They shrug, and in consolation offer me some of their sunflower seeds and take me to the Kremlin. Outside its walls men with scythes trim the weeds, a quiet slicing that doesn't distract from the en-trance tower and its sculpted angels honking on golden horns. Inside are several churches topped with dazzling onion domes.

Meanwhile, my guides are climbing over old bronze cannons and yelling "Boom!" They could care less about the biggest church, Ospienski, so I alone enter the massive square building surrounded by cedars. Inside it's dark and heavy with the sweet stink of incense, with a stupendous iconostasis: dozens of moody paintings depicting the hard times and miracles of Jesus.

As churches go, Ospienski is a tad depressing, but at least it survived the Bolsheviks. Ivan Pavlov would have been pleased. He risked his neck defending both science and the right to worship, although he was himself an agnostic. As for the Bolshevik social experiment, he sassily announced that "We live in a country where the state is everything and the man is nothing." If he had not been a renowned scientist in his seventies, Pavlov might not have survived his words.

I pay off my three guides with ice-cream cones. Back at my hotel, bartenders are pouring Johnny Walker into heavy tumblers. Women outnumber men, women with painted faces, waiting, waiting. . . .

That may explain the mirrored ceiling in my room—I believe I've rented a kind of fitness center. The TV weather lady—displaying gorgeous maps with smiling suns in the general direction of the Caspian—inspires me to check out and hop on my bike. At a kiosk I pick up some ramen noodles, yogurt, and beer. Back into the farmland I ride, repelling a frothing dog attack with a squirt from my water bottle and a couple of rocks. At sundown, still close to the city, I pick my forest camp with extra care, avoiding even a footpath. Solitude is my wish. The last thing I hear is the dew falling plip-plip from the toothed leaves of alder.

For a wake-up, I prefer birdsong to gunpowder, but the next morning it's a shotgun that eliminates the need for a rousing cup of coffee. Hunters, I guess, out in the sunflower fields, and there's little to do except shake the dew off my bag and slice up a banana into a half-kilo of *The Taste of Sunny Fruits* yogurt. My spoon makes it only halfway to my mouth before I hear a rustling in the brush. It's an old couple in rubber boots and canvas coats slinking through the forest, carrying pails and poking with sticks under leaves. Mushroom hunters. They nearly walk through my camp, yet scarcely glance at me while they forage with a determination that means winter's coming.

Yet today is warm and blowsy, the autumn weather the Russians call Woman's Summer. I share the road with other bicyclists and tractors towing disk plows and huge wagons full of cow manure that slops over, giving me an added challenge. I'm acclimated to the load and can steer with the slightest dip of my shoulders. After the first awkward days of the tour, the machine and I are mates again. Like the wife who finishes her husband's sentences, my bike seemingly anticipates my intentions.

Although I'm passing farm towns, where the yards of the old homes are endlessly mowed by a tethered cow or a goat, there are also 1970s housing blocks. During that decade S. V. Shevtsova wrote in *World Magazine* that "Soviet construction is well on the road to solving the housing problem— something never before attempted by any society or country. It is acquiring increasing know-how on the problem faced by all mass production countries—that of combining beauty and utility."

Well, maybe utility. The farmhouses slump in a kind of dying glory, but the late-Soviet-era apartments were ugly from the get-go. Concrete joints are sloppily patched, rebar is poking from the landings, and huge exposed heating pipes with tattered insulation run down the streets. An administrative building is topped by a loud sign urging the residents to *March On!*

But just down the road, when I stop to talk to a pair of girls selling potatoes from a roadside bucket, I get a chance to visit one of the apartments. I need water, and the girls' mother invites me into their place. It's a nicely padded pad. Rugs on the walls, gas stove, color TV, and, most important, a bathroom with hot water. The pipes that are such an eyesore are actually the main attraction of Soviet apartments—there's a central heating plant in every sizable town and city, and all winter long it provides abundant hot water.

Judging from the bright paint and flowers in front of the crooked old homes with lace curtains in the windows, their owners are proud to stay put. They are brave. I admit that after a few Russian winters of chopping wood, bringing water in from the well, and stomping through the snow to the outhouse I, too, might accept a warm apartment, even if I did see

March On! from my window. Besides, when I stop at a nearby store I see that new propaganda has replaced the old. It's a huge poster for Stimorol Original Chewing Gum, showing devastatingly handsome men and their lithesome playthings chewing Stimorol on palm beaches.

Blessed by a tailwind, I ride sixty miles through flattish farmland and isolated clumps of forest, reaching the town of Ryazhsk well before sundown. It looks good, small and quiet, and I find a hotel equipped with the essential desk and electricity for my electronics. There's no hot water, but with the thin mattress and thick silence it's not so different from camping— there's nobody but me in the hotel. I go for a walk in the last warm slants of sunlight, past the flowers kept in the square beneath a larger-than-life aluminum statue of Lenin. Kids use the heaps of raked leaves to bury their Barbie dolls. Barbie rests in peace for just a moment, then bursts out for a change of wardrobe.

Dinner is at the sole café/bar, where I attract a pair of eighteen-year-olds, Arthur and Sergei. They want to try my pipe tobacco. Without the pipe. They roll it into big clumsy tubes of newspaper, then happily suck as the embers fall onto the table. In return for my gift, they twice shoo off undesirables who desire my company. "Drunks," says Sergei. "Prostitute," says Arthur as they walk me back to my hotel. "Bums," says Sergei as we pass in the park what appear to be some gypsy women in the shadow of Lenin. "Ryazhsk not so good," they say in concert, echoing the lament of small-town teens around the world. "Nothing to do. Only Mafia has money."

Russians love this word *Mafia*, which seems to mean any sort of corruption, with possibly violent consequences if you resist. I catch the scent of Mafia the next day, while riding to Michurinsk. I pass a dozen little towns where people are shoveling manure into their home gardens and selling mushrooms from baby buggies. But when I reach one named after the thirteenth-century warrior-saint Alexander Nevsky, I see that something is up. It reminds me of a certain place in Mexico, a town called Cosala, which seems richer than it should be. Likewise, Alexander Nevsky is bedecked in too many flowers. But it's the cops driving BMWs that really make me wonder.

On the other hand, the city of Michurinsk isn't faring so well. Three hundred miles south of Moscow, home to 130,000, it looks as if it has been hit by a bomb that killed only cars. I've been in auto-free cities before, but only where the people ride burros. Michurinsk seems a city in hibernation. I ask a man in the street for directions to a hotel, and to my surprise he replies in English. After a few questions about my tour, he tells me with hesitant pride that he's invented a way to fix a flat bike tire with neither tools nor patches. This I truly want to know, but he excuses himself after delivering me to the hotel.

"I'll tell you tomorrow morning," he says.

HE'S WAITING FOR ME in the hotel café, a quiet place with fresh flowers in hacked-off soda bottles. Ryndiouk Konstantin. I like him straight away— he not only recognizes a genuine cactus in my Arizona postcard, but he also knows the Latin name of the saguaro. Over tea and hard-boiled eggs, this compact blond Russian of thirty-five tells me that he is not from Michurinsk, but from Dushanbe, Tajikistan.

Tajikistan borders Afghanistan and China. It is gorgeous country if you like arid valleys in the shadow of ice mountains. Along with much of central Asia, it was conquered by the tsarist armies in the nineteenth century during the Great Game, a race against the British pushing north from India. By the 1880s the Russian Empire had swelled to three times the size of the United States. The Bolsheviks divvied it up in 1924 into the former Soviet—but now independent—republics of Uzbekistan, Turkmenistan, Kazakhstan, Kyrgyzstan, and Tajikistan. All are inhabited by Turkic-speaking peoples except for the Tajiks, whose roots lie closer to those of the Afghans and Persians. All made the 1990s move to independence without violence. Except the Tajiks.

"It is not a problem with the Tajik people," Ryndiouk insists. "I had many Tajik friends. It was the nationalists. They made a slogan: *Asia for Asians—Out with the Russians*. The riots began in February of 1992. It was a horrible time. Everywhere there was automatic gunfire, tanks, and burning buildings. Many people were killed, and soon my mother and sister flee to the only place Russia will allow them to resettle. Here—Michurinsk."

Ryndiouk stayed on with his tottering old man. He worked for an airplane leasing company, and once spent forty days in Nepal. He's intensely proud of this brief period—a regular, respectable job that required English, which he taught himself by listening to the BBC and the Voice of America. He still has the documents identifying him as an emissary of the company, and today carefully opens a little manila folder to reveal a few typed pages that survived, with charred edges, the riots that by 1997 had killed 60,000. Ryndiouk lost everything in the fires except these papers and his father.

"I had no money. No passport, no extra clothes. Only a backpack. I had to leave my father. The only Russians in Dushanbe now are those too old and weak to leave.

"I walked at night—it was dangerous during the day. I knew I had to cross two mountain *perevals*—what is this word in English? Yes, pass. Two passes. Forty kilometers each day for six days. Then I was rescued by an Uzbek that fed me and gave me a ride to the train to Tashkent.

"After I arrive in Michurinsk, I have my mother and sister and nothing else. No friends, no job. What do I do?"

What to do in Michurinsk? I know nothing of the economic statistics of this city, but only fifteen people are staying at its sole hotel. There are 150 rooms, and the place seems a vast dark catacomb. With a consequently low workload, the desk clerk, porter, and maid were all quick last night to find a place to store my bike, help me with my bags, and, by way of apology for the lack of hot water, give me the key to the only suite that has an electric in-line water heater. It took them at least ten minutes with the instruction booklet to make the heater work, but their efforts put a dent in the Soviet reputation for dour service.

Likewise, when I take a stroll with Ryndiouk to the bookstore, business is slim and we're helped immediately to an excellent map of the region. "Ten years ago," says Ryndiouk, "you could not buy a map like this. It was a military secret."

And the military did not trust their own citizens, who might let a map slip into enemy hands. There could hardly be a better measure of paranoia than a Soviet-era map: a chart of lies, with distorted distances and misplaced towns. Weather maps, too, were fictions, for even the temperature was a military secret.

We're the only customers at the Flamingo Café, where we lunch on goulash and potatoes while listening to the Beatles' "Yesterday." The meal is a treat for Ryndiouk—in four years he's never visited a Michurinsk café. I know why, and although it is perhaps cruel I bring up the future.

"You see that four years ago I work for the airline, leasing planes. Three years ago, I was a teacher in Michurinsk, for fifteen dollars a month. Now I sell herbs. Who knows what work I'll have next year? I live in today."

When it's time to part ways he says, "Wait—I forgot to explain my tire repair." With pen and paper he shows me how you drill an extra valve hole in your rim, then install two tubes within one tire. If the outside tube goes flat, you pull out the thorn or glass, inflate the inside tube and ride on. He's really a very clever man.

Back in the hulking cinder-block hotel, I return to my writing. When I need to send off a story to Discovery, I can't get a bearing on the satellite from my room. I end up in a stairwell with the phone balanced in a window opened to the night sky. It's 1 AM, and I fear the consequences if the night watchman happens upon me in this compromising position: huddled in the dark, face lit by the computer screen, tapping in a password to access the satellite phone.

Nobody comes. Until the next morning. I suspect trouble when the hotel clerk asks for my passport and visa. "What are you doing here?" Journalist. Bicycle tourist. She returns my documents and says, "Wait in the café."

Only fifteen minutes later they show up. A young woman and a young man, smartly dressed, she in a plaid skirt and silk blouse, he in a black suit and sporting a little walkie-talkie. They flip open wallets to reveal badges that identify them, I suppose, as official officials. "Visa, please."

In a holdover from the Soviet era, when there were only a handful of "open" cities, the visa allots very little space to the trip itinerary. I'm passing through dozens of towns and couldn't possibly list them all. The man scans the little blue visa and says, "No Michurinsk." The woman says, "Problem."

Please wait, I say—and I trot off to fetch from my room my emergency documents. I return with the papers and fan them out across the table, as if I were revealing a four-of-a-kind. They can't beat the hologram seal of the Russian Consulate, the wink of very official permission. They can scarcely believe it, but it's true—the man works for an American company, yet he's riding a bicycle! They set me free.

I walk through the city, under the shadows of slow clouds, and find Lenin standing above the park. In a former movie theater turned teen disco, a big mural features the Soviet symbols of progress—the dove of peace, the man of industry, the woman carrying a sheaf of wheat, the scientist holding in his palm a whirl of electrons, and the cosmonauts of the future. In the city museum there is an entire hall devoted to Ivan Michurin, the plant breeder whose name the city adopted in 1932, despite its having been known as Kozlov for four centuries.

Born in 1855, Michurin was a man of little education but considerable skill in crossbreeding fruit trees to survive the Russian winters. He was also a crank who rejected Mendelian genetics—the basis of inheritance—as well as the concept that competition provides an advantage to some individuals and not others.

Michurin should have become a footnote in Soviet history. But the notion that an organism's destiny was a matter of environment, not heritage, was adopted by a Bolshevik named Trofim Lysenko as a uniquely communist approach to agriculture. History, finally, was irrelevant. And without competition, there would be no "class struggle."

Lysenko made his career by eliminating all methods but the Michurin method. This was during Stalin's reign, so "eliminating" meant just that—scientists who begged to differ were sent packing to Siberia, or shot dead for "trying to create a condition of famine in the country." The science of genetics was dead until Stalin himself was dead.

Russian science eventually recovered, but like an old sailor tattooed with the name of a woman who left him long ago, the land does not forget. When I pedal back into the countryside, I pass subtle reminders of Lysenko's campaign against science. It's bright and breezy, with scudding cumulus, and I'm riding by a tree plantation. The pines are tall but skinny as flagpoles, because they're planted too close together and are hungry for light. It was Michurin's idea—he called it cluster planting. Lysenko, with Stalin's blessing, took Michurin's doctrine and in 1949 devised "The Great Plan for the Transformation of Nature." The trees were supposed to cooperate, with most seedlings sacrificing themselves for the good of the species, allowing a few to grow thick and strong.

Millions of rubles and hours were dedicated to the creation of vast forests. But trees knew nothing of class struggle. The Great Plan was a great flop because each tree looked out for itself—naturally. In the end it was not ideology but the forbidden genetics that controlled the urge to grow and reproduce.

Such urges are not unique to plants. At day's end, after reaching the city of Tambov and finding a hotel, I head out for an evening stroll. Just outside the entrance is a small park casually occupied by women either chunky and vivacious in an omnivorous way, or very skinny and even more plainly hungry. One of the latter quickly recognizes me as a solitary male. She sidles up and asks something in Russian. I don't understand.

"You give me cigarette?" she says in English. She's no more than twenty. "Where are you staying?"

I gesture to the hotel.

"This is not a good hotel."

That is true—but it is the only hotel.

"Let us go sit on that bench over there."

I look over *there*, to a lonely park bench in the shadows, and I get the willies imagining thugs dropping out of the trees. Or, less painful but more embarrassing, she'll propose something I must refuse.

I like light, I say. We can sit here, on this bench.

"It is dirty here." But still she sits. She smiles. Her lipstick has left red slashes on her gold tooth, like a vampire. "You must be cold in that shirt."

No, I feel just fine, thank you. And I have other shirts, very warm shirts, in my room.

She runs her nails through the ruff of her coat and says, "I have fur of cat. Not house cat. Forest cat." She purrs and drops her chin into the fur, up to her lips. "It feels good."

Umm . . . I bet it does. But I really must be going. I'm a bicycle tourist, and I need to sleep.

"I understand. Good night."

I like to think it was the bike that saved me.

ON A HAT-AND-GLOVES MORNING a day south of Tambov, I pedal an empty blacktop past road signs that ask the driver to *Look out for pedestrians at bus stops* and *Please don't light the forest on fire with your cigarettes.* Less common are signs that say where the road goes, so I'm lucky to have the fine map from Michurinsk, and without trouble I reach the town of Znamenka. The sole store is decorated with the familiar posters for Stimorol Original Chewing Gum. I love its classic appeal: it's what adventurers chew in the jungle, in rapids, on sailboats.

I opt for the semi-famous "Tula" gingerbread. Just one sweet cake has calories enough for at least ten miles of pedaling. Unfortunately, I've fifty miles of open farmland to the next store. I pass a sugar-beet factory the size of a steel mill and a half-dozen villages, but no stores—only tilted houses with peeling paint, and people leading bulge-eyed cows into barns or chopping wood with the measured determination of a marathoner.

I break open my emergency rations of Delta airline peanuts and cookies. Still hungry, I stop at a field of dried and bent sunflowers. The seeds are good, shell and all, but not as easy to get at as I'd hoped. A living sunflower beckons your touch, but a withered sunflower is as friendly as a cactus, with each seed topped by a prickle.

This is the province of Tambov, where people know hunger. Starvation, actually, following a drought in 1920–21. America and western Europe were aware of the famine, but as H. G. Wells wrote in his *Outline of History,* "None of the tolerance that had been shown to the almost equally incapable and disastrous regime of the Tsar was shown to the Marxist adventurers." At the time, the only crime of the Bolsheviks against the West was their utter rejection of capitalism, but that was enough. While Russia starved, the West acted slowly or not at all, with fingers crossed.

Lenin, the earnest revolutionary who dreamed of a just society, had in 1918 declared "war communism," a policy that entitled the Bolsheviks to snatch a portion of every peasant's harvest for the cities. After the drought reduced the people of Tambov to hunting acorns, the Red Army unwisely persisted in taking the acorns.

Alexander Antonov, himself a revolutionary who'd fought the tsar, massed an army of tens of thousands of famished locals into the "Green

Army" representing the Union of Working Peasants. The Bolsheviks, hinting at the lethal bureaucracy to come, responded with the "Plenipotentiary Commission of the All-Russian Central Executive Committee of the Bolshevik party for liquidation of banditry in the Tambov Gubernia." The Red Army cut the Green Army down, with artillery, armored rail cars, and, most horribly, poison gas.

My hunger is just a little thing, a tightness as I ride past fields of black clods bordered with yarrow and blue asters. I can see the town of Uvarovo long before I reach it, a tight cluster on a low mesa dropping on one side to the Vorona River. Along the shore, willows toss in the wind.

In the oldest part of town (Uvarovo dates back to 1699) is the most decrepit hotel yet, a sagging shotgun cabin of seven rooms. After I ring the buzzer and the woman recovers from her surprise, she leads me to the "administration." The floor is freshly painted, and sunlight shines through lace curtains onto a vase of daisies. Her name is Tanya, and she somewhat gravely explains that the room will be twenty rubles a night—between one and two dollars.

Of course there's no hot water. There's not even water. Tanya must fetch it in a bucket. But it's only fifty feet to the outhouse, and meanwhile Tanya warms up a couple of gallons of water with a hotplate so I can sponge myself off. She cooks my ramen noodles, too. Brings me a table lamp, while rambling softly in Russian. Tonight there's no place I'd rather be.

With my east-facing room I expect an early rousing by the sun, but the next morning it's suspiciously dark. Pull open the curtain: rain is thrashing the streets. Feel the glass: it's freezing.

Tanya asks me to fill out the usual registration form. What, I ask Tanya, is the name of this place? Hotel, she says. What day is it? she asks. I don't understand. She points to a calendar, I point to the day, and she fills out half of the form before giving a little shrug that means, What's the difference? She points to my birth date and indicates that she was born the same year. We grew up with the same fears, which happen to be detailed in the only official poster in this hotel. It's instructions on what to do in the event of a nuclear war. Duck and cover, except in the Russian version you end up in a cellar with a barrel full of potatoes.

When the rain gives up I leave Tanya with an Arizona postcard and a little fanny pack I brought for just this purpose. It's not her birthday, but it's close enough. Like me, she's a Sputnik baby, 1957. Unlike me, she's staying put in Uvarovo. I ask her how far it is to the next town, Borisoglebsk. But she's never been there, and doesn't know the way.

TWO MILES OUT from Tanya's hotel is a sign no larger than a loaf of bread. Café, it says—and an arrow points to what looks like a prefab warehouse but is immensely attractive when it's 40 degrees outside. It's dark and quiet, and for my pleasure the owner hits both the light and the music. I have a tomato salad and tea while listening to the disco hit "I Need a Superhero Lover." After my eyes adjust to the 25-watt bulb, I see that the walls are covered with Formica and shower curtains—all the easier, I imagine, to hose off after a boisterous wingding.

When I'm back on my bike and riding all day through one-cow towns where everything is so tired that the power lines are actually holding up the utility poles—well, then it's easy to get the impression that there's no reason for celebration in Russia. But people aren't just sitting around, waiting for a miracle. In a town not quite as big as its name, Novonikolai-nevski, I find the only café occupied by a party. I sit outside and bide my time, calculating that if any mother spies this skinny bicyclist . . .

Bingo. *Come inside and eat all this extra food! It's a wedding party!*

Actually, it's the wedding rehearsal dinner, but my Russian is so lousy I don't understand. So I'm surprised when, the next morning, the bride's uncle finds me—in the only hotel in town—and escorts me back to the café and the big event. Newlyweds Ina and Volodya are young and blond and happy. The bride's mother, Lila, and her grandmother, the babushka, get to work feeding me while the others pass around a bottle of champagne for everyone to autograph. I'm soon surrounded by slabs of roast beef, eggplant topped with chives and red peppers, garlic bread and carrot salad and grilled fish and pickled watermelon. And that's only the plates I can reach.

A toast is made, and the vodka vanishes. An accordion player starts squeezing some life out of his instrument. Everyone else is fancied up in suits or dresses; he, true to the international dress code of accordion players, appears to be from a neighboring planet. But he can make music. A woman sings, the old folk sigh, and the teens yawn. The tempo picks up as the bride and groom cut their cake and hand out slices in exchange for dropping some rubles into a hat. Another toast, and a woman starts dancing on a chair. I'm asked to make a toast. To the new wife and the new . . . but nobody hears the part about the groom. The party is taking off.

My glass is refilled by Sasha, a doctor with the hands of a serious gardener. He speaks enough English to make a toast, "America and Russia—friends!" Obviously, I have to drink.

Natasha is one of the women who speak to me from a distance never greater than six inches. Her face is flushed and her eyes are wide, but she's just friendly. "Please," she asks, "please for the newlyweds . . . " She flips through the pages of my dictionary and finds, to my horror, the word *sing*. "Please sing for the new man and new wife."

I'm no singer, but after a few toasts I'm ready for the "Star Spangled Banner." Yet at the moment the only song that comes to mind is "I Need a Superhero Lover." The lyrics are within my grasp ("I need a superhero lover, super lover, super lover!"), but the audience reaction could be less than favorable.

Natasha is pleading "Sing, sing!" when the babushka decides that it's her duty to feed me. She butts in to say, *Sing? He needs to eat!* And not only does she set down another plate of veal cutlets, she actually forks one up and stuffs it into my mouth. I am so grateful. Natasha gives up and joins the dancing.

Ten minutes later, while the babushka is delicately sucking the meat off a chicken skeleton, I'm yanked out of my chair to join a dance that is just four women and me. They hold their hands high and snake them around like gypsies, they stomp their feet, they sing. When the song ends they explain it to me in English. "No love! Yes love! The story of life!"

The accordion gives out. The tape deck is commandeered by a young man in black, and the speakers jump with Disco Collection #1. The young will forget our parents' songs, and everything else will change, too.

Except weddings. No love, yes love, the story of life.

WHEN THE WORLD is wrapped in what looks like ice fog, it's hard to leave the great hot feast of a Russian wedding and pedal on. But I must reach the Caspian sooner or later. Probably later—I'm addled by too many toasts to the newlyweds, and can't find the little road out of town. It's shown on the map as a thin gray line, a reflection of the mapmaker's doubt that the road exists.

So I take the train, the slow and rocking local to the next town, which the map shows connected to a thick yellow line I hope is an actual road. The town is Frovolo, and it's the train conductor's hometown. He promises that the hotel is only a hundred meters from the train station. He's right—and he knows exactly where to find me the next morning.

Andrei wants me to come to meet his family. I want to take advantage of a sudden increase in temperature and ride on to the town of Log. Andrei wins, and in his 1994 Lada, which looks like a 1974 Datsun, he takes me to his home.

Andrei's wife, Irana, and her sister Natasha are young and supple and earthy in the Russian female way, with gold teeth and hair dyed in colors I'd believed were limited to minerals, like oxidized copper and gypsum crystals. The house was built in 1940 of what appears to be corrugated roofing. There's no plumbing. Nothing fancy, says Andrei, but it's rent-free: the house belongs to his grandmother, a nameless babushka who seems to live in the kitchen outbuilding.

The living room is intensely packed with oriental wall rugs and big black puffy armchairs and the usual color TV and VCR. Andrei pulls out a stack of photographs eight inches high, and I settle in for pictures of his red-carnation wedding, pictures of toddlers in sailor suits, pictures of pure white people on a Black Sea beach, and pictures of people buried alive in fur hats and thick coats, balanced atop snow drifts. I ask, Siberia? No—here, Frovolo.

Time to head south, but then Babushka silently delivers pickled mushrooms, dumplings, sour cream, and crab salad. Presumably she's taking very small steps in her shapeless house dress reaching to the floor, but the slow gliding effect is of an electric grandma on hidden wheels.

A feast wouldn't be complete without a toast or two, maybe three. Then back to the photo archive—still three inches to go. There are so many baby pictures that my heart flies back to my family in Tucson, and when my eyes begin to cloud I must excuse myself—how can I explain that I miss my son? But they understand—Andrei has two children in school. When it's time to go, he says, "Good-bye—and please take this for your son."

It's a foot-high stuffed pink bunny, wearing a polka-dot bow tie. Very nice, I say, but where do I put it? When I ride off in the direction of Log, the pink bunny is standing tall on my sleeping bag.

I'm out of the fertile black earth country and happy to be riding through a lumpy sandy land, with hunches of scrub oak on the rises, and poplar tracing the watercourses. The wind, a surprisingly warm wind out of the southeast, swells until it overwhelms. In one hour I pedal three and a half miles, which must be a flatland low-speed record. I stop, exhausted, on the shoulder near a dump, and stand amid a scatter of broken bottles. A bus passes and thirty heads turn in spontaneous synchrony, staring.

Yesterday I was merely odd; today, with the big pink rabbit on my tail, the Russians assume I'm nuts. I desperately want to ride on, past melon fields and goat herders—the enticing signs of aridity—but I admit defeat and retreat to the Hotel Frovolo. I ride the same three and a half miles in only nine minutes, with hardly a turn of my pedals.

I've grown surprisingly fond of this cold-water hotel that falls dark after the tea pot blows a fuse. I hear nothing but the radio in the beauty parlor next door, tuned to a smoky lilting sax carried on the wind.

It blows through the night and into the morn. Anxious to beat the winter, I pedal out of town, around roadkilled hedgehogs, and into a dust storm. Hungry for a shish kebab, I turn too quickly into a roadside eatery and fail to spot a slick of sheep fat. The crash leaves the uncaring rabbit unscathed, but the wind will not stop and I end up on the train, humbled, alongside quiet men with sand under their nails and sacks of melon between their feet, and schoolgirls clutching Spice Girl notebooks. We all rumble and nod into Volgograd, a city reduced to rubble by one of the most terrible battles of WWII.

Volgograd was reimagined and rebuilt by Stalin's team of Soviet planners. This does not sound like the recipe for a pleasurable place, but I'm learning, and a change of heart comes easy for a man who hasn't had a shower in four days. Freshly scrubbed after a night at the frankly regal Intourist Hotel, I stroll the esplanade that embraces the immense sweep of the Volga River with a chain of linear parks. Kids flit by on in-line skates, sober adults walk drooling basset hounds, and the semisober sit at sidewalk cafés with big mugs of beer. The 1950s housing and shops, built of stone blocks or a reasonable facsimile, are the next step in from the river, and the factories and busy roads are set well back. I really could not have picked a better place for my computer to break down.

It's only four keys that refuse to work, but I'd never realized the importance of O and L until I need them. (The semicolon and dash I can do without.) In a mild panic I visit the American Business Center. They summon computer repairman Alex Shopochkin to my rescue. I tell him that if he fixes the computer I will put him in my story and a hundred billion people will know of his technical savvy. He replies, "And if I can't fix it, I think I will still be in the story." This guy is smart—he's certain to fix it.

Meanwhile, the staff of the Center, which helps American companies set up shop in Russia, delivers glum news on the economic scene.

"After the crisis hit," says Karina Ray, "the Pall Mall minivans disappeared. They would park on the street and open up the doors and blast music out the back. They had black lights inside the vans—and even underneath. They'd attract attention, and the Pall Mall girls would hand out cigarettes. They target young men, and light the cigarettes for them."

Cigarettes are the first taste of America for many Russians. The apartment blocks at the edge of Volgograd feature ten-story-tall Marlboro men, and when I visit the central market I find an entire aisle lined with towers of cigarette cartons. "Cossack" smokes are only 15 cents a pack, yet American brands are selling briskly at $1.60.

It's the busiest market I've seen since Moscow. Now I know where Russian women buy Blondex hair color, where girls get the picture pins of Leonardo DiCaprio, and where men pick up *Speed*, a tabloid reputed to promote safe sex but whose current cover shows a defenseless man in a steam bath being assaulted by three lasses armed with tiny towels and loofahs.

The meat market is slice and whop and long steel tables laid out with cows reduced to a leg, a head with a blank eye, a pair of bull balls. Less disturbing is the domain of the sunflower seed vendors—just follow the sparrows to the mounds of seeds that apparently induce calm not only for the chewers but also for the sellers, who recline in various states of repose on big burlap sacks. Everyone else is busy selling, a scene with the promise of becoming what Maurice Hindus saw here in 1923, when the market "teemed with caravans of carts, drawn by ox, horse or camel. . . . NEP had struck its stride, and trade was booming in the bazaars and shops."

The NEP was Lenin's New Economic Policy. It was capitalism. Lenin called it a "strategic retreat"—putting communism on hold for five years.

It was a wily move, and Joseph Stalin was just as effective as his predecessor. Volgograd was once called Stalingrad, after the man who, like Lenin, knew when to back down to achieve a larger goal. Stalin allowed the temporary resurgence of the church during WWII, if only because the people are more willing to die for their country if they believe heaven awaits. Russia's dreadful losses during the war are remembered in the monumental statues of Volgograd—a bare-chested man heaving a hand grenade seems to stand on every other street corner. The Battle of Stalingrad was the fulcrum of the war—the Germans lost over 300,000 men, and the momentum shifted to the Russians.

To walk through Volgograd today is to confront the paradox of Soviet communism—how things got better and worse at the same time. Stalin exterminated millions by starvation and gulags, and for the survivors Stalin built the lovely Intourist Hotel and the comfortable city of Volgograd.

Even Volgograd's old state cafeterias are the nicest I've seen, with one featuring perhaps the world's only aluminum bas-relief of dumplings. They look like the plump clouds that slide over the city at dusk. There's a silken breeze off the Volga, and the riverside parks fill with families and lovers and drunks. Teen girls in clunky black shoes walk arm in arm past the most stirring Battle of Stalingrad monument, the blasted shell of a flour mill.

But tonight it is easy to forget the war. Especially if you're staying at the Intourist, the first place outside Moscow where I've encountered actual tourists. Not many. In the lobby café there is a fleshy German man, ruddy with booze. On his knee sits a woman, a slinky giggler half his age. After I take a seat he points to the café's matron and says without prompting, "This lady can get you anything you desire in Volgograd."

He's repulsive, but it's true that the Russians seem extra-considerate of wandering men. It's 10 PM when the Welcome Wagon rings me in my room. This mystifies me. It's a big hotel, and there are a lot of empty rooms. How, I ask the caller, how did you know that I was in this room?

"I did not," she says. "I call all the room numbers. Are you sure you do not want a sleeping woman tonight?"

I'm sure. I have a wife.

"And I have a husband. But I understand. You are good husband. Good night."

The nicest prostitutes! I like feeling wanted, but I have a late-night appointment with the computer fix-it man, Alex Shopochkin. He delivers my laptop in perfect order, but also delivers the less happy news of his current employment. His job as a computer specialist at the Imperial Bank vanished with the ruble's crash. The bank is history, too. He's fed up with Russia. "I want to emigrate," he confides. "Russia is no place for people. History, yes, politics, yes—but it is no good for people."

Not everyone agrees. In the lobby café for breakfast, I meet the buoyant Alex Limanov. He likes what he calls the "Stalin baroque" architecture of the city, yet doesn't mind covering it with ads for his Danish employer, Stimorol Chewing Gum. "We do not sell just chewing gum," says Alex. "We sell fun. Our ads show the jungles, the ocean, the beach—Stimorol *is* adventure. Teenagers like it very much."

But, I ask, who's going to buy chewing gum if Russia runs out of money? "Russians, as you know," says Alex, "have special training to survive. I would not say I'm happy about this crisis. I'm just saying we have to find a way out, to find the right tool to fix the Russian economy."

It's easy to be optimistic in the dining room of the Intourist, with crisp linen and Turkish coffee under enormous hanging brass lamps. But Alex has fears, too.

"Corruption is very flexible. In an authoritarian regime there will still be corruption, because *nobody will have to explain.* In an open government, there's less opportunity for corruption."

Back at the American Business Center, deputy director Galina Tokareva is evasive when I ask about corruption. She scolds the national banks that are "involved in securities gambling rather than in direct investment." She dismisses Russia's capital: "Moscow is a parasite. It sucks the life out of the provinces." But when I ask for her vision of the future she says flatly, "No comment."

Not every Russian is a pessimist, I say—and I cite Mr. Stimorol Chewing Gum. Galina comes back with "A pessimist is a well-informed optimist." And then she offers a joke that she claims is very popular among Russians but will probably make no sense to me.

"A hedgehog is taking a walk in the forest when it meets a frog. It's just sitting there in the middle of the path. The hedgehog says, 'You're so *ugly*, so *slimy*, so *green*. How can you go on with your life?' 'Never mind,' says the frog, 'I am not feeling well. Usually I am white and fluffy.'"

White and fluffy Russia will have to wait a bit longer. Galina's joke reflects the sentiments of the poet Yevgeny Yevtushenko: "To give time for new kinds of political leaders to be born in Russia, ones not chained to feudalism at birth, we will have to wander long in the wilderness, and resist the temptation of hoping for some sort of homegrown Moses to lead us to the Promised Land. We received freedom as a desert, and we must learn to plant trees in it."

Volgograd's desert is more than metaphor—it rains only about eleven inches a year. Yet on the morning I leave, the sky is clotted with clouds like steel wool. I wrap my gear in plastic bags, but the pink bunny—which I'm now resigned to carry all the way to the Caspian—will just have to face the elements, perched atop my sleeping bag.

Only a hundred feet from my hotel I ride past a wedding party taking the customary photos of the bride and groom under the chestnut trees in Fallen Heroes Square. It's easy to spot their sedan with a pair of giant wedding rings atop the roof, and it's likewise easy to spot a bicyclist with a stuffed rabbit. Within twenty seconds the party has thrust a shot of vodka into my hands. To the newlyweds! I drink and sputter, and they howl and give me the antidote, a slice of bread and salami. Then someone gets an idea: *Look! A present for the bride! A pink bunny!*

A minute later I ride away, rabbit-free, to take the ferry across the Volga. The temperature is dropping fast, drawing puffs of vapor from every soul. The river is a dull reflection of the muddled sky, but the long and thin sand islands are fringed with autumn cottonwood gilded like church icons. The ferry is packed with commuters, a literate group that hardly looks up from their novels and newspapers.

On the far shore I pick up two apples from a vendor who refuses my money. It's not the first time, but it's the first time the gift is from a Kazak. The Caspian Sea is not only the lowest point in Europe but also its frontier. The rim of Asia is just over the horizon.

I DON'T REALIZE how cold it is until I stop at the hotel in Leninsk and discover that my right foot is numb. When the receptionist sees me hobbling, she invites me behind the desk to warm myself with her little electric heater. She's a sweetheart, and for all I know she lives here, cooking on a hot plate and spending her hours in the lobby with the buzzing TV and the philodendrons and palms. It is a strange thing to come out of the gloomy blue chill and find these tropical plants, but the hotel keepers like defying the odds.

It's possible, too, that the plants are in a sort of suspended animation, neither dead nor alive. A little Russian hotel is very tranquil, and it's easy to imagine falling into such a state. I no longer bother to ask if there's hot water. I use my stove to heat up a pint for a bandanna bath, then head out to find dinner.

As usual, there's a kiosk cluster near the statue of Lenin. They all carry ramen noodles and Turkish candies and Stewardess cigarettes. For young men coping with a growth spurt, there are luxuries like nail clippers and naked-lady playing cards. An old woman dodders up to the kiosk and shows me a comic-book tract from the Jehovah's Witnesses, pointing to a picture of a lamb and a lion lying together. If I really spoke Russian I'd mention that this is a potentially fatal gathering of carnivore and herbivore—but she only wants me to accept Jesus.

The next morning I ride down to the shore of the Akhtuba River, the Volga's fraternal twin, which runs alongside its larger sister for several hundred miles, the two intertwined by dozens of distributaries, where water fans out from the main channels. Between the two rivers is neither land nor river—it's the Water Meadows, a constellation of hundreds of oxbow lakes with pastures and farms among them.

The Volga, like the Colorado, is one of the most intensively plumbed rivers in the world, engineered into a staircase of hydroelectric dams and reservoirs. So it's a shock and a delight to see that the Russians—the same folk that murdered the Aral Sea by water diversions—have mostly preserved the Volga's wetlands by faking the spring flood each year, opening the penstocks at Volgograd's dam and inundating over a thousand square miles.

It's a miasmic land, a good place to hide. The Meadows have been part of Russia since Ivan the Terrible kicked out the Mongols in the late 1500s. But the tsars weren't so popular after it was declared, in 1649, that serfdom was hereditary—once a peasant, always a peasant. Serfs recognized a raw deal. Some ran away. Many were Cossacks, and the bands of rebel serfs hid from the sting of the tsar's whip in places like the Meadows. In the 1670s they stopped hiding, and around 20,000 of them went on the offense, led by Stenka Razin, who gained a romantic reputation as a sort of Robin Hood. It was the first serious anti-tsar civil war. The rebels took control of nearly the length of the Volga—until Razin was caught, brought to Moscow, and dismembered.

The Russians seem to prefer me whole, but sometimes I wonder. Leaving Volgograd, I was warned that Communist Party members of the Duma are stirring up anti-American sentiment by blaming Russia's problems on the dollar. When I stop in the Leninsk market to buy a pound of big purple grapes I'm suddenly Mr. Capitalism, in the flesh. A knot of vendors closes around me with aggressive shouts of *America dollar! Dollar up, ruble down!* I worry most about the growler with an earflap hat, a man with "1960" tattooed on his hand. His birth date, I figure. When he was young he surely learned how Russia was the first to launch a man in space. Now he's hawking a stack of Chinese pots labeled, in English, "Happy Lady."

After some ruble waving the anger sputters out. A hungry cyclist must be a pitiful sight. Within a minute I'm gobbling grapes and accepting a gift of two tomatoes.

It's a ten-aspirin ride to Akhtubinsk, where I finally ride out from the under the lid of clouds. There's a big modern hotel, which means it's destined to collapse in the not-so-distant future. The bathroom bidet is connected to nothing, and the wall tiles are falling off, leaving a spectacular 3-D landscape of grout.

But there's a café. I order in my usual way, simply pointing to whatever someone else is eating and saying, One of those, please. This works beautifully, and tonight the other diners invite me to sit with them.

The four men with big mustaches and smiles are on their way to pick up sixteen tons of salt from a dry lake about sixty miles east, then haul it six hundred miles to their homeland in the Caucasus Mountains. Sounds like a lot of work, I say with a *Whew!* and an emphatic mopping of my brow. They shake their heads—*No problem. We're up at dawn. We don't drink. We're Muslims from Dagestan!*

Dagestan is one of the twenty-one Russian republics that are something like reservations in the United States—the federal government gives autonomy and a hunk of money to those minorities swallowed by the empire. Ebadula, Omar, Magomed, and Koorban are very hospitable. They don't yell or cajole me to swallow vodka. They're impressed by the jottings I made in my notebook before leaving the United States, and they now believe that all Americans know that Dagestan's president is Magomedali Magomedov, and its capital is Makahchkala. It's a good thing they can't read English, because the rest of my notes read, "Dagestan is Russia's most politically violent republic. Fourteen politicians and businessmen murdered in the last two years. The mayor of the capital is in a wheelchair from a car bombing."

Ebadula none-too-subtly points out Russians at another table and does a remarkable job of pantomiming his cultural perspective. A Russian drinks and gets crazy. A Dagestani is pure. A Russian man doesn't care if you borrow his wife for sex. A Dagestani man will cut your head off. Don't believe it? He invites me to see for myself, carefully printing his address in my journal, dressing it up with a sketch of snow-capped mountains and soaring birds.

I'm impressed, but I needn't visit Dagestan for a taste of a country that would earn a high Scrabble score (if proper nouns were allowed). Today's ride along the desert rim of the Meadows passes within fifteen miles of the frontiers of the newly independent nation of Kazakhstan to the east, and the Russian republic of Kalmykia to the west. The influence of the tsars never extended much beyond the Volga and the Meadows, and with the fall of the communists the low stubble of desert grasslands to either side of the river is again the domain of Turkic-speaking herders. As I ride, it seems that nebulous sheep are always disappearing over a swale along with the sound of the herders on horseback, jangling their noisemakers and hooting.

With the sun low and the indolent smoke from fallow fields hanging in the poplars, I drop into the riverside town of Kharabali and see that the sheepherders live here, with the Russian farmers. They die here, too, and rest under tumbleweeds in graves marked by the crescent moon of Islam.

Two worlds, Jesus and Mohammed, wet and dry. In the Water Meadows the cows plod with tails that look like heavy clubs but are actually masses of cockleburs. Just beyond the reach of the river the land is clean grit and prickles of rigid brown grass. I only wish I'd been here a month earlier. When I duck into the comfort of a truck-stop café in Syeleetrenoy and hear the wind beating the building, I don't want to go back out there.

But I'm very close to the Caspian. So close that three Kazaks and a Russian drop in and throw down on a table a three-foot-long sturgeon and invite me over for a closer look. I've never seen one, except on the label of a jar of caviar. I tap on its head; it's an armored fish. There's no dorsal fin but instead a long row of finned plates like a stegosaurus. Sterlatka, they call it. One fisherman whips out a long knife and slices off a piece of pink flesh with yellow fat. It dangles from the knife as he lifts it to my face and says, *Eat.*

It's remarkable how very quickly the eye and the brain put together a list of Things Worth Noting. That's a terribly sharp knife. No obvious skin infections or lip ulcers on the fisherman. The fish appears very fresh.

So I eat and manage a look that says, "Wow, that's tasty." They slap me on the back and send me on my way to the last city on my route, Astrakhan.

ADVANCE BILLING CAN make a skeptic out of any traveler, particularly if you've visited the region of Iowa that likes to promote itself as "Little Switzerland." The city of Astrakhan is called the "Star of the Desert" or the "Gateway to the Orient," but I don't believe it until I see it.

Forty miles north of Astrakhan, I see it: oil derricks and gas flares rising above sand dunes and double-humped Bactrian camels. I stop for a camel photo, but this is no tourist beast, and it lets loose a tremendous honk that rocks me back on my heels. It's hobbled, thank God, so I'm not afraid to camp nearby. I can prime my stove without attracting attention— it looks like just another gas flare from the refineries on the horizon. It's the warmest night in a week, and I'm glad to have eked out a lead on the Russian winter.

Unfortunately, it's only a eight-hour lead, and I wake in the morning to a cold tickle of rain on my eyelids. I pack in a flash and split for the city as the distant smokestacks of a refinery fade in the mist. It's a bleak ride. Crows with gray shoulders like epaulets jauntily pick at the ribs of a roadkilled horse. The Volga wetlands are laced with power lines under a hydrocarbon sky, but I can still make out the colors of the land. The higher ground is home to silky hummocks of grass, the bottomlands blush pink with ripe seedheads, and the channels are lined with tasseled reeds.

The French novelist Alexandre Dumas came this way in 1858. Dumas was excitable (his *Adventures in Czarist Russia* is jumping with exclamation marks) and sometimes gullible—he swallowed the accounts of sheep with tails so fat that they were trailed by a little wagon to carry the tail. But it's true that he passed a "Chinese pagoda" just above Astrakhan. It was actually a Buddhist shrine built by the Kalmyks, who still live west of the Volga.

All the Soviet Union suffered during Stalin's reign, but the south was hit the hardest. The Kalmyks, descendants of the galloping Mongolians, say they fought with gusto against the dirty Nazis in 1942. Stalin claimed the Kalmyks welcomed the fascists with tea and butter. Both sides agree that in December of 1943 trains began arriving in Kalmykia. Jostling lightly on their couplings behind the engines were an extraordinary number of cattle cars. They arrived empty and left full, destined for Siberia. Within months the entire population of 170,000 Kalmyks was gone.

Stalin died in 1953, after three decades of rule. In 1957, 6,000 Kalmyk survivors were allowed to return. The rest vanished, hollow-eyed, into Soviet history, as did the Ukrainians who resisted Stalin's drive to bring all farms into the fold of state collectives. Stalin seized their harvest and let them starve. Around 14.5 million died. Stalin himself believed the figure to be around 8 or 9 million, but as he once said, "A single death is a tragedy, a million deaths is a statistic."

I don't expect to find much of the old ways of life during my storm-driven sprint into Astrakhan. With snapping mongrels at my heels and a superb wind on my tail, I whiz past the plywood slums and concrete apartment blocks into the city center. The oldest buildings have ornate wrought-iron balconies reminiscent of another delta city, New Orleans. But the buildings are vacant, the balconies collapsing. The cathedral hasn't fared much better—the communists turned it into a bus station.

Yet the central market thrives. Overflows, actually, into the streets, where perfume and pomegranates are sold from stands barely twelve inches from the steel whir of the passing trams. Inside, Kazaks with faces round and flat as coins are spooning out carrot salad and skewering lamb on shish kebabs. Ladies under headscarves are yelling "Chipsies," which I mistake for *gypsies* until I spot the sacks of Lay's potato chips. Like a teen drawn to a horror movie, I aim for the meat market. As hoped and feared, the Russians are dismembering cows with huge and horrible axes atop tables made of tree trunks, big ones, bound with iron hoops.

Zesty markets are not uncommon, but Astrakhan's is the first I've seen since Turpan, China, that is well below sea level. This fact I recall after I get a room on the third floor of the Hotel Lotus and open both a Delta Beer and the wonderfully detailed map I bought in Volgograd.

The Caspian Depression is a flatland without peer. The Volga drops only three feet during its fifty-mile run from Astrakhan to the Caspian, a slope of precisely 0.72 inch per mile. That's ridiculously flat. If you tossed a paper airplane off the top of the Empire State Building and it dropped in elevation at the same rate as the lower Volga, it would fly 20,000 miles before touching down.

The map intrigues me and disturbs me. The northern coast of the Caspian isn't a coast at all. Like the Water Meadows, it's neither land nor sea. It's a hundred-mile-wide swamp. There will be no seashore or any alternatives. To the east of the delta is Kazakhstan, where the Caspian sea lions had just that summer chomped on forty unwary beach lovers. Luckily, I have no visa. To the west is the Russian Republic of Kalmykia, whose president, Kirsan Ilyumzhinov, claimed to have been abducted by space aliens. "We flew to some kind of star. They put a space suit on me, told me many things and showed me around."

I wouldn't mind warming up on a nearby star, but Kalmykia borders Chechnya. That settles it: always the prudent chicken, I will stay in Russia. Besides, there's one place on the map that's caught my eye, a place both low and high.

IT's A FRIGID MORNING—and I'm still in my hotel room. It's warmer in the seventh-floor café, but the place is packed, and I must share a table with a young shark in a deluxe suit. He's silent until he tells me that he doesn't like the look of my handlebar bag on the table. Move it. Sure, I say—if you'll move that ugly cell phone. He puts it in his pocket and shortly exits. I finish my lemon tea and zip out of town on high hopes and a joyous tailwind.

Just beyond Astrakhan's surprising little suburbs of neat two-story brick homes is the water world of the delta. I pass an occasional roadside memorial to drivers who made it no farther, but there are hardly any cars today. For company I have canals and fallow rice fields and unmoving cows. Perhaps they're frozen. The sun is blinding but impotent.

It's farmland all the way, irrigated by the Volga but shunted by earthworks in so many directions it's not clear what's river and what's canal. The single village I pass, Syemiboogri, is built on a subtle rise reached by a floating pontoon bridge overlain with a slapdash collection of sheet metal. That's not as frightening as the attack geese that rush out from under a cottonwood but fail to reach me before I park the bike and trot into the town store. Inside, a half-dozen men are talking about the recent cold snap. The clerk reaches into a freezer and gives me a bottle of frozen water. Russian joke.

The town is ready for the winter. Watermelons are stacked in sheds. The haystacks are as big as the houses, which still manage to put on a pretty face with fancy windows—although it's usually just one pretty face, facing the dirt street. The other three sides look as beat as I feel.

But I've only twenty miles to Tishkova. The pavement quits, and I bump along on gravel as a little bus with classic dingle-ball windshield trim passes. Its placard says Tishkova-Astrakhan. Good—I'll be on that bus tomorrow, heading back to Astrakhan, then home.

When the sun is low the big reeds cast a long shadow, and in search of warmth I ride on the wrong side of the road, in a thin strip of sunlight. Then I see what I've been hoping for, what my map showed as the only hill of any significance, three hundred feet long and fifty feet high and as close to the Caspian as possible without swimming. Its slumping sides appear, despite the cold, as if they're melting. It's a regular mountain in these parts, and it's the end of the line for me.

The hill is above the wetlands, connected to the road by a raised isthmus of desert, powder dry. The delta is equal parts water, mud, and reeds, but in truth the northern Caspian gets only about eight inches of rain a year. I ride off, cross-country, and make it halfway up the hill before I notice that this is no ordinary heap of dirt.

It's the ancient shore. The Caspian is a capricious sea, with a sea level that has fluctuated wildly throughout geologic time. I don't know when its waters last lapped up against this hill, but I imagine there's at least a few thousand years of history poking out. Crawling on my hands and knees, I find a tibia from a deer-sized animal, a gleaming mussel, a piece of charcoal, and a pottery shard, presumably from a time long before the communist revolution and the tsars. Suddenly Russian history seems a blink in time, destined to be covered in silt.

And just as suddenly the sun is almost down. I push the bike to the summit for my view of the sparkling Caspian. Instead I see a swamp. I'm not disappointed—after all, I'm standing on the highest point on the lowest point in Europe. Until the wind saps my heat and I hustle down for the shelter of a single willow tree at the edge of a lily-pad marsh. I put up the tent and fire up the stove for a pot of steaming ramen noodles.

Geese honk overhead in the dying light, and unseen birds clamber through the reeds. I climb into the tent and fluff up my sleeping bag. With my little lantern I study the map and smile. A month on the road. I've grown fond of sweet tea and sunflower seeds. I grew up listening to America's version of the venomous communists, and I came to Russia like a tenderfoot in the desert, seeing signs of snakes everywhere. In the end I found free tomatoes and apples—and a pretty good wedding, too. No love, yes love, the story of life.

For dessert I have a cup of instant "Super Coffee—True American Taste" (made in Singapore) and a shot of Astrakhan vodka (the lowest booze in Europe). The air is literally freezing—my thermometer reads 28 degrees. But I'm pleased. There's something I like about the low points of the world. Gravity rules, and all things come to rest. No farther. This is the place.

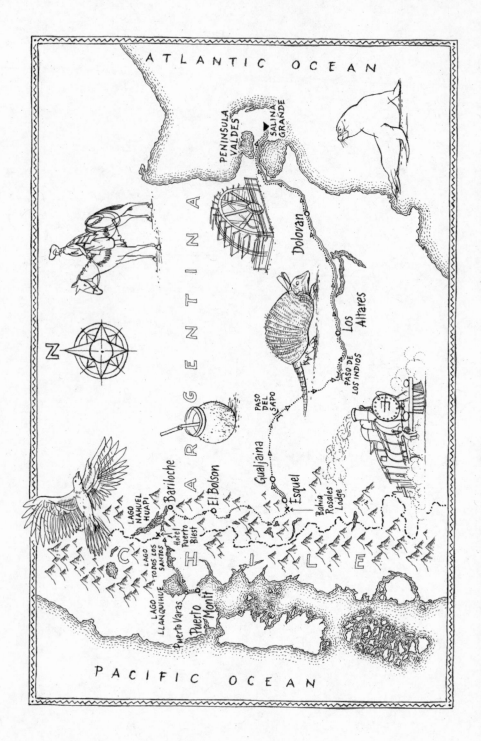

ATLANTIC OCEAN

PACIFIC OCEAN

PENINSULA VALDES

SALINA GRANDE

Dolovan

Los Altares

PASO DE LOS INDIOS

PASO DEL SAPO

Gualjaina

Esquel

Bahia Rosales Lodge

El Bolson

Bariloche

LAGO NAHUEL HUAPI

Hotel Puerto Blest

LAGO TODOS LOS SANTOS

LAGO LLANQUIHUE

Puerto Varas

Puerto Montt

ARGENTINA

CHILE

N

SOUTH AMERICA

*Light your pipe and be silent.
There's only wind and smoke
in the world.*

—Irish proverb

CHAPTER 7

Tucson to Puerto Montt
It All Comes on Ships

SHUT YOUR WINDOW SHADE, the passengers grumbled on the flight home from Russia. They were glued to the video; I was frozen to Greenland and a flotilla of icebergs sailing off its shattered coast. Trying for a compromise, I covered my head and window with a blanket. *Like a child,* my wife would say when she was wishing I wasn't.

Then I was home, relishing the glow of reentry into the familiar. On the first Monday morning after my return, I trotted outside to the curb with my toddler in my arms, taking care not to catch my bathrobe on the prickly pear cactus. Rudy had wakened only moments before to his favorite alarm, the diesel growl of the garbage truck. Now he stared in astonishment as the hydraulic claw snatched our trash can. He gave the driver an apple, and we scurried back inside for the thrilling ritual of the hissing espresso machine. Then I set him free to wobble and drool where he pleased while I sat on the couch, the late October sun warming my shoulders, and fished for compliments in my e-mails from the Caspian ride.

Some were sweet.

> Dear Jim, Thanks for the ride from a Grandmother
> in southeastern Ohio. Come and sit a spell. Sincerely,
> Wanda

Some were not sweet.

> You have Titanium balls. Keep kicking ass dude.

And some wanted advice.

> Hi Jim. I've been preoccupied with the thought of cycling
> across the country for a few years. Do you have any advice
> on how to get The Discovery Channel to pay for it?

He'd neglected to supply his name. It made no difference: Discovery was
no longer sending me fruit baskets. The flood of internet money was drying up, just when the future of my little quest for the low points was at the
tipping point—three down and three to go. Recalling the editors' earlier
aversion to Africa, I opened my atlas and cautiously prepared and mailed
my proposal for the ride to Salina Grande, a pit in Patagonia, the tail of
South America.

The place called Patagonia is not a country but a remoteness. It is cantilevered so far into the vast southern oceans that if you sail due west from
the Pacific coast you'll simply circle the planet without landfall until you
return to Patagonia. In doing so you will have traveled from Chile to Argentina, where Salina Grande was sunk near the Atlantic coast. I decided
to do the same: from the Chilean Pacific to the Argentine Atlantic, except
that I would go overland, across the Andes.

While I waited for Discovery's decision, my bicycle was stripped to
the frame and a new downtube welded in place. When the phone finally
jangled with a job offer, it was Sue Rutman of Organ Pipe Cactus National
Monument. She needed a botanist who didn't mind being alone in the
desert, somebody to map the vegetation of a half-million acres of people-
free southwestern Arizona.

Somebody had to. I pulled the cylinder heads off my derelict Jeep and
lugged them to a machine shop for a valve job. A month later I was hiding from a dust storm under a hackberry in Growler Wash. I walked a lot
that winter and spring, stopping to poke at slow ants and to mull over

why certain plants lived *here* and not *there*. I slept on the sand under the weightless stars, the only sound the diligent throb of my pulse.

The blaze of summer holed me up at home. Snaggle-toothed Rudy needed a live-in playmate; he was denied the breast, and within hours (it seemed) Sonya was pregnant again. The celebration was doubled after a call from Discovery: Salina Grande was on.

There are guidebooks galore on the Patagonian Andes, detailing the many lodges for those aiming to reel in a trophy trout. But scarcely a word has been written on the Argentine desert between the Andes and the Atlantic, and I considered myself lucky to discover G. G. Simpson's *Attending Marvels*, the account of his 1930 paleontology expedition in Argentine Patagonia.

Now I knew why hardly anyone lived in Patagonia. Simpson wrote of "a barren outer world where the ruthless, the nerve-wracking, the terrible wind blows incessantly."

The wind is my most feared enemy, and I could only hope that Simpson was exaggerating when he claimed that "some go insane. I cannot erase a horrible picture from my mind—two men in straightjackets lying neglected on the beach, writhing and shrieking. Later they were loaded like two logs into the boat to Buenos Aires. They escaped from Patagonia."

I was going in. A big box from Discovery arrived, with satellite phone, computer, and digital camera. The gear weighed the usual twelve pounds, but the contract that tagged along had grown. To help translate it, I brought the paperwork over to my friend Jim Boyer, a writer and climber and, at the advanced age of thirty-five, student of law. Before we studied the fine print, we rode our bikes up A-Mountain (aka Sentinel Peak), swooshed back, drained a quart of Pabst, and talked about books and women until, two hours after sunset, I remembered I had a wife and son. The contract could wait a day or two.

Two days later, amid the pines on the north slope of the Santa Catalina Mountains, a piece of climbing gear gave way under Jim's weight. He wasn't particularly heavy, but he was a hundred feet above an outcrop of granite knobs.

A friend rappelled to the scene of the accident and found golden lichen and purple larkspur, and honeybees gladly swarming on the scatter of Jim's skull.

I was horrified—at the loss, and the way he was lost. I'd long been afraid of heights. For the next month I would wake from falling dreams with a gasp. It wasn't insomnia; it was cold fear and hot tears.

Then it was October, and spring was surely waking the southern tip of South America. At the airport Sonya held Rudy in her arms and number two in her womb. Nobody had to say *be careful.*

When I woke in the night and slid over to a window seat for a look, we'd already crossed the Amazon and the equator—yet half the journey remained. Surprisingly close to the plane were the ice mountains of Peru, the Cordillera Blanca. This I knew from studying maps with Jim four years earlier, as he prepared to climb Nevado de Alpamayo. Now I sat blinking in the moonlight, thinking of life and death and especially that moment between.

How long will your heart persist beating after your brain is gone? The question was not the stuff of sweet dreams, and in utter self-interest I diverted my attention to the Sky Mall catalog tucked in the seat pocket. It seemed a kind of sacrilege, but it did the trick. Soon I was wondering if anyone actually slipped their credit card into the AirPhone to order a $250 Stainless Steel Kitchen Garbage Can from Denmark while flying along the rim of South America.

I dozed and woke and looked out onto a desert. It was the color of bones, with long smooth ridges and moon-shadowed canyons running from the Andes to the Pacific. I nodded for another two hours, then woke as the Boeing 767 throttled back over a valley of vineyards and eucalyptus muted by a flowing fog. It was morning, and the airport was Santiago's. I changed planes and continued south to Puerto Montt—still Chile, and still between the Andes and the Pacific, but now the mountains were very close to the sea. The land was greener and steeper, with rivers foaming through canyons of black rock. An oval lake lay at the foot of a sleeping volcano shaped like a science fair project.

The clouds suddenly thickened, and the jet landed in a blur of nimbostratus. The air was 52 degrees, and the rain was colder—time for a taxi. A blue Hyundai took me and my box through a dripping forest and down a hill into Puerto Montt.

The lobby of the Hotel Pérez Rosales was clogged with military men in dress uniform with gold braid looped through one epaulet. The soldiers were reminders of an ugly past. In 1973 Chile's socialist president, Salvador Allende, died during a coup led by General Pinochet. Over the next decade, thousands of Chileans were killed by the Pinochet junta, a brutal purge of a democracy made possible by U.S. money and brains. "I don't see why we need to stand by and watch a country go Communist," said Henry Kissinger.

Anxious for exercise, I went for a walk past old homes with clapboard siding like fish scales. The wind came up, and I ducked into a furniture store that would look like most other furniture stores if it did not possess a gigantic window overlooking the harbor. I took a picture of the many tin roofs in the slanting rain.

An unsmiling man in a navy blue polyester suit appeared. He clutched a walkie-talkie. I gave him the grin of the harmless tourist. He was immune. "Sir," he said, "it is prohibited to photograph furniture."

Despite my familiarity with the Spanish language, the Russian security apparatus, and Egyptian customs, I was slow to recognize the danger of being arrested for Chilean furniture espionage. I asked Mr. Security if he believed I was working for another furniture store. He repeated, "It is prohibited to photograph furniture."

No problem, I said.

I walked out into the mists and wood smoke. I felt like a foreigner, without a name for the hanks of dried kelp sold in the plank-floor market. The dried innards of clams, strung in garlands and hung from rusted hooks, looked like little shrunken heads. Fish hawkers arranged the day's catch and yelled, "*Merluza! Congrio!*" Fish have no eyelids, and although dead, they looked startled to be away from their watery home.

When the tide went out, so did the old people, raking through the muck in search of dinner. On a black sand beach they clomped in rubber boots, drawing rude squirts from the razor clams, which were dispatched by a quick trench with a short-handled hoe. Anything is fair game—keyhole limpets and mussels, wedge clams and the carnivorous snails called *el loco*—and any restaurant will serve up the diggings.

The meal is called *curantos*, and when it arrived at my table I felt a tad queasy. Surrounded by a wrack of steaming bivalves, the centerpiece was the world's largest barnacle, eight inches of *Megabalanus*. I boldly forked out the guts. Barnacles are related to lobsters, I told myself, but taxonomy meant little to me when confronted with the mucilaginous blob on my plate. I quivered, and so did the barnacle.

My first and last *curantos*. Living off the sea was a Chilean habit, and the tradition lived on in a new way in stores like Piwonka. It was not a grocery (unless you count the sweets) or an automotive store (although you can buy jumper cables) or a hardware store (ignoring the screwdrivers). Piwonka's owner, a well-preserved lady named Elma, revealed without hesitation her simple business plan: "We'll sell anything. It all comes on ships."

No larger than twelve by twenty-five feet, Piwonka was a glittering cave of what can be had with just a little cash. Duck under the Big Wheels and soccer balls hanging from the ceiling and negotiate the ten bikes on the floor and behold the dazzling selection of Hi-Output Key Chain Lasers and Ninja Crossbows. There's sensible fare, too, like the 3-D Last Supper Clock and actual telephones and plastic flowers. Close inspection showed that many trade names had mutated during the long Pacific voyage. Rugrats were Ragrats, and Barbie was Barbara. A few made-in-Chile products struggled for brand identity, but they'll have to do better than Never Ending Toilet Paper.

Chile refills the ships after unloading their Piwonka fare. At the commercial harbor sat a great pyramid of wood chips destined for Asia. A queue of new Mercedes tanker trucks were one by one fitted with fat yellow corrugated hoses that ran out to a ship. Pumps whirred and the trucks squirted thousands of rainbow trout smolts into the ship's holding tank.

An agreeable man in nice loafers, Mr. Alberto Navarrete of Ventisqueros S.A., orchestrated the operation while smoking unfiltered Camels and answering his chirping cell phone and my questions. The freshwater youngsters, he said, were heading for adolescence in a cage submerged in a nearby sea channel. He gestured south, to the thousand miles of largely uninhabited Pacific coast between Puerto Montt and Cape Horn, a place fractured and flooded into an archipelago of fjords and islands flailed by incessant rain and blizzards. The trout won't mind. They will live in floating cages and be fed, like most industrialized livestock, with a spray of food pellets. A year of gluttony follows. The little trout swell from four ounces to fourteen pounds and then it's over: netted, beheaded, gutted, filleted, and bound for the United States or Japan.

It was a brilliant system, but disturbing, too. The food pellets were made from fish once considered not worth pursuing. Now the stinkfish and bottom suckers of the oceans would no longer be left alone—they, too, would be pursued and caught in the great nets, dried and ground up and fed to these shining tasty trout.

The weather disagreed with me. I would be aiming east, over the Andes, and I waited two days for the clouds to lift. When a morning broke clear, I packed my bags and pedaled through a city intoxicated by the sun. Couples smooched on the wharf. Young men went shirtless and goosebumpy. Men in suits whistled as they walked past Piwonka and Nueva Piwonka Numero Dos.

I stopped in Piwonka to say *adios*. A woman had just bought the 3-D Last Supper Clock.

It's beautiful, said the deeply satisfied customer.

And it was only four dollars. I shared her happiness, but for different reasons. No wind, no rain, no worries.

CHAPTER 8

Puerto Montt to Salina Grande

This Wind Is Just an Everyday Wind

THE GERMANS WERE HERE. Every guidebook makes mention of the brave Europeans who settled southern Chile, yet none admits that the Germans are hardly evident today. Where are the Germans? I ask a fisherman wearing a ratty sweater that may actually be an old net. He stops painting his little boat a giddy green and says, "Not here in Puerto Montt. You need to go to the country, toward Puerto Varas."

That's fine, because Puerto Varas is on my way to the Andes. I turn from the sea and pedal inland, toward the ice volcanoes that float above the thick marine air. It's a switchbacking climb out of Puerto Montt, past yipping mutts and black taxis and kids booting soccer balls. A light plane drones overhead, towing a banner promising, *Ray-O-Vac is the battery*. When I pass the last house and hit the old dirt road to Puerto Varas, I smile and stop and scribble in my notebook: I'm on my way to the Atlantic, pedaling across Patagonia.

I bump along, cookpot banging in a pannier. Rocks pinched under my tires go zinging off at slingshot speed into the ex-forest of tree stumps. Some of the stumps are ten feet across, and very likely the remains of a tree called *alerce*. It's the southern hemisphere equivalent of the redwood.

Both *alerce* and redwood are evergreen conifers, both live ridiculously long and grow to fantastic heights, and both are worshipped by naturalists and loggers. Chile declared the *alerce* the national tree in 1976, after realizing that only 15 percent of the original forests remained. Cutting was strictly prohibited unless the tree was already dead or burnt. The loophole was promptly exploited: burn or girdle a tree, wait until it dies, then haul out the chainsaws. So it went for almost three decades, until Chile finally banned all harvesting of the *alerce*.

But these *alerce* were cut long ago (the wood does not rot), perhaps by the missing Germans. They came to Patagonia at the urging of Chilean immigration offices that were set up in Europe after 1850. Chile, officially and freshly independent as of 1811, wanted someone to settle the land and build a nation. A new nation, that is. Around a million people called the Mapuche already lived in the south, but the government did not consider them a model for future development, despite their obvious vigor. In 1541, the Spanish explorer Lopez Vaz regarded the Mapuche as "the most valiant and furious people in all America." The Incas, in contrast, were dandies in feathered plumes. And just as the Mapuche had repelled the Incas, they roughed up the conquistadors. The first Spanish governor, Pedro de Valdivia, was not merely humiliated in defeat; the Mapuche gouged out his thumping heart and made lunch of it.

The Mapuche had a thing for raw freedom, and for three centuries the Spaniards failed in Patagonia. Their foes were brilliant guerrilla fighters, having practiced on themselves for several thousand years. They had no urge to write; oratory skills were so esteemed that history never died. They disciplined naughty kids with a dose of the hallucinogenic and occasionally lethal blossoms of *floripondio*, great drooping trumpets colored lemon and red.

Yet the Mapuche were not indestructible. Ground down by three hundred years of war, they were further weakened with booze brought by the Europeans. The new Chilean government saw its chance to displace the Mapuche with someone willing to live under the flag of Chile—otherwise, Argentina might claim all of Patagonia. The Chilean army did its work, and the Germans came. (Some Swiss, Dutch, and Italians did too.)

The Germans cleared and claimed their homesteads and presumably founded the "German Club" restaurant I find along the main street in Puerto Varas. Unfortunately, it is closed. There's not a German in sight.

Onward, along the shores of Lago Llanquihue, under gathering clouds. The road is paved and busy with people on their way to fun, towing Jet Skis and dirt bikes to and from vacation homes and hotels with names like Enchanted Lake and Hidden Cove. Between windrows of cypress and eucalyptus (another immigrant) are gray gothic farmhouses, huge homes with ornate gables and creaking wind vanes in a breeze that is beginning to worry me. In very green pastures the beasts of Patagonia slobber and chomp and train their indifferent eyes on the solo cyclist. Dairy cows, I presume; one farm has an old sign proclaiming, *We use a Girton Milk Tank.* There are indecipherable German signs, too: *Ist gesund und schmeckt gut!*

Volcan Osorno, 8,600 feet high, disappears and reappears behind fast clouds. It's huge and pointy and perfectly buried in snow down to 4,000 feet. When it begins to rain I'm relieved to see a sign for yet another German Club.

This one is open and looks vaguely Bavarian, although I've never been to Bavaria. In the parking lot is a BMW. The staff, however, is definitely Chilean. I order a bowl of asparagus soup and ask my black-tie waiter Carlos if any Germans are about.

"There are none. This is a restaurant with German food."

Where can I find them?

"I would look in Puerto Varas."

I was there, and didn't see any. What do they look like?

"They are big and have blond hair."

And they can be found in this region?

"One was here very recently."

Do you know where he or she lives?

"Not here—he was a tourist."

I visit the bathroom, and it's clear that Germans were here. The place is suitable for surgery, blindingly lit by miniature spotlights. And there's a Siemens hand dryer tagged, *Made in Germany.*

The rain quits but the clouds won't. The yellow lupines along the road are a fair substitute for the sun. I pass an encouraging sign: *Lots for Sale, Call F. Gunther*. A growl of thunder keeps me moving. I spy a little sign that says *Kucher*, pointing to a lovely old two-story home. Out front there's one of my favorite species, a silver-crested porch sitter—a female in a peach cardigan.

Hello, I say—What's a *kucher*?

"It's a pastry, of dough and fruit and baked in an oven. Like a tart. It's German."

And are you German?

"Three generations back. Now I'm Chilean, of course."

Of course. I want to know more; she wants to feed me *kucher*. There is no greater stimulant to the mothering urge than the sight of a skinny bicyclist. The *kucher* is wonderful. Raspberry, and baked in a wood-burning stove.

Her name is Magaly Brimtrup Birke. She still speaks German, as does her husband, Orlando, as did her predecessors in the late 1800s. She gestures toward the perfect pastures and the moo cows and says, "This was all a forest then."

Some trees survived, including a surreal araucaria in the front yard. This is a conifer whose repeating form, branching like a snowflake, gives it the look of a pagoda tapering to a point fifty feet high. The leaves are like pine needles except wider and creased into inch-long daggers. It's the oddest tree—and, says Magaly, it used to be the most important tree. The Mapuche ate the seeds. "They lived off those trees."

The Chilean government gave title to thousands of square miles of Mapuche lands to the settlers, lands that, a century later, they hoped to recover with the election of Salvador Allende. The landowners hoped otherwise. With the reign of Pinochet, land reform died—along with anyone who stood up for the people who ate the seeds of the araucaria. Magaly says, "It was a lot of work to cut down all those trees." She's still working. Chickens, ducks, and a stupendous garden with two hothouses for tomatoes. Is she tempted to sell out to holiday subdivisions?

"No. We like the tranquility, and we're doing fine by renting some cabins we built by the beach."

One more thing, please: what do you call the plant with the trumpet-shaped, hanging yellow and red flowers?

"Floripondio," says Magaly. "But why are you writing this down?"

I'm writing a story. I think it's about Chile and Germans.

"And you didn't visit the German museum in Frutillar? Shame."

I promise to visit next time, with my wife, who speaks German simply because she likes German. Magaly is touched, and that's good for another hunk of *kucher* for the road. It goes well with the ChocMan XL candy bar, Cristal beer, and empanada meat pie I pick up in the next town. Beyond, the road climbs past cliffs of volcanic rock, homogeneous and smooth, a frozen wave of ash. Lago Llanquihue falls behind as the road turns to gravel and parallels the Petrohue River feeding the lake.

The valley tightens. Nobody lives here. The river plunges over ledges of polished stone. There is absolutely no way to cross without a bridge, and there is no bridge. The only way is to follow the river, into the Andes.

IF MY WIFE is right on these matters, the patter of rain on my tent this morning is wonderful for my skin, plumping it with moisture. But the humidity is terrible for my map, turning it into a limp rag that tears in my hands. In truth I hardly need it. From my camp, there is only one way over the Andes to Argentina, the Paso de Pérez Rosales. The road over the pass is mapped as a lonely noodle, twenty miles long, connecting a lake in Chile with a lake in Argentina. It does not connect to any other road. Only ferries cross the lakes, and they carry not cars but only people, who are shuttled in minibuses over the pass, twice a day. The rest of the time the pass will be mine.

I refuse to emerge from the tent until the trills and sliding whistles of birds signal that my chance has come. Outside, shags of moss hang from branches and upholster the earth. In the drab cold I don't expect to see a big green and red Tarzan parrot—but there it goes, squawking as it flaps toward the glacial gloom of Volcán Osorno.

The gravel road to the lake has been wiped out and rebuilt in two places, the victim of landslides off Osorno. When Charles Darwin poked around Chile in 1832, the volcano was "spouting volumes of smoke." It's quiet today,

vaguely opalescent in the watery light, but it's plain to see that Osorno created the lake at road's end. It dammed the river with a steaming torrent
of ash. The river rose into a lake and topped the dam and chewed it away
until Osorno blew again and made the dam higher still.

In the contest between eruption and erosion, the volcano appears to be
winning: the lake, Todos los Santos, is over a thousand feet deep. It's also
twenty miles long and narrowly tucked between mountains so steep it's
no wonder that the ferry *Esmeralda* is the only way to the other side. The
tourists on deck are fairly chipper considering the curtains of rain sweeping the lake for two hours. Between announcements in Spanish, English,
and German, the ubiquitous *Four Seasons* plays over the sound system,
but everyone is hoping for just one season, the dry season. The tours begin in Puerto Montt, which is fairly wallpapered with posters advertising
this route, posters picturing frozen volcanoes and mossy forests under a
cloudless sky.

Lies, all lies. There is no dry season, only a less-wet season. Each year
brings 160 inches of rain—yet I, too, stand patiently on deck and wait for
Osorno to reappear. So does Mr. Hideo ("It rhymes with video!") of Osaka,
who faithfully records the waterfalls that slide out of the mountain clouds,
sluicing down gorges directly into the lake.

At the far end of the lake is an old hotel, three stories of stucco under
a hipped roof that would not look out of place in the Black Forest. In the
tastefully rustic lobby, a tour group of California oldsters swaps stories
of "treks," which I believe are "hikes" in places where people don't speak
English. One sturdy fellow is crazy for Argentine Patagonia.

"The archaeologists find dinosaurs out there, you know. It's better than
the Gobi Desert. They've just discovered that very big dinosaurs, say forty
feet long, come from eggs no longer than *this*."

He holds a thumb and finger five inches apart. The audience, not clear
on the concept, listens for the import of these five inches.

"That's not nearly as big as you'd expect from a forty-foot dinosaur!"

"Eighty feet!" interjects another man.

"Yes, eighty feet—that's even more amazing."

But it's not as amazing as the sudden flood of sunlight through the windows. I ignore the little fact paddling around in my brain—160 inches of rain—and give in to the urge to leave the hotel and find a camp.

A kind waitress wraps up two ham-and-cheese sandwiches for me. That should do me for dinner and breakfast, then I'll pedal over the Paso de Pérez Rosales into Argentina for lunch on the shore of Lago Nahuel Huapi. The pass is only 3,300 feet above the Pacific—hardly a workout for a real he-cyclist.

The road is deep black gravel peppered with smooth cobbles, and I must deflate my tires for traction. All is gorgeous for about ten minutes, the snowfields bronzed and the waterfalls so high and thin. There are several abandoned homes and apple orchards, so somebody must have stood here in the sun and thought: this is the place. A pasture to park a cow; inviolate citadels above.

Where did the settlers go? Insane, I'd guess, from the drip and plop of rain. The clouds, loitering on the summits, spill into the valley and hasten the coming of night. With the pastures now behind me and forest on all sides, I'm lucky to find an open spot on a gravel bar above a looping stream, and get my tent up just as the rain comes down. The hell with flood danger: I'm dry for now.

The first sandwich is gone in thirty seconds. I'm eyeing the breakfast sandwich when I remember my Emergency Soup. I fire up the stove and open the tent zipper for a bit of fresh air. Mosquitoes sneak in, and while I'm slapping about my ears, the noodles boil over and a cloud of steam fills the tent. My glasses instantly fog over. I grope for the roaring stove, kill the flame. The mosquitoes are thrilled by the mist and resume the attack. Lacking repellent, I rely on an internal remedy: a half-liter of red wine.

Two hours later, life is much improved. The rain's stopping. The stream purls by with restless liquid sounds. Frogs croak amiably, hoping to get lucky. And when I open the tent and look to the sky I see that my night wish has been granted. Above the Andes is a terrific blaze of stars.

It's as cold as a meat locker in the morning, yet bordering the stream is a shock of bamboo twenty feet high. During a walk that will be shorter than anticipated, I discover that bamboo is friendly only when encountered post-harvest in Polynesian restaurants. Living bamboo is impenetrable.

The rest of the forest is a confusion of moldering logs and a tangle of creepers encircling the lichen-mottled trunks of the beech trees called *Nothofagus*. Duck under a branch, and with the faintest vibration the dripping mats of moss release a thousand droplets. It's always raining in this rainforest, and I bet the first Europeans to come this way must have despised this wall of murk as much as I do.

They were Spaniards. They weren't sure where they were going, but knew what they hoped to find. It was 1621, and the legend was already a century old.

In 1528, Francisco Cesar and fifteen men set out from somewhere in the moist heart of the continent, to find a city where the roofs were plated with pure silver. Another account has Cesar setting out with four men in search of the "White King," an uncommonly generous ruler who made gifts of gold and precious stones. The details vary, but the ending is the same: the survivors laid eyes on an "Enchanted City." They swore it was true.

It sounds like nonsense, but only a few years later Pizarro proved that the Incas certainly had gold and knew a thing or two about master-planned communities. As the years passed the legend of the Enchanted City swelled and metamorphosed into a place where even the furniture was gold. Some called it El Dorado.

That was enough to propel Diego Flores de Léon and a crew of forty-six from the Pacific into this canyon. I imagine they avoided the bamboo by thrashing up the flood channel of the Rio Peulla. Perhaps they rested here. They would ultimately fail in their quest, but at least they could have enjoyed this excellent camp, with a flattish rock for a seat where I eat my slim breakfast. I'm not game for another walk in a place where you stumble in the dimness and try to guess whether that orange blob is a fungus or a slime mold. Too wet to catch fire, this forest simply grows deeper and blacker until an old tree dies and falls over and creates an open space in the canopy.

But not on the ground. Mr. Darwin, always ready for an alternative to being seasick aboard the HMS *Beagle*, penetrated the forest near Puerto Montt and encountered "a mass of dying and dead trunks." "I am sure," he wrote, "that often, for more than ten minutes together, our feet never touched the ground, and we were frequently ten or fifteen feet above it, so that the seamen as a joke called out the soundings."

I've got it easy: a road along the canyon bottom, without traffic. The clouds are back, low and gauzy and clinging to the canyon walls, but it's not raining. I pedal and stop where I please, keeping an eye out for a hummingbird called the green-backed firecrown and its favored treat, the drooping blooms of fuchsia. Instead I find a marvelously hairy tarantula and the utterly smooth trunks of a myrtle tree. Both spider and tree bark are the color of cinnamon.

The only bird I recognize is the caracara, a kind of falcon that has abandoned the hunting lifestyle in favor of the already dead. A large and patient bird, it sits on a branch and stares at me with head cocked. Waiting.

I wait. I want it to fly away, so I can snap a photo.

The caracara waits. With dark wings folded over its white body, it's a dignified character, not counting its huge horrible bill that appears dipped in blood. I wait until I remember that I don't have any lunch, and that the caracara is hoping that I am lunch. I throw a rock. The caracara takes wing, slowly and audibly, with a span roughly equal to the length of my bike.

The bird is waiting just around the corner, where the single rutted lane abruptly leaves the river bottom and switchbacks up to the Paso de Pérez Rosales. It's almost noon and the sun has struggled free, yet the day is still cool and I'm panting little clouds of vapor as I climb. Work makes heat and I strip off my shirt. Well short of the summit I experience what marathoners call "hitting the wall," the overwhelming urge to stop moving.

I stop. Digging through my panniers in search of food, I find only an ounce of grated parmesan cheese and immediately pour it down my throat. It's like eating sawdust. Two minibuses carrying ferry passengers trundle past in the opposite direction. The tourists gawk. Some, in an apparently reflexive action, videotape me. They'll regret it. Glistening with sweat, my beard flecked with cheese, I look like I've been pursued by bloodhounds for a week.

Running out of fuel is a rare and unwelcome experience. I look down as I push on, thinking of anything but the mountain—old girlfriends, new candy bars, and a salt lake called Salina Grande. I nearly miss the sign at the summit saying, *Welcome to Argentina.* Semidelirious but still in the saddle, I keep moving.

After all, I have my own foolhardy quest. And my own tale, which I swear is true, of the far side of the Andes:

East of the cordillera is a country that is all downhill. From the snow mountain with three peaks, descend to the lake like a radiant jewel. There on the shore under a cloudless sky is the Enchanted Hotel. There you will find smooth white basins of hot water to soak in and a table to sit at and fill your plate and glass for as long as you like. And you will be the only guest.

"Do you know why there are no blacks in Argentina?" asks Alfredo Pentke.

He runs the Hotel Puerto Blest on Lago Nahuel Huapi. The hotel is a thirty-room wooden three-story from the early 1900s. The tourist season begins next month, and I alone am seated for dinner. Pentke has joined me and soon revealed his German ancestry. His hotel is hidden fairly deep in the backcountry, and I've no idea if he is a friendly Nazi or a history buff.

"There are many blacks in our neighboring countries. But here in Argentina they were killed by the wars and the gauchos. The gauchos hated them."

The gaucho is the Argentine cowboy, the free-spirited redneck of the pampas and Patagonia. That they might have terrorized black people is entirely believable if you've read Jose Hernandez's 1872 Argentine epic poem, *The Gaucho Martín Fierro.* Stiffening his resolve for a knife fight against a man darker than himself, Fierro recalls:

> *God made the white, and Saint Peter the brown.*
> *At least so I've heard men tell.*
> *But the devil himself he made the black.*
> *As coals for the fire of hell.*

I expect Pentke to carry on in this vein, but he has other ideas. He orders a bottle of Humberto Canale Cabernet. "It's local, good, and only four dollars a bottle."

A mushroom omelet is served by a proper waiter. Pentke tells me proud tales of his family, and I do the same. He asks of the flowers in the Andes, and his curiosity warms me. Steak and fries arrive. Pentke pours another glass of wine, pulls his chair closer, and tells me of Argentina's troubles over the past century. It's a frank and generous recounting, with a single exception. Pentke makes no mention of the decade that began with yet another military coup in 1976. Like the Pinochet in Chile, it was the worst of times.

Leftist rebels kidnapped or assassinated those on the right. The military did the same to the left, but with a martial zeal for torture and execution that made them far more effective. Somewhere between 10,000 and 30,000 people were "disappeared." The word is exactly right, for many were pushed out of planes over the Atlantic, their arms and legs churning uselessly until they hit the water and truly disappeared.

Dessert is peaches and cream and the clink of spoons on china. The military ruled, says Pentke, until "the Malvinas disaster brought a new call for elections." The Malvinas are forsaken islands of rock and bog, thinly peopled and hundreds of miles off the coast. The British call them the Falklands and have claimed them as their own since 1833. The Argentine military invaded in 1982, hoping a surge of patriotism would bolster support. They were wrong. Hundreds died on both sides. Argentina lost.

"It was very bad for the Argentine military," says Pentke, finishing off the wine with a smile that suggests that what is bad for the military is, in the end, good for Argentina. Today, the most sadistic and least cautious officers from the Dirty War are "behind bars, or in America, or staying low." After several presidents and economies staggering under inflation of up to 3,000 percent, Argentines are still searching for stability, for money that doesn't fade to nothing by year's end.

Then they can come here, to the Hotel Puerto Blest, where dinner ends with a lute and a recorder on the stereo. I climb the stairs to the final bath of the day, with the window open to the shush of an unseen waterfall.

THE FERRY TO Bariloche is a big boat, a hundred-foot catamaran powered by twin 900-horsepower Detroit Diesels. The same informative sign assures

the passengers that the *Condor* is built with "nine watertight compart-
ments." If this stirs sunken memories of the *Titanic*, you can ascend the
carpeted spiral staircase to the bar and soothe your nerves with a shot of
Old Smuggler whiskey.

Plenty of passengers do. Late in the afternoon, they're no longer awed by
the dark mountains ramped with pointed trees and snow, and not bothering to video the waterfalls that crash down every valley and dive into Lago
Nahuel Huapi. The mood on deck turns contemplative, which is similar
to bored except under pleasing circumstances. The sky is a firm blue. My
bicycle is lashed to an anchor on deck. Eastward, the land dries and the
forest opens in the rain shadow of the Andes. The snowfields shrink until
they persist only on the shady south slopes.

Bariloche is a high-dollar resort of bombproof chalets behind one-ton
gates, where not-thin people in velour warm-ups jog or at least shuffle.
For the proletariat, a package tour parade of double-decker buses runs
between the Wonderland Hotel and Little Red Riding Hood Ceramics. In
the town center the preferred building materials are timber and stone, a
rustic motif so pervasive that even the phone booths are miniature log
cabins.

Bariloche is the first place I can buy Captain Black pipe tobacco. It's
where I slip under the covers at night with a small contented smirk that
means: *Ha!* No more rain. It's where I rise in the morning, attempt to
touch my toes, then snap open the blinds to see that it's still not raining.
It's snowing.

The streets are swept clear of humans. The snow soon turns to rain, and
the rain itself gives up when the clouds are flung to Paraguay by an extraordinary wind. The telephone lines tremble and thrum, yet as soon as the
sky is clear the brave folk of Bariloche emerge. A girl wearing a relatively
aerodynamic beret is the only person I see attempting a hat, and she loses
it before my eyes. It sails the length of a city block before it touches down.
She doesn't bother to chase it.

I'd read that the furious Patagonian wind blew out of the west. Usually.
Today it's out of the northwest. This works while pedaling south, out of
Touristland and into a place where the people are darker and the cars are

older. The dump is announced by thousands of plastic bags snagged on fences and bushes, snapping like white flags.

It's easy to surrender when the road kinks west and into the wind. I'm aiming for the Atlantic, but the Andes won't cooperate. "Seventy kilometers per hour—very strong," says Roberto as he helps me load my bike into the trunk of his '89 Falcon. It's blue, like the sky is until a fresh regiment of clouds pours over the spine of the Andes. The sun is snuffed out and the land falls colorless.

Only ten minutes later the wind is fading, and it's good-bye to Roberto. The road turns south to hug the shore of a slender lake. Far above the water a toothy ridge of rock and ice rakes the clouds, which move so quickly it's impossible to know what's coming, sun or storm. All I can do is watch when a burst of wind and rain skids down the mountainside on the opposite side of the lake, a gray smear that bends the trees and spills onto the water with a sudden froth of whitecaps. The sound, a not-unpleasant whoosh, reaches me well before the wind itself.

Which arrives first as a tremble that may simply be my own fear, then a cold shove in the side that tilts but does not topple me. I squint at the Andes in shadow, at the ranks of dark pyramids ranging from hard black to rain-dulled gray. Beautiful and dreadful, they'll be at my side for the next two hundred miles.

> A stranger arrives. His name or business must not be asked, nor must he ask yours, unless there is some very good reason for doing so. He must be invited into the home and must at once be offered mate.
>
> —G. G. Simpson, *Attending Marvels:*
> *A Patagonian Journal,* 1934

THE LODGE COOK, oblivious to the cruel rain, is sweating over the stove. His name is Oscar, and he uses one hand as an ashtray and the other to hold the cigarette, stir a magnificent stew, and pick up from time to time what looks like a bonsai coconut with a silver straw to suck on.

It's not a coconut. It's a *mate,* which is pronounced "mah tay" and literally means "gourd," but more loosely describes the tea in the gourd, *yerba mate*.

I stick with a *café con leche*. Most Argentines insist *mate* is better. It provides not only a zesty pick-me-up but also sweet dreams. And unlike coffee, *mate* is often shared among friends in a communal gourd. I'd like to stick around and wait for the cook to offer a sip, but the rain stalls and I jump on the bike for my escape.

The Andes are still buried in storm, but still I make thirty miles. The rain piddles on my tent through the night. In the morning a blizzard is on my tail as I pant up a long grade to a another split-log tourist lodge with a perfect curl of smoke from the chimney.

A tour bus from Buenos Aires stops and the people pile out with their personal gourds and thermos jugs. They file in and beg, "Bathroom, where's the bathroom?" Increased urine output is another consequence of *mate*, but is generally construed as simply keeping your kidneys alert. On the other hand, these tourists are weak-bladdered seniors and may be more interested in *mate*'s alleged benefit of shrinking hemorrhoids while boosting the immune system. The gourds are passed among friends who take a sip or two on the slender *bombilla* before passing it back to be refilled from a thermos, swirling the mess of leaves. There are no tea bags. Some straws are filigreed silver with gold tips and some are gleaming stainless, but all are flattened and perforated at one end, to act as a filter.

The tour bus driver calls them away with a toot of his horn. It's still snowing. I read the provincial newspaper while sipping a coffee and enjoying its proven effects: trembling jitters to keep warm and oral pleasures such as a distinctive breath odor and, if I drink enough, a brown tongue. It tastes good, too.

Mate is said to warm you on cold days and cool you on warm days, an apparent contradiction that would be appreciated under the schizophrenic skies of Patagonia. When the clouds suddenly vanish I valiantly pedal on, but only ten minutes later I'm stung with sleet. I duck under a tree and waterproof my gear with plastic bags. Within a half hour I'm sweating madly under glorious sunbeams, and I need to stop and strip off the raingear and find a drink at the Cascada de la Virgin. A curio shop and waterfall in one, it has yet to open for the season. I ask the caretaker for water. He takes me to a spigot I hope is tapped into pure Andean spring water. (Although I smoke and drink, occasionally without bothering to get off the bike, I suffer healthy urges.) I fill my bottle and drink deeply before I notice the spinning clots of green algae. I ask, Umm, what's this? He looks and shrugs and says, "It's nothing. The water is clean."

It's downhill into the valley of El Bolson, whose welcome sign proclaims itself an "ecological community." It's the sort of place where people prefer their *mate* with a simple reed for a straw, paying homage to the native Guarani who first plucked *yerba mate*, the leaves of the holly tree called *Ilex paraguayensis*.

It's a friendly valley. I stop to watch a soccer game, taking a seat on the single long plank that serves as a grandstand. The satin-shirted players sprint through clouds of dust—it's hardly rained here. Who's playing? "Union del Sur and El Galpon," says my neighbor, passing me a quart of Schneider Beer. I drink, hoping the alcohol kills the algae from the Cascada de la Virgin.

At the grocery I stock up on apples, wine, instant cappuccino, soup, and an intriguing candy called Trembly Bichos, which means "trembling bugs." The check-out man is sharing a *mate* with a man named Nicanor, who tops it off with hot water. He recognizes a curious man and offers me my first *mate*.

The poorest gaucho would rather be trampled by his dearest sheep than drink from a Styrofoam *mate*. This taboo may collapse with time, but the gourd remains the traditional favorite. It may be intricately carved with geometries reminiscent of a Navajo blanket, or it may be jeweled like a Faberge egg. Some are painted with kitsch, or rimmed with sterling silver, or entirely sheathed in aluminum.

Nicanor's *mate* appears to be wrapped in leather. There is so much *yerba mate* in the gourd that it looks like a green froth of lawn clippings. It's not sweet. It's nearly astringent. Nicanor looks for approval. "Pretty good, eh?" Yes, I say, I like it. He smiles broadly and reveals pretty good teeth. "It's best when you drink it like this, from the testicle of the bull."

My Spanish fails me. I try to say, Sure, that's why it's still warm—but give up and only manage, You say this for fun? Nicanor slaps his thigh and takes the *mate* and says, "Look, here are the wrinkles!"

I can't argue: I've never been close enough to bull testicles to make a positive identification. But, I say, I thought *mate* was a gourd. "It *is* a gourd," says Nicanor. "The testicle goes around it, outside, to make it impermeable."

I believe him—but, I ask, couldn't you use intestines? Stomach? "No," is the definitive answer. "Bull testicle is the best."

He sees me off with the standard Argentine good-bye: "Luck. Good Luck." And it works. I find a perfect camp along a buttercup path. The Trembly Bichos are gummi bugs, which I like very much. The lullaby of a creek. And waking to see my favorite morning star, the sun.

It's time for a cup of coffee.

THE SCATTERBRAINED BIRDS know this much is true: it doesn't rain in paradise. A goose honks from the blue heights, a woodpecker spears a luckless grub from the bark, and a leggy plover called a teru-teru circles and cries out something that does not sound like *teru-teru*.

A call of pleasure, I guess—but then it dives at me and the bike. I forgive the nuisance. On this Sunday morning I've the blind cheer of a born-again Christian who sees everywhere the splendid handiwork of God. The long valley is tightly bounded by mile-high ridges, frosted with snow and so steep that the only way up is vertical rock or rubble chutes clinging at the angle of repose. Nothing lives on this moveable mountainside; the big fans of debris reach down to the very edge of the forest, the tall tight cones of somber green.

Where the slope gentles to something flat enough to cultivate and inhabit, the valley is bright with the baby greens of spring—the leaves of the skinny poplars that line the irrigation ditches. The water is shunted to little farms of black furrows flecked with young crops. Presumably the harvest is bound for the roadside stands of Bio-Andes Organic Vegetables.

Only two paved roads run north-south in Patagonia: one along the Atlantic, and this one. The Sunday drivers pilot thirty-year-old Ford pickups and burbling eighteen-wheelers and Mussolini-era Fiats. Traffic is tolerable, the heavens unblemished, and the teru-terus gone. Yet when I reach the junction with the scenic long-cut to Esquel, I pause. The detour is a hundred miles of dirt road striking off to the west, back toward the black peaks streaked with snow. The wrong way, of course, but the map shows the road eventually turning south again, alongside lakes I imagine as reflecting pools of the mountains. And although just yesterday morning I was cursing the Andes, today their beauty convinces me to take the long way to Esquel.

The hard-packed dirt road is excellent. It runs past split-rail corrals and through cattle pastures growing nature's answer to greedy cows: low tight mats of poisonous locoweed, pincushion grasses, and the clawed stems of roses.

A wrong-way wind picks up, fluttering a tattered shirt that's hung on a stick crucifix wired to a fence. I'm not a superstitious man, yet this Jesus scarecrow coincides with the road going to hell: deep gravel and steeply banked corners. Gravel is the worst: the slightest deviation from dead straight and the front wheel becomes a rudder. Just as a sailboat doesn't work in reverse, a bike cannot steer with a front rudder, which will promptly become a plow. To avoid being tossed over the handlebars I must keep the front wheel straight and light, shifting my weight behind the seat, all the while pedaling madly.

The gravel alternates with smooth stretches, luring me on into a forest of cypress and mushrooms. Very pretty, but the road is a trap, like falling for a woman whose sole unmentionable habit is not fully revealed until after the wedding. The wind swells and the road becomes a chattering washboard. Sitting is a nonstop spanking. Standing catches the full force of the wind. The only option is to pedal with head low and rear up, the profile of a pissed-off Arizona stinkbug.

The bike is taking it badly: one of the cargo panniers is rattling to pieces. I stop to fix it, in a brake of willows along a blackwater creek. A sweating horse is tied to a tree, and a gaucho is crouched by the stream. He can't hear my hello over the wind roaring in the trees. Oblivious to my presence, he palms up some water to slick back his dark hair.

I ride. Near a lonesome cabin a big hound charges out of the scrub. I leap off and drop the bike and grab some rocks. The beast halts under the dusty pines. I'm panting with adrenaline and anger. I don't want to hurt man's best friend. I want to kill him. Recognizing this subtle sign of exhaustion, I soon stop for the night. But my sleep is haunted by my friend Jim Boyer. He's falling again. And again.

There's no wind in the morning when I push on, but the road is lousy and Jim won't stop dying. The things I cherish about cycling—the time to think and an always open window on the world—have turned on me in this particularly unkind way: the gleaming summits of the Andes remind me of nothing so much as places to freeze and fall and be finished. Unable to shake the dead, I avert my gaze and pedal until I'm rescued by the living.

THE FIRST VEHICLE to pass in three hours is a big-windowed Fiat van. Once I'm inside, the outside world collapses to a moving picture beyond the hypnotic swing of the pine-tree air freshener hung from the mirror. My rescuers are a pair of tour guides with a single client in tow, the seventy-four-year-old Alberto. He grins and says, in English, "I speak English like Tarzan speaks Spanish."

Then says nothing more as we cruise pass the skinny lakes I'd so desired. The van halts, and the trio invites me on a walk into the "Thousand Year Alerce Grove." The rugged bicyclist is too beat to move. "Nature," wrote the poet Charles Simic, "is that which is slowly killing me."

They return in thirty minutes. A guide lights a smoke and explains why Alberto is still grinning: "We saw the giant woodpecker. Extraordinary. It was only ten feet away, and we got beautiful pictures."

Well. The van is very nice.

"Would you like some water? It comes from the Andes."

It's only a fifteen-mile ride, but it's nice to have company. The only thing better would be the company of a child, and that's exactly what I get when I'm dropped off at Bahia Rosales Lodge. There are no tourists on a Monday in November, only the delightful couple running the place, Viviana and Luis de Uriarte, and their toddler, Santiago. I recover—in bed, or eating stew, or sitting in a rattan chair and writing by the light of an unfrosted bulb—then continue south, along the pebbly shore of Lago Futalaufquen.

The dirt road is smoother but steeper, bulldozed through crumbling yellow sandstone and sooty volcanic bluffs. To the west, storms over Chile struggle to clear the Andes. When they finally push into Argentina, the clouds come with fantastic speed for something so big, a steely corrugated roof a hundred miles across. The little swallows, hardly a calm bird in the best of circumstances, duck and hide. I stop and brace for the wind, murmuring what has surely passed the lips of every Patagonian: *Not again.*

But the clouds evaporate and the sun returns, dazzling the chop on the lake. I hear, then see a young couple on bikes pumping up a steep grade. Each of us is glad to see another cyclist. They say they're on their way to the United States, and there's no reason to doubt them: Wilfred and Jikke wear biking shorts that can scarcely contain their tanned super-thighs.

I admire their rubber cargo panniers, and Jikke says, "Everything's waterproof—we're from Holland!"

But you sound like an American.

"I was in Tennessee for a year, in the prayer belt. I was in a student foreign exchange program. I lived with huge people. I learned all about fat food. What I like most about America are the fat-free cookies and ice cream."

When do you hope to reach Arizona?

"July," says Wilfred. "Is it hot then?"

I'll pray for you.

The road turns east at last, toward the faraway Atlantic, and within ten miles the beech forest is replaced by grasslands and big hopping hares. Trees persist only along the rocky banks of the Rio Percey, wands of poplar with leaves that flash silver undersides in the wind.

Sunset bloodies the west. In Esquel, a hotel room on the plaza rewards me with a view of the landslide mountains like slag heaps. The writing desk and hard bed are perfect. On the television, the Simpsons demonstrate a remarkable command of Spanish. In comparison, my cultural integration lags: I can't even tame the Patagonian shower, which has five identical knobs. I turn one and a hidden jet squirts me under the chin. With more caution I try another knob, and this time easily dodge the blazing hot water from above. I simplify the situation by assuming there are only two positions, on and off, for each of the five knobs. This means there are two to the fifth power or thirty-two possible combinations, one of which eventually delivers a warm shower.

The rest of Esquel is welcoming, with curb cuts for wheelchairs and mild-mannered motorists who wait for pedestrians. Mapuche boys hawk newspapers on the street. At an ice-cream parlor there's Cher on the radio, and a young lady wearing the standard ice-cream server smock. Her name is Monica. I ask for a single scoop of "Fruits of the Forest," then sneak in a question about my hoped-for route through the desert.

"It is very pretty in Paso de Sapo. Lots of rocks, but not many plants." Meanwhile, she's assembling not a single scoop for me, but a little Matterhorn. When, I ask, was the last time you visited?

"Umm . . . two years ago." Then she adds, sagaciously for her twenty-one years, "But places like that don't change."

Paso del Sapo doesn't change because it's a hundred miles off the pavement. I haven't forgotten my accidental self-starving over the pass into Argentina, and the next day I buy pasta, soup, cereal, powdered milk, cheese, bread, and cookies. I pick up fifty aspirin and a tin of hand cream. A bike mechanic oils my chain and envies my tires, each an uncommon 700 x 47. Such things don't come to Esquel. I post a letter in an office with a rattling teletype. In the bank, typewriters clack and rubber stamps thud. Old sounds, like the hoot of the steam train. Once it connected Esquel with Buenos Aires and carried Paul Theroux to the end of his journey from Boston, in *The Old Patagonian Express*. Today it runs just twelve miles, for the tourists.

When I load my bike onto a wooden carriage I'm surprised to see one of the Mapuche newspaper boys on board. He hops off at a place called Nahuel Pan. In Argentina, what little land the Indian is left with is not called a *reservation*; they live on a *reduction*: a picket fence and a half-dozen cabins. The gray-green plain clumped with sheep may be Mapuche land, but it's unlikely. Much of Patagonia is now owned by the likes of Benetton. The Italian apparel company has well over two million acres in holdings, mostly devoted to turning plants into wool—with the help of several hundred thousand sheep.

The train drops me off by the highway. The engine sneezes and huffs away. At the turnoff to Paso del Sapo I bump onto the gravel and ride for a minute before stopping to consider the expanse of sheep-clipped grass and dull green shrubs, each a congestion of bristled stems. Sheep-repellent, probably—but they attract me with the possibility of making first-rate pipe cleaners.

The wind is out of the WNW. That's good. Yet it's forty miles to the next town, Gualjaina, then sixty more to Paso del Sapo. Despite my infatuation with self-propulsion, I'm nervous. After a final look over my shoulder at the last mountains with snow I'll see, I slip my foot into the toe clip and ride, into thick air.

ON THE OPEN PLAIN is a gaucho, walking along the road with his head down and into the wind. He's a fine-looking sheepboy, dressed to kill, with a flat-brimmed black felt hat cinched to his chin and a silky red bandanna round his neck, a belt woven of many colors, and pleated baggy pants tucked into polished leather boots.

I ask his name.

"Gustavo."

Where do you come from?

"Out there."

Out there I see twists of wind sucking at the dust, and large birds tilting in the wind.

I feel guilty asking him to pause for a photo. Gustavo has no questions, while I suffer the usual city man's hankering for cowboy life—at least as I imagine it. The legendary Martín Fierro sang, "And this is my pride: to live as free as the bird that cleaves the sky." A century later Bruce Chatwin hitched around Patagonia and was favorably impressed by the gauchos' honest poverty. Aside from their "ponchos, their *mate* equipment, and their knives, the peons were free of possessions."

Gustavo says good luck and lowers his head and walks on. In ten minutes this shy man is a dot.

For a long time there is nobody but the whiptail lizards. The road is thankfully thin on the gravel. When a Ford pickup finally passes, its brake

lights flash on. It waits in the dust. The driver, who already has one passenger, wants to know where I'm going. "Gualjaina!" he says. "Let me give
you a ride up this hill. Then you can ride downhill to Gualjaina."

Their names are Jorge and Juan. They deliver gas cylinders for stoves,
and drive for five minutes before Jorge suddenly slaps the dash and yells,
"*Piche! Piche!*"

It's an armadillo trundling across the road. Juan mashes the brakes
and we slide to a halt, with Jorge climbing over me trying to get after the
creature. Juan is already in pursuit. The armadillo skedaddles through the
brush and Juan dives for it. Nothing.

Jorge's lunge is on the money. He cradles the armadillo upside down.
It's the size of a football. Topside, it actually looks like a football, except its
leathery shell is gray. But underneath it is merely hairy and hence quite
vulnerable, with four frantic legs, tiny eyes, and a pointy snout.

"It's a male," says Jorge. "It's a fat one," says Juan, and suddenly I know
the fate of the armadillo. As Darwin wrote 170 years ago, "It almost seems
a pity to kill such nice little animals, for as a gaucho said, while sharpening
his knife on the back of one, 'Son tan mansos' (they are so quiet)."

Jorge finds a saw in the back of the truck and slices the armadillo's
throat. Ten seconds of blood darkening the dirt, and the armadillo is still.
"Everybody," says Jorge, "eats armadillo."

They're nice guys—they don't cut my throat. They drop me off, and a
brisk tailwind shoots me toward Gualjaina with such speed that I reach
the town's single long dirt avenue well before sunset. I park my machine
between a pair of Ford Falcons. Since I'm packing enough food to survive a
nuclear winter, it's no surprise that Gualjaina has a grocery filled with all I
needlessly carried. To give my visit the appearance of purpose, I buy a beer
and a banana. Outside, a mess of children stare goggle-eyed at my amazing
bicycle. The store's owner comes out and says, "Travelers are welcome to
spend the night at the police station—and they have a shower."

Thank you, madam. But I seek the company of willows and waterbirds
by the Rio Chubut.

Not far from town I help a man put a wheel back on his wagon. It's old
and held together with wire. The equally worn-out horse is instructed to

stand still. A silent wife and small dirty children stand by a stack of fire-wood they've offloaded to lighten the wagon. "*Uno . . . dos . . . tres!*"—and the wheel slips onto the axle.

Camp is where the green river is coaxed into a bend by a cliff of lumpy red rock. I spritz open the beer and wash my feet by poking around the polished stones in the shallows. In the cutting aridity, my feet dry in a minute.

There are many pretty rocks on this earth, but only the rare ones are known as precious. So nice, it is, to be at last in a place where water is precious.

THE WIND COMES in the night, at first a hollow roar, then bullying down the canyon and burrowing under my tent so the floor flaps like laundry in a gale.

At dawn the birds are glaring at me, as if I kept them up all night. A lazy caracara, perched on a snag like a claw, waits. The ibises are bashful and fly away, calling out with what sounds like the cry of monkeys in jungle movies. But the nervous teru-teru actually comes for me, shrieking mad and so close I see its red eyes. I win the stare-down: my sleepless eyes are redder.

The wind is on my tail but so ferocious that by noon I can hardly stop, much less turn around. The road never leaves the river for long, and to-gether they drop into badlands of colors like melted purple crayons. In a reedy meander a flock of flamingos sieve the shallows with their big goofy bills. Another bend in the river and the badlands are replaced by seamless bluffs of monolithic ash flows. It's a tough rock: a lone butte stands like a hitchhiker's thumb, in defiance of both wind and river, three hundred feet tall.

The wind is loud. It blows across my open water bottle with a moan that changes pitch with the water level. Only when I get coasting along at 20 mph on a good stretch of road does the wind quiet in my ears, and only then do I hear the wind in the cliffs. Sometimes it is like a waterfall and sometimes like a cutting torch.

When the land fades behind a wall of dust I'm relieved to find an old stable to rest in. I lie back for a minute, counting the fox skins that hang from a rafter. An hour later I wake to a cry of surprise from a gaucho atop a fine pony. Jammed under his belt is a foot-long knife. I hop to my feet and tell him who I am and where I'm from, and he does likewise. Fermin Espinosa, he says, not bothering to introduce his soundless sidekick, an antique peon with rawhide hands.

"I come from Gualjaina, but now I am from this ranch. The Three Brothers."

He reconsiders. "No. The Two Brothers."

He shows me the little ranch house with a beehive bread oven, built of mud. The house is smartly equipped with a windmill for electricity. Switches of poplar, ripped off by the wind, sail past. Some are sliced into kindling by the blur of the windmill blades.

"This wind," says Fermin, "is just an everyday wind. You should be glad it's not *really* windy."

The everyday wind is mostly at my back, but it's hard to be glad. Every two or three minutes there is a big blow and I'm not merely shoved along but engulfed in a cloud of dirt and little stones that pelt my back and click off the lenses of my glasses. With this velocity and viscosity, the wind is like water, with sudden eddies and riptides, and it is all I can do to keep the bike on the road. Sometimes I can't. Blown into the desert, I hang on, legs splayed wide like outriggers and feet ripping through the spring flowers in billows of dust and pollen. Easing on the brakes, I stop and suck for air through the bandanna round my face until the wind drops to a mere 20 or so mph.

Late in the afternoon the wind vanishes. The dust settles and from the murk emerges the river canyon, walls of sandstone branded with ripple marks from a now-dead sea. The side canyons, deep in alluring shadow, are fenced off as natural corrals. From the barbed strands the gauchos have hung the carcasses of coyotes—a warning to the enemy of sheep.

The wind returns and carries away all notions of hiking into one of the canyons. All that matters now is reaching what appears, a few miles ahead, to be poplars in long windrows that bow, then relax.

In time-honored rural tradition, most every house in Paso del Sapo looks to be either going up or coming down. Outside a whitewashed church topped by an ugly concrete bell tower, a gaggle of young nuns tell me exactly what I want to hear: there is a place to stay right next door.

It's a house, a little clean white cube. I knock. The door opens and the matron immediately gestures me inside, saying, "Close the door before the flies come in!"

I'm looking for a room, I say. I'm tired.

She takes a good look at me and says, "You look dead."

Fortunately, I've landed in intensive care. Ms. Nilda Sierra's two-room inn is a spic-n-span expanse of white tiles. When a fly manages to buzz in, she takes aim with Raid insect obliterator, followed with a spritz of Blue Sea air scent.

On the counter by the register is a sign: *No Torn Money*. I wash my socks in the shower and Ms. Sierra strolls outside with me as I hang them from the clothesline. She's friendly but impatient with my Spanish, preferring volume over clarity when she speaks.

"A man went down the river on a raft a long time ago," she yells as she hands me a Patagonian clothespin, a clamp with the spring of a bear trap. "He was very fat, and looked like a toad. So came the name, Toad Pass."

Paso del Sapo. Back inside, she keeps a running tab of my bill, inking a new figure on her palm as I drink and eat. But I've no stomach for my fried slab of meat. During the night I wake a dozen times, stricken with a deadly thirst and rising fever. Ms. Sierra is not exactly sinister, yet as I lie unhappily on the lumpy bed I get the irrational idea that she has stuffed my mattress with dolls.

When I wake at dawn to rain battering the roof, I know there will be no bicycle escape from Paso del Sapo. I ask Ms. Sierra to call the local gas station and spread the word that a sick tourist is willing to pay cash for a ride to the pavement at Paso de los Indios. It takes three hours for a pair of Sapo boys with crude tattoos and easy grins to drive me the distance.

There are no Indians in Paso de los Indios, only a truck stop and wool depot and school serving the sheep ranches. There is no river valley. I've arrived during the glory of spring, yet there are only small thorn bushes decorated with plastic bags shivering in the wind. The depot is corrugated steel and big enough for a soccer game if it were not stacked with man-sized bales of wool, each weighing 260 pounds. There's another stack, too: the skins of foxes, guanacos, and pampas cats—all destined to be collars and cuffs.

As usual, I'm the only guest at the inn, but the adjoining bar suffers no lack of business. Men in black berets and rope-soled slippers raise heavy tumblers of red wine and slap cards onto a stained bar. They regard me with caution. Perhaps I still look dead, although my fever has cooled. The adobe walls, painted the same faint green of the scrub, are sixteen inches thick, and at night I hear nothing in my room but the faint round-the-clock clatter of the diesel generator that electrifies Paso de los Indios. Satellite TV arrived last month, bearing the global gift of Chuck Norris.

I pass on the tube but take a dinner of mutton. In 1930, G. G. Simpson stayed at a mud-brick inn near Paso de los Indios. "Provision for dinner at this hotel consists of a live sheep, and permission to use the stove."

THE EXQUISITE SILENCE of morning can only mean that the wind is gone. But where? Somewhere it waits, ready to pounce on the foolish and bat its victim about playfully before delivering the final, spine-snapping coup de grace.

Such are the deeply wary thoughts of a recovering cyclist, pedaling east with low hopes. Five miles out of Paso de los Indios, the highway slips back into the Chubut River canyon. This far from the storms of the Andes, the river is a thin scribble of water in braided channels between sand islands and willows. To either side are sheer walls built of pebbles and ash that restrain the river within a mile-wide floodplain. Where the road closely approaches a cliff there is a sign advising the tourist: *Photo Panorama*. Some have stopped and spray-painted political war cries on the blameless stone.

I pray, in my godless way, for no wind. Argentines hoping for the un-likely have their own approach: they leave a roadside offering of a plastic water bottle on certain hillocks scattered throughout the country, including one by the Rio Chubut.

The water is for Deolinda Correa. She's not a virgin or a saint recog-nized by the Vatican. She was a mother, with an infant, trying to reach a husband who was, depending on the story, either unfairly drafted or unfairly jailed by evil Argentine authorities in 1840. Like Jesus, she suffered in the desert. When she was finally felled by thirst, she gave her life so another may live, which is why her son was found alive—a suckling at the breast of a corpse.

A miracle! say the believers. And, hoping for their own miracle, they leave a water bottle for *The Deceased Correa*. It's a slapdash veneration that ends up looking like a small dump. The shrine by the Rio Chubut is a single candle in a blue wooden box surrounded by an enormous heap of Fanta, Sprite, and Coke bottles.

For my money, I'd rather believe in the blood-sucking *chupacabra*. I'm certainly in the right habitat: few people and plenty of unattended livestock. The *chupacabra*, unlike most large carnivores, has defied extinction and instead recently extended its range over the whole of Latin America, clear up to my Tucson home. So it should be no surprise that I've seen one, with the wings of a bird, the scales of a reptile, and the appalling fangs of a vampire. Or at least that's how it looked in the drawing made for me some years ago by a miner prospecting on the Mexican border. The *chupacabra* had menaced him only the night before. I did not mention that the drawing strongly resembled one of the gargoyles of Notre Dame—how could this lonely miner know of such a thing? But then he shook the drawing in my face and hissed, "This is one fucking bad French bird."

Now, on the banks of the Rio Chubut, I choose my camp with careless disregard for the *chupacabra*. The real creatures of this world hold mystery enough, dashing through the brush as I lay out my sleeping bag. I catch a glimpse of one. "Elegant-crested Tinamou" says the bird book. *Martineta*, say the Argentines. But it sure looks like a racing chicken with a long neck and a ridiculous plume atop its head.

There is no wind. A large animal, unseen but probably a horse, splashes across the river. I sleep, then wake to find the moon down and the stars startling. Were there this many before? The Milky Way arches from horizon to horizon. Looking up at this incandescent donut, anything seems possible, from *chupacabras* to time itself curved by an unimaginable gravity until it runs in a circle like a snake swallowing its tail. But when I look to the side, at the grasses gone to seed, there is unexpected satisfaction in a world where time runs one way, and tomorrow's wind can never undo this day of calm.

COFFEE TIME, and the caracaras are watching me again. I wish they would get a job. Darwin noted that "these false eagles most rarely kill any living bird or animal," yet they are hardly a cheering presence. They possess several habits whose appeal is likely limited to teenage boys and Darwin, who called them "a bird of very versatile habits and considerable ingenuity." By "versatile" he means that they like to snack on the scabs on the backs of horses. By "ingenious" he means that the caracara will leisurely watch vultures gorging on a dead sheep. Only when a vulture leaves does the caracara take wing, relentlessly pursuing the vulture until it vomits the carrion—then it's mealtime for the caracara.

I have a ham and cheese at the Los Altares gas station/café, a 1960s extravaganza of wood and glass and concrete in a dozen intersecting planes. The man in charge is briskly attentive to his patrons, cruising the dining room with an eye for detail.

"What is that?"

He's pointing at the electrical cord for my computer, which I'd plugged in without first asking.

"This is not a dump where you can do whatever you like. Do you not have any respect for property?"

Not enough. I soften him with an apology. He deserves it for doing a bang-up job of running this outpost. It's swept. All the lights work. There's a mechanic, dressed in overalls the blue and yellow of the Argentina flag, waiting in the nearly greaseless greasepit for your car to wheeze or knock.

Locals ranchers, in wool slacks and shoes caked with dung, tank up on gas at two bucks a gallon, then step in to refill their *mate* thermos. When they spot me they invariably say, *Welcome to Argentina! We saw you in the newspaper!* They show me the story: a German cyclist is heading south to Tierra del Fuego. Sorry, I say. I'm going to Salina Grande, only a couple hundred miles east.

Outside, the flag of the Automobile Club of Argentina is beginning to flap in the wrong direction. I hurry to pack, and notice that I'm being watched by a group of young men idling by the gas pumps. Some have asymmetrical faces, permanently quizzical yet at the same time lacking the look of intellect. I'm not sure of them, and fear that some have seen the computer go into my bag, making clear a connection between me and money that I'd rather remain unknown.

Too late. Here comes the one with a florid face of a boxer, wearing blue plastic flip-flops. He gets what he wants from me: name, origin, and occupation.

I get the same. Abel Escobar, chief of this eighteen-man sheep-clipping crew and their antique Mercedes bus. I'd seen similar buses, parked near fences draped with drying laundry.

"We're all from Rio Negro, in the north of Patagonia," says Escobar. "Every year we head out in August, and we return in December. We travel the same route, the same ranches."

I hit him with a barrage of questions.

How long to shave a sheep? "Three to four minutes."

How much wool? "About four kilos a sheep."

How many sheep a day for the crew? "Twelve hundred."

Whose clippers? "Ours. They're in the trailer behind the bus. Each is $800." Like a proud dad, he shows me a photo of the clipper. It's like a dentist drill, with an articulated arm delivering the power.

The men take a picture of me—not the German, but better than nothing. I ask the crew what they do when the season is over. They look to Escobar, who shrugs and says, "No work." He looks down and toes the gravel and waits for disapproval from the man from the country that never stops working. I tell him that six months is enough.

"Yes!" cry the men. "Enough! That's the way to live!"

Knowing when to quit is an acquired trait in Patagonia. I'm getting the hang of it, pedaling through the morning during the lulls in the wind, and giving up once it really starts blowing. Then I seek shelter behind a boulder that had fallen from the canyon wall, unwrap and eat a rapidly desiccating sandwich, and remember G. G. Simpson again.

His pilot once tried to land a light plane into a typically fresh wind, and found to his horror that although they could dive with enough speed to approach the runway, when level they could not fly fast enough to reach it. Time after time, the plane would plummet to the end of the runway, only to bob like a bumblebee with its engine roaring as the wind pushed it back before they could touch down. Of course they finally did land. And only one person died.

I hitch. A 1978 Ford pickup stops. The dashboard is home to socket wrenches, hand cream, and several hundred anxious flies. The driver is a creased and fit man named Mr. Hector Tolosa. He wants to know, "Are you the German?" Sorry.

In the center of the seat is a tall Basque with a severe expression on a face as long as a goat's. He wears clean jeans and penny loafers and a silk bandanna held by a silver ring. Yet he is a working man, with a ranch on the far side of the river. When we drop him off he must scull across in a little boat.

Here the canyon is lava spills over pink badlands. Mr. Tolosa points out a seam of coal. I crane my neck to take in the big fangs of rock under a sky of water colors. Sensing my affection for the land, Tolosa tells me his secret, his hidden canyon from which he pipes in the water to his ranch house.

A white house with a big garden. An aged, limping lady greets us at the screen door. Tolosa kisses her, and for a moment I ungraciously assume that he married the last woman in Patagonia. "Sir, my mother."

Oh. I meet his trusty helper, too, a man so old that it's unlikely he's much help. I'm invited to stay, but the story deadline clock is ticking, and I must try for another ride.

No problem. It's another 1978 Ford pickup, its windshield laminated with decades of insects. "Are you the German?" Sorry.

Twenty miles brings us to a gas station in Las Plumas. Two women are enjoying the dusk in the windbreak provided by the station. The younger says that there is no hotel in town.

The older retorts with authority, "Yes, there is."

"Well, it's not much of a hotel."

The building is a Frankenstein of adobe, red brick, concrete block, and cut stone. Dinner is cooking in the courtyard, the eternal flame burning under the splayed carcass of blackened lamb impaled on what looks like a sword. In the bar, a cluster of protein-poisoned carnivores clamor for more *vino tinto*—until they notice me, after which they fall silent.

It's not much of a hotel. I alone sit on the verandah and sniff the moisture aloft on the east wind. It's the Atlantic Ocean.

ALONG THE FINAL STRETCH of the Rio Chubut, the valley opens wide and runs true to the sea. To one side of the highway is a pale desert of pebbles and stiff bushes shading the spring yellows of mustards and the curls of heliotropes. To the other side are irrigation canals and alfalfa fields and the town of Dolovan.

The Welsh built Dolovan. The first of them came in 1865 on the brig *Mimosa* out of Liverpool. Just as the Chileans welcomed the Germans, the Argentines gave land to the Welsh on the condition they would hoist the local colors. Eager to shed their hated English overlords, by the First World War about three thousand had made the voyage, trying to build a new Wales. Then the Welsh stopped coming.

I imagine that they built the stern chapel and slow waterwheels. The red brick building straddling a canal surely must have been a mill; today it wears the sign "Oasis Disco." Hundred-year-old willows give shade to pickups with doors open and speakers thrusting with industrial rap. This is one of the most effective Malusa repellents known, and I pedal on, along the edge of the pebbly desert and into thickening humidity. The river valley is bounded by natural levees of low crumbling hills. As the valley widens, so does the road, busy with air-conditioned tractors and cars driving to video stores or industrial parks of giant metal sheds.

Before leaving home I'd read up on the Welsh and thought I'd invest a day in tracking them down. Now, with eight hundred miles behind me and Salina Grande only a day north along the coast, I'm looking for nothing more than a pit stop.

But I'm a lucky man. The owner of my bed-and-breakfast in the town of Gaiman is Gwyn Jones, a thirty-seven-year-old in a BBC Radio Wales T-shirt. After I shower off the Patagonian grit, Gywn invites me to boys' barbeque night. "Bring a knife and a cup. The Golden Rules of the party are no talk about women, politics, football, or the English. And no portable phones, either, or we would never get around to singing our hymns."

Welsh hymns, I suppose—something to remind them of Wales, because Patagonia sure doesn't. The first settlers were led to believe that the valley of the Chubut was rather similar to their homeland. Captain Fitzroy and Darwin, aboard the HMS *Beagle* in 1832, noted driftwood and wild cattle on the Chubut delta. In the 1862 *Handbook of the Welsh Colony*, these observations became "tall strong forests," "luscious pastures," and "herds of animals."

The 1865 settlers found driftwood on a nude floodplain. The Welsh were so ill-equipped for the desert that it took them two years to discover the principle of irrigation. They'd thought the soil was bad.

Today there are traffic lights at the end of the earth. The lower Chubut Valley is thoroughly inhabited by over 100,000 people. Of these, men surnamed Hughes, Evans, Humphries, and Jones have come to the *asado*, gathering in a one-room shed with a fireplace, a grill, and a single bulb on a wire. Although most of them are of mixed blood, the flag of Wales is tacked to the wall. A four-liter jug of wine sits on a rough table scattered with breadcrumbs and big knives. Most of the talk is in Spanish, thank goodness. To my ear, the Welsh language is hungry for vowels, and it's no wonder that nobody but the Welsh are willing to keep the language afloat.

The sound of knives sharpening on whetstones means that the meat is ready. Gwyn stabs a hunk and points with his dripping blade. "One man—there—is half Tehuelche Indian, and he speaks Welsh. The Welsh probably would not have survived without the help of the Tehuelche. Things went badly at first, and the Tehuelche showed them how to catch animals like the guanacos and rheas. They had to learn to throw the *boleadoras*."

Nowadays nobody hunts with tethered stones. But they are still celebrating their feast with song. The guitar comes out, and after the Argentine ballads come the Welsh hymns. *Hallelujah*, they cry—and the chorus responds, a bunch of half-breeds singing in Welsh. Maybe it's just the wine, but tonight that tottering language sounds not just fully alive, but beautiful. It sounds to me like the dream of a Welsh Patagonia came true, and I tell my host exactly that. Gwyn says, "For the moment. Come back in fifty years and see."

I keep my true Patagonia thoughts to myself. I don't want to come back. The winds have pared me down to a single desire.

PENINSULA VALDÉS is an unlikely piece of earth, shaped like a hatchet. The handle is a narrow neck of sheep land with the strong blue Atlantic on either side. The head of the hatchet is fifty miles wide and fortified with white sea cliffs. It is the last place in South America I would expect to find a great dimple, 138 feet below sea level—Salina Grande.

Pedaling out from the mainland, I see no hint of a hole—there's just a thin black road bordered with knee-high bunch grasses, and the expanse of low, tight shrubs beyond. The land is flattish, just sandy enough to have been humped up by the wind into hillocks ten and twenty feet above the horizon.

With little traffic, I'm free to stop and poke at the dried husk of a tarantula, then stop again to feel sorry for half of a green snake. On the roadside is another sloppy shrine, a mess of water bottles beside a splintered wooden sign that simply says *Deceased*.

For the wildlife still alive, Peninsula Valdés is a preserve. I pay the entrance fee at the visitor center, climb the concrete observation tower, and put a peso in the spotting scope. It's very good, zooming in on the lumps of sea lions hauled up on the sands. Unlike television sea lions, they decline to mate or fight. They don't even move. Above a little island of rock plastered with guano are thousands of white birds spinning like confetti. They do nothing but mate and fight.

Once I'm back on the bike, a north wind boots me in the side all the way to the town of Puerto Piramide, tucked in alongside the bay where the handle meets the head of the hatchet. I head for the shelter of the first hotel. The wind huffs all night and into the morning. Breakfast is six hours (the wait staff is very accommodating) of coffee and writing and glancing up to find the sea still troubled by the wind.

Although the wind will not quit, the asphalt does, only a few miles out of town. I stick to the tracks where truck tires have spat out the gravel. A helpful sign reads *Avoid Sudden Turns of the Wheel*, and I abide. Then, without my permission, the side wind shifts to my back. The sun, also behind me, floods the sandy swales and even the sheep with a marvelous green-yellow light. I feel the pendulum of luck swinging my way.

Yet there's always the suspicion that good weather won't last in Patagonia. "To this day I don't know whether I love it with all my soul," wrote Simpson, "or hate it with all my heart. Or both."

A blue truck stops, out of courtesy and curiosity. The bed of the Chevy holds the four-wheeled ATV of a modern sheepman. He's a smiling dad with two sons who appear to be exact shrunken copies of their father. They want to know where I'm going.

I tell them: to the lowest point in all of South America, Salina Grande.

"Yes! It's forty-two meters below sea level. You must look carefully for the turn, just after you first see the low."

The "low" is a great bowl ten miles across, several hundred feet deep, and rimmed here and there with sandy bluffs. The turnoff is obvious. The two-track road is smooth, and soon I'm close enough to see that the bottom of the bowl appears to be filled with the sky. The splendid illusion spurs me on, although there's no need to hurry. It's only a few miles, and there's a good two hours before sundown. A pair of guanacos, slender humpless camels, spy on me, but they're not very good at hiding. A lime green lizard shoots across the road like a party favor, celebrating my arrival. I take the hint and stop for a festive drink of red wine.

But like many an excitable man, I suffer from premature celebration. Only a mile from the salt lake, I catch the sputter of a poorly tuned engine. It's a pea green Peugeot pickup truck. The rancher inside is not smiling.

"This is private property. A tourist can't come here."

It had never occurred to me that somebody may actually own Salina Grande. I'm too dumbfounded to deliver my life history, and it's just as well: he may think me a dangerous crank on a whacked-out mission. Instead, I meekly ask Mr. Fernandez for permission to camp by the salt lake.

"But what if you start a fire?"

No fires. Promise.

"If I let one person camp, I'll have to let others."

I explain that this salt lake is like no other in South America, but he's already loading my bike into the truck. "You cannot stay here."

Can I stay at some other place on Salina Grande?

"You can go to the next *salina*—Salina Chica. It looks the same. There are three or four *salinas*, and they all look the same."

He drives me back up to the main road and offers to take me to Puerto Piramide. I decline, saying I'd rather head downwind. The truck heads toward the mainland, the clatter of its diesel engine fading until there is no sound but the wind.

I figure Mr. Fernandez isn't the owner of Salina Grande but works there under strict orders to eject all tourists. It won't be his fault if a single man fails to heed him, and instead finds another road to the Salina, five miles east. Keeping in mind that Mr. Fernandez may at this moment be preparing his Elmer Fudd musket with a load of salt intended for me, I sweep away my tire tracks at the turnoff. A branch from a shrub with leaves like arrowheads does the job.

This road is five miles of dips puddled with gluey clay. I charge through, only to bog down in a sand trap. I drag the bike. Nothing can stop me now that I see that the lake at the bottom of the *salina* is no longer the color of the sky. It's a shocking pink and blue, and it's edged in brilliant white.

I reach the shore thirty seconds before the sun drops below the horizon. The full moon is rising over a shore of pure salt. The pink comes from the sort of algae that gives flamingos their color.

There is an abandoned saltworks, reduced to foundations, and a wood-slat cabin that rattles and moans in the wind. I find a better camp in a sandy hollow rimmed with plantains, their stalks like cotton swabs. Out of the wind, I devour a ham sandwich and get to work on the wine, then lie back and listen to the whistle of a bird and the slap of waves on the shore.

Later, my spirit buoyed by the wine, I stand to face the wind and see the moonlight on the salt. I take a stroll, and crystals pop underfoot like glass ornaments. I'm happier than I should be. Patagonia had beat me, from the dripping Andes to the blasted desert. Yet when I turn to see the light from my lantern, I understand that this is my reward—a single yellow flame at the bottom of South America, with Mr. Fernandez nowhere to be seen.

AFRICA

*Hyenas are ugly animals that smell
bad and eat animals killed by other
creatures. They make a sound like
the laughter of an insane person.*
—Art Linkletter's *Picture
Dictionary for Boys and Girls*, 1961

CHAPTER 9

Tucson to Djibouti Town

Usually in Afternoon We Are Eating the Khat

"So WHERE ARE you headed off to this time?" asked Dr. Pellerito. "Step on the scale. Let's get your weight and height."

Djibouti, I said. It's in Africa, a little country between Somalia, Ethiopia, and Eritrea.

"Africa? Malaria everywhere. One hundred fifty-five pounds—same as before. AIDS, too. Even the monkeys have AIDS. Five foot ten. Good." He gestured to a chair. "Have a seat and tell me what you need."

Dr. Pellerito's little office was packed with pharmaceutical samples and leaning towers of magazines ranging from *Sports Illustrated* to *Diabetes Self-Management*. A plastic fig tree languished in a corner. The walls were shingled with snipped-out cartoons taped atop older cartoons taped atop the oldest cartoons.

We talked about malaria. Dr. Pellerito, looking professional in his white lab coat and neat beard, listened carefully and said, "So you don't like the Lariam? It's the antimalarial recommended by the County Health Clinic."

Yes, I said, but it gives me nightmares. I'd much rather try the new drug, Malarone.

"OK with me." He found a pad and pen advertising Zoloft and figured how many Malarone to prescribe. "Twenty-five. Alright—what else do you need for Djibouti? What about wild animals?"

Not many, I hope. I only worry about the hyenas.

"Well, a hyena can eat you."

I'll carry a pointed stick.

"They run in packs. You might get the first, but others will be right behind."

He was right, but he was being playful, too. He took my blood pressure. "I don't know how you do these trips, but I suppose you're used to it, camping alone all over the world. How do you pick these places like Djibouti? Are you carrying something for dysentery? Amoebas?"

I checked my kit and said, I've got some Flagyl, but isn't that for *Giardia?* The lowest point in Africa is in Djibouti, a salt lake called Lac Assal. It's like Death Valley, except deeper: five hundred feet below sea level. And it's right on the coast, where the Red Sea opens into the Indian Ocean, across from Yemen. The sea doesn't rush into the pit because they're separated by a volcano that last erupted in 1978. Can I take Flagyl for amoebas?

"You can, but the dose is tripled."

How do I know if I've got *Giardia* or amoebas?

"That's right—you won't know. Why the low points? Most people go up, not down—or is that your point? Something different?"

Actually, something warmer. Someplace I can ride my bike. Unless I've got dysentery.

Dr. Pellerito discovered a cache of the anti-diarrheal Imodium. He gave me enough to plug the Nile.

"That should do it. What about the roads in Djibouti? Do you have any general antibiotics?"

I checked my kit. Nope, I said. I don't expect many paved roads. There's only one city.

"How about some Ciproflaxin?" He tossed me a box of two five-hundred-milligram pills. Then another box. "Do you have a rearview mirror?" Another box.

I stuffed them into my kit, forgetting to ask the dosage. I said that I had a mirror, but I survive by assuming that *nobody* sees me.

"That's what I do when I'm jogging. Need some antibiotic cream? Band-Aids?"

Sure. Thanks.

"I wouldn't turn down free Band-Aids, either." The sterile-until-opened Band-Aids were relics; the wrappers immediately peeled apart. Dr. Pellerito knew I didn't care. He wrote a prescription for my bee-sting allergy injector, shook my hand, and said, "Djibouti. You're set. Have a good trip."

I PEDALED HOME and promptly recorded my visit with Pellerito. I kept a list titled "Warnings and Encouragements." Nobody was indifferent when I mentioned my plan to pedal through Djibouti.

Mother-in-law Rosa set down her glass of *vino tinto* and gasped, "Oh, God."

Graduate student Andreas, a German who boarded with Rosa, confessed, "I want a Hemingway experience: crawl and shoot, crawl and shoot. And a big safari camp with lots of drinking."

Neighbor Dave, after correctly parking his garbage can for curbside pick-up, said, "Djibouti, Africa? That sounds scary. If it's in Africa, you think strife and very big animals."

Sister-in-law Ingrid stirred her green tea, smiled, and said, "I love that name, *Djibouti*!"

Bike mechanic Tracy looked down, spun a pedal, and hooted, "Ohhh, boy!"—a polite substitute for "You're nuts!"

But nobody had actually heard of Djibouti, much less visited. Locally, the closest I'd gotten was a chance encounter at the post office. A woman was searching for a priority-mail envelope while I calculated the postage for the birth announcement of my daughter. I guessed, from her sunken-eyed supermodel cheekbones, that she was from the Horn of Africa.

Elfy was a microbiologist from Ethiopia. After some talk about life on the high plateau, I asked about her neighbors down in Djibouti. She sealed her big blue envelope and said, "These people—before the man gets married, he must kill another man and cut off his sex."

I said that I'd read of the practice in the 1934 book by L. M. Nesbitt, *Hell-Hole of Creation*, and found this frankly discouraging.

"Oh, but they are a pleasant people. It's a tribal thing."

Elfy had never visited Djibouti. Tucson was scary enough. "My first night in the city I hear all the sirens and noise and think: this must be a very dangerous place."

She was right, of course: every year over a hundred Tucsonans were mortally squashed in car accidents or shot dead. But it was hard to ignore the bit about the castrators, especially after discovering that Wilfred Thesiger said much the same in *The Danakil Diary:* "They invariably castrate their victim, even if still alive."

I tracked down and called a Swiss photographer who'd recently worked in Djibouti, and asked about Nesbitt and Thesiger.

"Rubbish!" said Mr. S. "It was very rewarding for them to say they had been to a place that is so dangerous. Everyone repeats this. Rubbish!"

That, I said, is a relief. Mr. S. carried on. "Djibouti is a little bit insane. There are the Legionnaires and the prostitutes. It is part of the charm. Of course there are occasional knife fights and murders, but it is not so bad as Detroit."

I called the Djiboutian embassy in Washington.

"Do you have bicycle experience?"

Yes, I said. Last year I rode in Patagonia, and the year before, Russia.

"What about the security in Russia? You must be careful in such a place."

He didn't mention *Hell-Hole of Creation*, leaving it for me to ask, What about the security in Djibouti?

"You should not have any problems. Usually in afternoon we are eating the *khat*. It is a plant—a stimulant like coffee. It's just a pastime, usually from one to around seven o'clock."

Should I try the *khat*?

"This would be very interesting."

Djibouti should be very interesting.

"When you go there you won't feel any stress—you'll just enjoy it."

There was stress. The Discovery Channel took action to staunch the cash hemorrhaging from its internet venue, eliminating the most costly feature stories and half the staff. As a writer, I was unemployed, and now Djibouti was not only a hole in Africa, but also a hole in my wallet.

I chewed this over until the bad news came out looking good. Had I not been well paid for the first four trips? Now the money I'd saved would pay for the last two. In this ceaselessly optimistic view, I'd merely collected up front. Better yet, no job meant no computer and telephone. Free at last.

And best of all, my wife still supported me. Sonya not only understood but shared with me the urge to move, see, and wonder. Some see it as pathological; we saw it as life. It would also be nice for her to have me out of the house for the month.

She did worry for my safety. *I* worried for my safety. Only a month before my departure, Al Qaeda terrorists blew a hole in the USS *Cole* in Yemen, only thirty miles across the Red Sea from Djibouti. Still, nothing was exploding in Djibouti, not even the volcano guarding Lac Assal. The port of Djibouti was ranked by the *World Survey of Climatology* as the hottest city on earth, but anything was better than the winds of Patagonia. As for the estimated 20,000 prostitutes, that was a risk I would have to face.

Djibouti might be uncomfortable, but it was unlikely to actually kill me. Besides, if I was to ride to Lac Assal, it was now or never. I was forty-three, squinting at fine print. Although I'd skipped the stage in life that includes matching silverware, I had matching children. They sat at the dining table on the evening I prepared my final notes and maps. My brother John came by and polished off a bean burrito. He looked over my shoulder and said, "It's not a good sign when your guidebook comes from the CIA."

Sonya asked if I'd bought life insurance yet. I pulled out my policy and began to read the fine print, realizing only now that there would be no benefits if I expired due to a hernia, fowl-herding by plane, or suicide bomber.

Silence. My brother and wife didn't find Djibouti very funny. Then my boy Rudy suddenly cried, "She's spitting up!"

It was baby Rosita, making full use of her esophagus while flapping her arms. Despite the clear danger, Rudy was attracted by the spectacle. He moved closer to see for himself. She grabbed his hair and hung on like the bite of a gila monster. "Ahh! She won't let go!"

I was glad for the distraction, and for the feeling that at least the little ones wouldn't fret over my absence. I disentangled the two and brought them to bed. Just before Rudy slipped into sleep, he squeezed my hand and asked, "Why is Africa so far?"

THE TENDER WARMTH of Tucson in November was replaced by ice rimming the window beside seat 27A. The lady in 27B wore a purple fleece jacket with a Praise-the-Lord pin. She made faces at the Sky Mall catalog, pointing to the French Professional Hose Nozzle and asking, "Does anybody buy this stuff?" But mostly she studied the "Disciples" curriculum for her Bible study group.

I mapped the landscape in my journal, recording how the Rio Grande floodplain is revealed in a thin scrawl of mesquite. As we approached Cincinnati, the sun sank into a lush and ludicrous red. The jet dropped into a boil of cumulus, and the wings bent and unbent like a soaring bird's. Beneath the clouds it was night. We came in low over cars crawling like glow bugs alongside the great black belt of the Ohio River.

"*This*," said my neighbor, "is the part when I pray a lot." We touched down. "And this is when I say, 'Hallelujah! Thank God!'"

Two jets later, six miles above the Red Sea, my seatmate Sohail Malik excused himself to visit the bathroom. He was a dark-suited banker from Pakistan via London, and I didn't expect him to return wearing nothing but a pair of sheets and a look of complete contentment.

He graciously explained that wearing the *ahram* is required of every pilgrim, rich and poor, heading for Mecca. "Your right shoulder must be exposed. You wear no other clothes but these." He practiced his prayers until we approached the port city of Jeddah. When I invited him to look out the window at the place where he would begin his journey, Malik leaned over and said, "Beautiful, really beautiful."

It was dusk, and I saw many cars on a freeway under the pumpkin glow of sodium vapor lamps.

"They say that Eve is buried here."

He showed me the little scissors that he would use to ritually cut off a lock of hair after seven round-trips around the black cube of the Kaaba. We landed and he exhaled. "Now we are entering God's house. There is nothing to worry about, for God will take care of me."

As for me, he cautioned, "You bring in the white sugar, you are beheaded immediately. Do you know this word? I mean narcotics."

The flight crew locked up the liquor as we idled in Saudi Arabia. Small silent men in green overalls cleaned the plane. Nobody boarded. The remaining Djibouti-bound passengers—French heading for their former colony, and Africans—buckled up as the Airbus bellowed into the night and sped along the length of the Red Sea. The water was black, and where the blackness opened wide into the Indian Ocean, a peninsula of lights jutted from Africa.

The airport was small and neat. I traded $20 for Djiboutian francs so worn they felt like tissue paper. I held one banknote to the light. It depicted three camels pausing to consider the leaves of a thorn tree. The watermark was of two long knives and a spear.

The taxi driver called the city "Djibouti Town." His Peugeot wagon was equipped with mysterious red lights behind the dash vents, so instead of air conditioning there were slashes of red across my chest and the seat. I pointed and shrugged, Why? The driver swung his shoulders, grinned, and said, "Disco."

It was 10 PM. Occasionally the headlights caught a few people chatting by the roadside, men with high foreheads shining with sweat. Some stood like flamingos on one leg. From this statistically meaningless sample I imagined Djibouti as a nation of skinnies. But I could not imagine a disco in this dark and sea-damp city.

Ahmed drove slowly. We passed an even slower moped buzzing like a hornet. The little scroll of Arabic that hung from Ahmed's mirror hardly swayed until we stopped at the Djibouti Palace Hotel. There were street lights here, but none illuminated the hotel behind a low white wall and several trees with trunks painted white. Satellite dishes atop the third floor were visible, but little else. It looked a little like a whitewashed castle, but more like a place to be interrogated.

Such is the nonsense that occurs to a man who's flown over 9,000 miles without realizing how strange it can be to arrive, in the night, in a little postage stamp of a country. I dragged my bike box through the front door of the Palace. Two young men sitting behind the counter hopped up and exclaimed in concert, "Malusa!"

Apparently, few people call from the United States to arrange a reservation. Actually, none. I was the only tourist.

Ahmed—the clerk, not the driver—checked me in. He gave me a stiff towel, a bar of GIV Beauty Soap, and a roll of pink toilet paper, and escorted me to room 9. It was clean. Ahmed immediately whipped out a TV remote, turned on CNN, then pointed to a sign. It was the air-conditioning schedule. Cooling was available only from 9 PM to 9 AM and 1 to 4:30 PM. The rest of the time you really should be out doing something.

I asked Ahmed, via my fingers walking along a city map I'd photocopied, where I might visit tonight. He indicated the Menelik Plaza of the European Quarter—only a few blocks away.

The sidewalk was potholed and clumped with fruit skins and crumples of newspaper in languages I didn't recognize. I saw no one but a few sleepers in the shadows until I turned a corner and came upon abundant non-European life in the European Quarter. The buildings were French antiques with warped shutters. The second floor overhung the first, making an arcade with arched portals onto the street. I stopped for a sidewalk sweeper, and on the opposite side of the street a pair of shutters opened and a lady beckoned, *"Mon cheri! Mon cheri!"* I sheepishly waved hello and good-bye. I didn't want to hurt her feelings.

Blending in with the locals was, for chromatic reasons, out of the question. Men in plastic sandals and secondhand slacks greeted me in French. I managed to say hello in Arabic, and this made them smile. I peeked into a bar and ducked out before the prostitutes latched on. I was wondering where the French lived when a young African approached and offered himself as a guide. In good-enough English he said his name was James, and immediately made clear his personal situation.

"No work in Djibouti."

I believe you, I said.

"Tomorrow I bring you the *khat*. Very nice."

Thanks, but no thanks. And I don't need a guide.

James would not abandon me. He pointed out the sign for the Restaurant Bon Coin: a cowboy roundup amid saguaros. He brought me to a souvenir stand selling "Harley Hog Wild" belt buckles. I offered to buy him a mango juice. He declined sullenly, then trailed me back to the hotel. At the entrance he made his bid for one thousand francs—about $6.

"I want a beer."

I said that I wouldn't buy *myself* a beer for a thousand francs.

"I stand here and ask you: why don't you give me the money? You have money. I don't."

It is that simple, I said, but I didn't come to Djibouti to give my money away. I did not want you to follow me. I offered you a mango juice.

"OK—five hundred francs. With this I can buy a beer in a store."

No.

"OK—I will take two hundred francs for the mango juice. I do not like this drink."

I gave him two hundred francs. He fingered the money, then burst out, "I am good man for you, but you are bad! I protect you. We walk past the people waiting for you. The Mafia. Without me, they get you"—he made a sudden stabbing motion—"with the knife."

He turned and vanished. The clerk Ahmed just shrugged. His cheek bulging with *khat*, he sat on a rug and watched MTV.

I retreated to room 9. The night went poorly. It was not the jive talk of James that bothered me, but the mattress. Like a black hole, an invisible ring of gravity sucked me into a pit in the center. I woke with an aching back to discover that mosquitoes had feasted on me. I shambled over to my first-aid kit and got out the Malarone. I didn't want to forget my morning pill and have malaria spoil my Djibouti holiday.

THE AIR CONDITIONER shuddered to a stop at 9 AM. Under a cloudless sky a pretty girl with braids jumped rope on her way to a school behind an iron gate. A yellow tabby slunk along the hotel wall. It was the thinnest cat in the world.

I dressed for success, with money stashed in three places on my body, and strode out into the early heat. Nobody but me wore a hat. Jeeps and green-and-white taxis and minibuses cruised the Boulevard du General de Gaulle. The minibuses had sassy names, like Texas or Cobra, splashed across the windshield, but if you wanted to know the destination you had to listen to the young man hollering out the open door. I understood only one locale: "*Rimbaud!*"

Arthur Rimbaud was a French poet and a sensation. First published in 1870 at age fifteen, he pursued the "systematic derangement of the senses" with the aid of absinthe and hashish. Thus primed, he spouted glowing verse like *The Drunken Boat*. His drunken lover shot him with predictably poor aim, but good enough to inspire Rimbaud to write *A Season in Hell*. Soon afterward, he quit writing and began the long wandering that would lead to Djibouti in 1885.

Except there was no Djibouti yet, only the condensing ambitions of French colonialism. The British had a colony in Yemen, the scalding port of Aden. The Italians were grasping for Eritrea. But the French had not built Suez only to let others be the gatekeepers of the Red Sea. They acquired their own colony, French Somaliland, bit by bit, and peaceably enough with payoffs to the appropriate sultans.

The future nation of Djibouti was in the right place, and not only because every ship had to pass within ten miles. To the west, high above the desert, the landlocked Ethiopians wished to continue business as usual, bringing coffee and slaves to the sea and international markets and taking home all sorts of interesting merchandise. When the soon-to-be Emperor Menelik of Ethiopia desired guns, he swung a deal with an ex-poet turned arms dealer who'd recently moved to French Somaliland. Rimbaud promised to deliver 1,755 rifles and 750,000 rounds of ammunition.

With one hundred camels, he did—yet failed to turn a profit. He tried general trading, but then a kind of cancer began to eat his knee. He returned to France on a stretcher, where the bad leg was sawed off. Two years later, at thirty-seven, Rimbaud was dead.

"I loved the desert, burnt orchards, tired old shops, warm drinks," Rimbaud imagined while still a teen in France. Today it was not hard to find a warm drink in a tired old café. The sun was turned away with heavy drapes. There were no lights, and the waitress brought me not only the menu but also a flashlight. She appeared to be wrapped head to toe in a sheet of silk. She served Ethiopian coffee the luscious black of crude oil, then returned to her preparations for the afternoon *khat* chew, placing sumptuous cushions around a platter of teacups and a cone of incense in a burner hewn from coral.

Rimbaud Plaza was just beyond the European Quarter, where the arcades petered out at a big white mosque with a single thick minaret like a lighthouse. To the south was a tornado of pigeons and honking minibuses surrounded by hundreds of market sheds of blue steel and hundreds of other vendors in pools of shade beneath ragged umbrellas. I weaved through the noise and flies and escaped into the alleys of the African Quarter. Looking for nothing, I paused near a row of knee-high aluminum jugs of cooking oil, chopped dates, and a frothy liquid. The vendors were ladies in billowy dresses in splashy patterns with matching head scarves. I said hello in Arabic. They responded, then asked, *Where are you from?*

America, I said. I don't speak French. Tourist. Seventeen days in Djibouti, to see Lac Assal.

Cries of amazement bought the alley to a standstill. The women wanted me to have a drink of the froth. It was camel's milk. I declined, and a sleek man wearing a sarong butted in and said in English, "These ladies, Somaliland. Me, Somaliland. We British Africans. Not African.

"Look, nose. Not like this." He squashed his nose. "Look, hair. Not like this." His fingers curled into claws. "Hair like this." His fingers relaxed.

They were refugees from the civil war in Somalia, a country united by a common language but split by ancient grudges and the last century's colonialism: some parts were British, some Italian.

The cook at the nearby Maskali Restaurant was a refugee, too. The Maskali looked like it was built in a day from plywood and corrugated steel, but it was freshly painted the pink and blue of sororities and swimming pools. The obvious owner, in a spotless white gown and skullcap, stood at an entrance decorated with Mecca postcards.

Inside were a half-dozen men at four tidy tables with napkins of sharply folded newspaper from Malaysia. There was no music or TV. There was one lunch: oven-charred fish, mystery soup, and flatbread dripping with honey. As soon as I finished, the man next to me handed me a small leafy branch. He'd been waiting. Now his eyebrows arched in expectation. He smiled and revealed green teeth. Dessert was served.

KHAT IS THE NAME of a little tree. In Djibouti they say "cot." It grows in Arabia and Africa, where its leaves are chewed with varying degrees of fervor among those who find its effects pleasing without knowing or caring that the reason is a molecule called cathinone. It's a member of the large and happy family of alkaloids, recognizable by their sturdy ring of carbon atoms with a nitrogen atom tucked into the circle or hanging off to the side. The list of desirable alkaloids is a who's who of addiction: nicotine, cocaine, morphine, codeine, mescaline, caffeine, and, lest you think you are immune to the allure, aminophylline from cocoa. The cathinone in *khat* is structurally related to ephedrine, a stimulant first discovered in a plant that grows in my Arizona home: Mormon tea, one of the genus *Ephedra*. Besides helping the Mormons wake up, ephedrine makes my bee-sting allergy injector tighten up my blood vessels.

But as any allergy medicine makes ambiguously clear on the warning label, its effects can improbably be both stimulant and sleep-inducer. In the case of cathinone, the United States Drug Enforcement Agency sternly warns that "widespread frequent use of *Khat* impacts productivity because it tends to reduce worker motivation."

But the Maskali cook, Nasir, implied the opposite. "You eat this, you become fresh," he said in fine English.

I looked at the men sitting beneath a painting, in a serious wood frame, of nineteenth-century frigates locked in sea battle. Nobody was actually *eating* the *khat*. They looked as if they were storing walnuts in their cheeks. I followed suit, stripping the leaves from the stem, chewing the mass, and tucking the cud into my cheek.

Very fresh, I said.

"Yes, it comes every day on a plane," said Nasir. A young man, he had excellent green teeth and powerful shoulders. "Nine thousand kilos. Just don't drink beer with *khat*, or you will be finished."

Speaking of beer, I said, is there a bar where I could buy one? I mean, if I wasn't eating *khat*.

My question provoked grave frowns and whispers. I looked up to see a poster of the genealogy of the Prophet, with Adam at the trunk and Mohammed as the shining terminus of the highest branch. Suddenly I felt subterranean—as if I'd asked for a date with Satan.

Nasir delivered the verdict. "We do not know about the beer. This is not good for your spirit."

Tea was served. Several more sprigs were produced. My beer blunder was forgotten as we resumed "grazing the salad." The *khat* went to work, and I was consumed by a humming curiosity. The men taught me the Somali words for *water, thank you, wife,* and *may I take your photo*. I passed around my driver's license. One man discovered that the letter I in "ArIzona" was actually a saguaro cactus. This, we agreed, was fascinating.

Khat was achieving its contrary promise: a relaxing stimulant. With the drool of a baby but the wisdom of a sage, I casually circulated my passport among the total strangers. They were gracious, and they were very curious. With Nasir as translator, I answered the usual family questions: children, wives, brothers and sisters. Nasir told of his father, killed in the civil war, and his brother in Los Angeles.

A couple entered and ordered lunch. The woman vanished into the ladies-only room. Nasir invited me into the kitchen. "Watch," he said as he split and gutted a foot-long *arabi* in ten seconds. "This is what I would like to do if I make it to the United States." The gleaming white flesh he slathered with a sauce. "I want to work in a restaurant with my brother." He hooked the fish with an iron claw and dropped it into a hole in an earthen oven.

I mentioned that blackened fish is very popular in the United States, and in inadvertently raising his hopes I earned another fish for lunch, on the house. I followed with an offer to buy the next round of *khat*. Nasir took me out into the market and around a corner piled with big blue plastic jugs. People were picking up for the afternoon. A woman shooed flies from the mounds of sticky dates before wrapping them in a hobo bundle.

A man with buttered hair trotted past holding a clutch of long wands that flexed with each step.

"The toothbrush plant," said Nasir. The banana-sized bundles of *khat* lay under wet burlap on a wooden table belonging to a young woman with skin the color of tobacco. Nasir greeted her. Fatima's gold hoop earrings swung out from her head scarf as she leaned forward to pick a bunch. It was carefully swaddled like the baby Jesus, except in plastic wrap and crisscrossed strings. Three bucks for a day's chew.

Back at the Maskali, the chatter had subsided. I donated the *khat* and excused myself before I became hooked within twenty-four hours of my arrival.

I wandered back through the now-calm Rimbaud Plaza. With the men dispatched by *khat*, the market was inhabited mostly by women washing the sidewalks or dampening the dirt. Along Boulevard Thirteen was a music shop selling the same tunes that drifted from the minibuses, with snake-charmer horns and strings echoing the lament of a melody, or a piccolo and twanging guitar chasing the happy slap of bongos. I bought one of each, and was instructed to wait while the owner copied the original onto a cassette.

Waiting was easy. It was no hotter than Tucson in September. There were no sirens in Djibouti Town, no guns, no bulletproof glass. It was not as if there was nothing to steal. Earlier, at a money exchange in Menelik Plaza, the man in front of me had exchanged $1,600, yet other than a screen there was hardly more security than at a lemonade stand.

The sun vanished and life returned to Rimbaud Plaza. The call for prayer wailed over the square. The European Quarter was cooling down and lighting up. I hesitated at the sort of place I'd avoided the night before: the Club de Rire, whose sign was a man in a bowler hat that spouted party favors. From behind its doors—black, with pink ladybug polka dots—came the click of pool balls and the snicker of women.

I heard someone yell, "Get out of here!" Instead, I went in.

"AMERICAN?" guessed the smiling doorman. "Yes, we have Americans! Over here, by the pool tables."

There were two Americans and six women at the pool tables, big American sailors, one named Jack and a younger one whose name I didn't catch. Jack was built like a sack of grain and clutched a vodka tonic. The younger man leaned unsteadily on a pool cue pressed into service as a third leg. He blurted, "Where you from?"

I told him.

"Get the fuck out of here! You're kidding! What the fuck are you doing in Djibouti?"

His Heineken-carbonated brain was no match for my *khat* clarity. I calmly said, Tourist. Just curious, I guess.

"Get the fuck out of here! You're mad!"

Women outnumbered men two to one—and that was counting the French Legionnaires in the opposite corner. Both the French and the women wore tight clothes, and the effect was to make the women look less dangerous than the French.

The young sailor chalked up and missed an easy shot. A woman cleared the table. Apparently she had lots of practice.

I asked Jack, What's that guy's name?

"I can't remember. It's a big ship, an 880-foot tanker converted to hauling grain for the UN. I work on the bridge. He's a third-class engineer."

A woman approached and immediately sized us up. How did she know where her chances lay? She ignored me and Mr. Wobble and headed straight for Jack. "You big tired man, need to relax."

She was maybe twenty, in second-skin jeans, clingy tank top, and lipstick. She was not bashful. She ran her fingers lightly over her breasts, where her shirt said *Sports Girl*.

"Look. Sports Girl. Me Sports Girl. Sports fucking."

Her method was a bit aggressive, and Lord knows what circumstances in life had brought her to the Club de Rire. At the moment, however, none of this mattered. In the airy recesses of the male skull, her words and actions neatly pole-vaulted over all other thought processes and landed precisely on the neural klaxons whose job was to alert those parts of the anatomy that really wouldn't mind a bit more exercise. Sports Girl knew she had our complete attention. She smiled and did a hip grind and took advantage of the moment to wheedle a Heineken out of Jack, meaning he agreed to pay for what she would fetch.

"I like this," said Jack, delivering bits of autobiography over the howl of music. "Merchant Marine. Was in Yuma not far from Tucson for nine years. Ex-wife still there."

Sports Girl returned with the beer. She took a swallow with a needlessly complete lip lock around the neck of the bottle, then put one leg up on the pool table for the sole purpose of demonstrating her remarkable flexibility. I thought, She really *is* a Sports Girl.

Jack rambled, "I've gone back to Yuma, but prefer this."

Sports Girl moved in. As if I were invisible, she kissed Jack and said, "*You* should come with me."

"But what would all my wives say?"

Her sports tongue ran a nice 360 around her lips, leaving a faultlessly wet O in its wake. She then issued an oral invitation that, despite my present agnostic condition, reminded me that if I'd repeated her words during my Catholic childhood I'd have been socked with a penance of one hundred Hail Marys, minimum.

Jack said, "I've got to work tomorrow. You'll keep me up all night."

He was a playful devil. Sports Girl grabbed a cue and worked on the geometry of a shot. Jack turned to me and said, "Most Americans never heard of Djibouti. If they knew the girls looked like this. . . . Of course, most are from Ethiopia. And my favorite, the best in the world, are in Novorossiysk. Black Sea. Maybe it's the rebel spirit, the first taste of competition. They wear see-through blouses. Beautiful."

Sports Girl didn't mind the competition. She turned to show us her rear, then bent over and backed slowly into Jack, like trains coupling.

Jack's eyes bulged, but he managed to hang onto his drink.

Sports Girl decoupled, turned, and admired her effect on Jack.

"Ha! You stand in attention for me!"

That was the last I saw of Jack.

THE NEXT MORNING I picked up the immense plastic telephone in room 9 and called a woman. I knew her only from a phone call months earlier.

While digging for information, I'd rung the only fancy hotel in Djibouti Town, the Sheraton, and asked if there was any tourist information they could send my way. A woman had said, no—but perhaps I would like some postcards from the hotel?

A month later I'd received an envelope with four picture postcards, each personally annotated by Roda Omar Hosh. One read, "There are two kinds of people in Djibouti, the Somalian and the Afar. The Afar are living in the north and the Somalian in the south, so the north is more beautiful.

"I hope you will appreciate all these pictures. I will tell you good-bye and see you soon."

This morning I told Roda I'd arrived, with my bike, for the ride to Lac Assal. I took the silence that followed as an opportunity to further explain that I would leave Djibouti Town in two days or so, and because Assal was only a hundred miles away I would also take side trips to the French enclave of Arta and to one of the oldest seaports in East Africa, Tadjoura.

Roda was appalled.

"You will ride a bicycle? By yourself? I thought you were going on a bus with other tourists. Are you bringing a *pistola* with you?"

No *pistola*, I said, although suddenly I wished I had a grenade launcher. I asked Roda, Should I worry? Has something bad happened to a traveler in Djibouti?

"Who knows what these people are like? And what about wild animals? If you sleep in the desert alone, they can eat you."

This calmed me: she had no idea. I promised to visit that evening at the Sheraton. Meanwhile, I packed a liter of Yemeni water and went for a walk. The fish at the Maskali was again superb, but when the *khat* arrived I headed to the Coiffure Vijay for a shave, thinking I'd better not show up at the Sheraton with a dribble of green on my chin. The dapper barber in a pearl-buttoned shirt was from Bombay. He unwrapped a fresh blade and assured me the razor was cleaned with alcohol. He said no more. There was no need to mention AIDS.

Only a block north of my earlier wanderings, I found the French Legionnaires, unsmiling men in silly white hats, in the Semiramis supermarket. Under vents blowing cool dry air was a faux country store, with wheels of

Roquefort and fruit bins made of rough-sawn wood, heaped with carrots and mangoes.

It all had come, as I had, on Air France. One of its thrice-weekly flights had arrived the evening I found Roda at the Sheraton. She was smart and trim in her uniform, retrieving a fax at the Business Center. The hotel was a tropical Arab fantasy of lattice ceilings and narcotic fans. In the casino, androgynous dealers flicked cards across green felt and sent roulette balls into orbit with a snap of their fingers. A gargantuan buffet was watched over by men dressed like jockeys in black-and-white checkered slacks and shirts.

Roda excused herself; the Air France passengers needed attention. Tomorrow there would be a conference on antipersonnel mines. Tonight, a steady stream of women headed into a reception room. At one end stood a pair of well-stuffed armchairs upholstered in gold, atop a platform with a backdrop of red velour and white lace bunting. A woman invited me in. There were a hundred women seated in rows, all ages and all done up expensively in shimmering fabrics and head scarves. A few wore full veils, but far more displayed henna tattoos in red and blue on their hands and feet—the marks of marriage.

More women arrived. With some discomfort I wondered what would happen when the men arrived and found two hundred women and me. Fortunately, the men were musicians, carrying a synthesizer and all sorts of drums. On the first note the women let loose with a trilling howl like Indians in an old western.

In rushed four more men, with video cameras and floodlights. The music swelled, an electronic pounding, and about a dozen women began to dance. I was hoping it was a coronation, but then a seven-tiered wedding cake arrived and was placed on a long table laden with pizza squares. I slipped out and found Roda at the gift shop.

"This is an Arab marriage," she said. "Afar and Somali marriages are similar—the differences are mostly the costumes. But always the woman has a party for all her friends. Not for the men.

"Usually we marry our cousin. My fiancé is the cousin of my mother's cousin. Often it is first cousin, and most always it is arranged. Mine was arranged by my family when I was sixteen. I'm twenty-two now, waiting for him to finish his studies. Some women don't like these arranged weddings—they escape to Europe, or America."

I asked, When is your wedding, Roda?

"In May." She paused and smoothed her skirt. It was already smooth. "But I will not be there. He loves me, and his family paid for me, but I do not love him. I have known him since we were children; we're like brother and sister, not man and wife. I don't want to be his wife for the rest of my life. Marriage should be for life, yes?

"So I will escape, too. Maybe to America. United States, or Canada. Perhaps you can give me an invitation so I can get a visa?"

I'm not sure it's that simple.

"I think it is if I have the money for a one-month vacation—then I never come back. I have a brother in Quebec."

An enormous hubbub erupted from the reception hall. Roda said, "Here comes the bride."

Besieged by the twin video teams, the newlyweds entered. Her hair was a tower of ringlets held aloft by invisible adhesives and a tiara. Her white gown had enough sequins to make Liberace self-conscious. A Cleopatra bracelet clenched her bicep.

The terrified groom, his pupils reduced to pinpricks by the lights, shuffled like a robot past the throng of trilling women. Five minutes later the couple reached their thrones, sweating madly, and exchanged leis of white flowers. Each of the two hundred women insisted on photographing the lucky couple.

No wonder Roda wanted to escape. I took a taxi back to the Palace and turned on CNN to discover that in 1994 Oman became the first Arab nation to give women the right to vote.

THE SHERATON was not alone on the northern tip of Djibouti Town. Most of the embassies were clustered nearby, perched on land's end like first-class passengers on the bow of a ship.

A listing ship, it seemed, after I screwed together my bike and rolled it outside. I had an appointment at the American embassy for a "security briefing." The miserable refugees outside my hotel posed little danger. Too wasted to beg, they lay with stick limbs folded in whatever shade they could find. The more fortunate had a scrap of cardboard to lie on. I felt like a king and a pig.

Dark clouds massed in the north. It was easy to recognize the embassy behind its concentric rings of concrete blast barriers, rolls of barbed wire, and an inner wall with a bulletproof security station. I was relieved of my camera, then I passed through a metal detector and a gate into a waiting room. For a minute my only company was Mr. Osama bin Laden, staring with oddly serene eyes from a poster announcing a $5 million bounty on his head.

Lauren May stepped in, shook hands, and introduced me to the security officer. He looked like a man who had a *pistola* strapped to his ankle. With my fine French map unfolded, he swiftly indicated the locations of land mines.

"Be on the lookout," he summarized in a square-chinned way, "anywhere north of Lac Assal and Tadjoura."

I mentioned that this would make camping tough.

Ms. May said, "There is nothing to do in any case in or around Tadjoura."

I said that the Djiboutians had been pretty nice.

"That's because you're not French."

Pedaling back, I realized that now I truly looked French, for they were the only ones with bicycles. The machines were locked outside the Semiramis market, where I picked up crepes, Laughing Cow cheese, and Madeleine rolls for the ride into the desert. Later, I stopped at the Three Stars café for a fruit drink. Distracted by Mariah Carey on French MTV, I neglected my usual practice of supplying my own bottled water. The drink arrived in an enormous sherbet glass, beaded with condensation, and after one sip my taste buds said, *Why not?*

Twelve hours later, in the predawn, I woke with a twisted gut that said, *How could you be so stupid?* I was packed and ready to roll, yet the only departure that morning would be the contents of my stomach and intestines, from both ends.

I slept fitfully until 2 PM. The spasms of fluid loss would not stop. I ended up in the office of Dr. Bruno dell'Aquila. The stacks of magazines and odor of alcohol were exactly like Dr. Pellerito's in Tucson, but this office had a poster proclaiming: *Don't Mutilate Women*. It was a simple gruesome cartoon of blood dripping from a blade and a girl's crotch, part of a government effort to curtail the Horn of Africa custom of female circumcision.

I waited twenty minutes. Dr. dell'Aquila wore very small black wire-rimmed glasses that would have been a mistake on me but looked suave on an Italian. After a brief exam he said, "This is very common this week—there is something going around Djibouti Town. It is likely bacteria, like *Salmonella*. You will get better in two to three days."

He prescribed four drugs for my relief. The Horn of Africa Pharmacy was across the street in a concrete cube. It could have been a brothel, but inside its electric doors the staff swiftly filled my prescriptions, and minutes later I stood speechless by the optical checkout scanner. Everything, from doctor to druggist, had taken less than $50 and one hour, without an appointment.

Recovery took somewhat longer, but at least I had a chance to visit the "Cultural Center" and discover another Djiboutian surprise.

"The Center has moved," said the woman behind a desk holding volumes of the French Civil Code and papers weighted by a stout shell shaped like a turban. A black robe hung from a peg. A Djiboutian lawyer, her name was Hasna Barkat.

What, may I ask, is your specialty?

She smiled at my naiveté and said, "Commercial. Civil. Criminal. Everything. A lawyer does not specialize in Djibouti."

How many lawyers are there?

"Twelve."

Twelve! In all of Djibouti?

"Djibouti is a small country. And it is not, as in some other countries, the first reflex of the people to seek a lawyer. If there is a dispute, it is brought to the elders."

These words made Djibouti seem so . . . civilized.

Yet that night my sleep was uneasy. It was thirty miles and a climb of 2,500 feet to the first town en route to Lac Assal—a long way for a leaky man. And although everyone from whores to lawyers had treated me well, I'd not ventured out of a tourist preserve of maybe three square miles. Like a deer in a national park without hunters, I was a coddled curiosity. *Look, honey, it's an American—and he's tame!*

The sunrise colored the bottoms of untroubled clouds. They were moving inland. I got on my bike and pedaled out of town.

CHAPTER 10

Djibouti Town to Lac Assal

Nobody Has Come
on a Bicycle

THE FIRST REFUGEE CAMP is strewn across a plain of fist-sized stones outside of Djibouti Town. It's hundreds of shelters built of any scrap of plastic, palm leaf, metal, or cardboard big enough to make shade, and held in place with cord and rocks. The French map calls this a "Spontaneous Habitation."

In occasional clearings by the road, kids chase cans or balls. I expect them to yell and wave when I pass. Instead they sprint for me. Out of the swarm of a hundred, one rushes up and grabs my brake lever and nearly topples me. Most of the kids scream and laugh and back off, but the bolder ones snatch up rocks, and in an instant I'm more target than tourist.

At the moment there is no time for fear, only self-preservation. I jump on the pedals. The bike is light—I've no computer, no telephone, no *pistola*— and the wind's up and at my back. One rock smacks my leg, and then I'm gone.

At a gas station I stop and, panting now with panic, tell my story to an Ethiopian truck driver. He shrugs. "There's nothing you can do. In Djibouti Town the people are good. These are animals."

He's going the wrong way. There are no taxis. On my own, I'm flying by the time the children in the next camp see me. Still, they try. Their best shot ricochets off the spokes. The next time I see a crowd of children ahead, on the right side of the road, I look back over my shoulder and see a truck coming. When it passes I duck behind it, picking up speed in its slipstream until a surge of adrenaline allows me to overtake the truck on its left, using it for cover as we pass the children. By the time they spot me and give chase, I'm out of range and only a few rocks skip past.

I'm too shaken to celebrate. I'm thinking of the parentless children in *Lord of the Flies*—but what were the refugee children thinking? Probably not much besides the thrill of hunting. *A new animal. Don't let it get away!* If they'd knocked me out, they might have gathered round in awe and poked at my sweating body with a stick. The very bravest might have touched my strange moon-colored skin.

After I've passed the last sorrowful shelter built of palm mats and the burnt flatbed of a long-dead truck, my fear deflates—after all, they were only forty-pound children with stones. Yet as I ride into the black rock desert I can't help but think that pedaling a bike through Djibouti is a ridiculous way to suffer voluntarily, as absurd as peeing into a water bottle at 20,000 feet because you'll freeze if you leave your tent.

At least the local herders should be in good cheer. Recent rains have persuaded the leguminous trees and bushes to let loose an extravagance of green, vivid against the volcanic clinkers. The sandy dirt is the red of Persian rugs. Lofty camels sway over the brush and strip the leaflets, while goats attack from beneath. The dry watercourses are trimmed with milkweed eight feet tall, with huge leathery leaves like oven mitts and big wrinkled seed pods constricted round the middle into a pair of hemispheres.

A cloud slides over the sun, and the gift of shade softens my temper. It can't be much over 90 degrees. It's Friday, the Muslim day of rest, with so little traffic that the policeman at the sole checkpoint is snoozing peacefully in his shack. The bike lets me slip past without a sound.

As I ride west, a steady climb brings into view the narrow Gulf of Tadjoura to the north, the milky blue light blending sea and sky. The black-top is smooth and bordered with the toxic purple blooms of nightshade and the brain-twisting white flowers of sacred *Datura*. Some forward-thinking soul has created a rest stop of a few shade trees by surrounding them with an anti-goat wall of fifty-five-gallon drums. Atop a power line is a long-legged buzzard with orange and white feathers and a slaughter-house beak, hooked and tipped with black. It turns and casts a baleful eye, and just like that I'm glad to be cycling through Djibouti.

As the road climbs, the bike slows, but a downshift keeps the pedals spinning at the same clip. A truck labors past, also downshifting, rattling with racks of returnable pop bottles and emblazoned with *This is the Fanta Moment!* I make do with Yemeni yogurt and oranges when I stop for lunch under a thorn tree. By habit I begin to clean up the orange peels before realizing that they'll be more appreciated on the ground. Pedaling off, I turn to see *This is the Orange Peel Moment!* The goats vacuum up the peels in ten seconds.

Ahead is a junction with a five-mile spur road to Arta, a summer retreat for those with the means to escape the heat of Djibouti Town. It's goat land all the way to the summit. The white flocks move lightly over the dark mountain, like sliding cloud shadows that expand and contract as they pass over ridge and canyon. At the mountaintop village of Arta, the homes are behind walls topped with broken glass embedded in the cement, or impenetrable hedges of red and white oleander, or an inspired trellis of bougainvillea and barbed wire. I push on toward a forest of antennae and spinning radar parabola, past a pair of massive gates with lion's-head knockers. The sign says, *Ambassador of France.*

I head to the Centre d'Estivage, a little hotel and a big white stucco bar and restaurant with a veranda onto a spotless playground and groomed volleyball court. The supervisor is welcoming.

"Nobody has come on a bicycle! Would you like to have lunch?" (Yes.) "And the evening meal?" (Yes.) "You can dream outside if you like, or you can dream inside, with bath."

I choose inside. This may be my last chance for a shower, for there will be no more French oases after Arta. Lunch costs the same as the room, but someone must pay for the signature white china, rimmed in blue. The hushed music I identify as a Rhinelander waltz without ever having heard such a thing. Likewise, the fixed menu is unrecognizable, but once the food appears I guess it's Petit Snippets Verdure and Jus L'Oink. With my diet of anti-*Salmonella* drugs, I don't chance the alcohol kindly offered by the couple with an infant at the next table.

"Bordeaux Saint-Emilion," she says. "Good with savage animals." Her name is Corinne. She's dark and lovely and the owner of some nose. The baby is enormously attractive to me in my child-deprived state.

"His name is Morvan. It is name from Brittany. 'Son of the Sea.'"

Son of the Sea is landlocked in a Chicco car seat. His crew-cut father wears an orange T-shirt, Camel Adventure shorts, and what is either a faint birthmark or a black eye. His improbable name is Claude Target and he is a Legionnaire, which means that his name might not be Claude Target. Anyone who joins this secretive arm of the French military may assume a new identity, to leave behind their possibly unpleasant past.

This I learned long ago from the *World Book Encyclopedia*. Its entry for the Foreign Legion began with a yawn ("one of the world's most colorful and gallant fighting forces") but led to an eye-opener: "Some of its members join to escape political imprisonment, others to avoid punishment, and still others to seek adventure."

This was a revelation no boy would forget: no matter how bad you were, there was a place you could go and be paid to shoot guns in the desert.

So Mr. Target has a perfectly good reason for being here. I'm more of a mystery, and he wants to know, "Why have you come to Djibouti?"

Tourist, I say—just to see Djibouti. Mr. Target honks an incredulous laugh and asks again, "*Why?*"

Why not? Except for the refugee children outside Djibouti Town, the people are very nice.

"Because you are not French! Where are you from?"

America. Arizona. I like deserts, and I want to see Lac Assal.

"Ahh! Now this is very nice. Spectacular. And very hot. It is one of the hottest places in the world. But not so far away is the Forêt du Day. *C'est fantastique*. Clouds and trees and animals." He growls. "Tiger."

It sounds as if you like Djibouti.

"What? I did not ask to go to Djibouti. Nobody asks for Djibouti."

But this is where many Legionnaires are posted. Why did you join?

"Adventure! Sensation! We just come back from desert school. Six days. Eighteen camels. We eat only banana and . . . *baaahhh.* . . ."

Goat.

"The goat. I have twelve years in the Legion. Many places I go. Bosnia, Desert Storm, Cambodia, Sarajevo, Chad, Congo, Senegal, Ivory Coast, Tunisia."

Mr. Target lights a Camel, tickles Son of the Sea, and pours both of us a glass of wine. This time I accept.

Mr. Target is too kind. The Legion is not known for kindness. Their training includes not flinching as a tank passes over you, a churning steel track on either side. They worship a wooden hand, kept in a glass box in France, that once resided on the arm of a Legionnaire captain who was killed in a 1863 battle in Mexico. The clumsy prosthetic was all that remained of a brave platoon that was hopelessly outnumbered yet refused to surrender. That they were duly slaughtered only enhanced the Legionnaire's reputation as men who fear nothing.

Mr. Target burnishes the tough-guy status by spearing and eating a wedge of extraordinarily stinky cheese. It's veined with busy mold and likely capable of crawling off the dessert tray. Its odor attracts two more Legionnaires and a bottle of cognac to our table. The man with a tattoo of a human skull with a goat horn for a nose notices my bike by the door.

"Why do you ride the bike?"

For pleasure, I say.

"I do not ride for pleasure. If I get the order to ride a bicycle, I ride."

And what do you do for pleasure?

"Fighting."

Son of the Sea begins to wail. Corrine says he needs to sleep. Let me try, I say—putting babies to sleep is something I also do for pleasure.

The mini-legionnaire is passed to me, and at once I'm happy and teary-eyed. I hum and pat Morvan to sleep in five minutes. I might have dozed off too if not for the entry of a man who satisfies all my preconceptions of a Legionnaire, tattooed to the last knuckle. He takes a look at the sleeping infant in my arms, backs off like it's a land mine, and says, "Baby. Mom."

I slip Son of the Sea back to Corrine.

Mike is, or at least was, an American. His wife, a round and red-faced Frenchwoman, joins us and helps herself to the cognac. Mike and Claude chat amiably—"Ha! Fuck you!"—before Mike turns to say, "Claude says you are a writer and something else? I'm looking for a writer. When I'm out of here I want to tell my story. Ten years in the Legion. French Guinea. Yugoslavia. Djibouti. All over the place. I got a story but I need someone to tell it."

Well, I'm not really *that* kind of writer. But I may meet one someday.

"Here's my address. Yours?"

We swap addresses, and he says, "I know Arizona. Yeah. Pen."

He takes my pen and scrawls a map on a napkin stained with cognac and coffee.

"Look. California. Arizona. Right. Yeah. Listen. Here. Marines—I was in the Marines. Here."

In Yuma?

"That's right. Yuma."

It's a lot like Djibouti.

"It's not Djibouti. Don't tell me Yuma is Djibouti."

I mean the desert.

"Desert. Listen. You're riding that bike through Djibouti?"

I am.

"Listen. You've got people who know where you are, when you are?"

The embassy knows my route, and when I should return.

"Listen. Here's my phone. 35135. Ask for post 2240. Wherever you are, the French will get you. Got that?"

Thanks. I'm hoping the only help I'll need is finding out where I can get water. Do they sell water in the village of Ouea?

"What? The village? Don't go there. If you want water we put some out at the gate to the post. How many liters? What time? Huh?"

His wife interrupts with, "Water at our house. You must come for dinner, and to stay the night."

She nods off, cognac in hand, before I need reply. I mention that it's no problem to carry water down the mountain. I could even cache a few liters in places I would return to after tomorrow's detour to the town of Ali Sabieh.

"Djiboutians steal it," says Mike. "They're watching you. In the rocks. Watching you. Last month, tell you, a Legionnaire died while driving to the post. Djiboutians found him. Took his wallet. Watch. That's the kind of people we're talking about."

It seems necessary for Mike to fear the natives, for he certainly wants them to fear him. He looks over the bulge of his considerable shoulder as another man enters the restaurant.

"Shit. That's the captain, and I want to kick his ass. So I think I need to go home."

He rouses his wife. She manages to repeat her offer of accommodation, then totters out the door.

I prefer to dream with bath, at the little hotel. Unlike room 9 at the Djibouti Palace, there is a toilet seat. With the windows open it's cool enough to appreciate the hot water. All is perfect, except that my time with Son of the Sea has intensified my longing for my baby girl.

And when I lie down for the night on the white cotton, there's the twinge of guilt. It's the kids from the refugee camp.

THE SOLDIERS are up with the sun for their *petit déjeuner*, the men looking less-than-savage in snug camouflage shorts, spooning up Rice Krispies and chomping on baguettes. I join them. After breakfast the generous commander makes a gift of three liters of French spring water.

The road plummets back into the heat. The country is long low plateaus, rimmed with modest cliffs or so wasted by erosion that nothing remains but a steep cone of boulders. In the valleys between, goats drift and pause and move on. Always there is a man close behind, sashaying easily through the brush, a long curved knife in his belt, and his hands loosely clasping a staff carried across his shoulders.

The goats are voracious, yet none chances a nibble of the squat tree with bark curling off its inflated trunk like skin peeling from a bloated corpse. I snap off a twig and catch the scent of church incense. It must be frankincense or myrrh, and it must taste awful.

A pair of fighter jets shriek past, leaving an exaggerated silence in their wake. When a whistling cry spins my head, I remember: *In the rocks. Watching you.* But it's only what appears to be a very big rabbit with no tail and little ears.

Except rabbits don't whistle. It's not a goofy-toothed bunny but a hoofed mammal with little fangs, the rock hyrax. There are at least a dozen among the boulders, brave as Legionnaires, daring me to stop and look.

On the blind curve entering Ouea, a truck accident has stopped all traffic. It's another Fanta Moment: children have come from their rock homes to hawk orange soda to the drivers going nowhere. Of course the bike can simply be carried around the wreckage, but not without attracting attention. When a boy dashes for me I reflexively fear another stoning, but he wants only to help push the bike up the hill. At the top wait girls whose round faces are dusted with yellow powder, like nectar eaters sprinkled with pollen. The children offer peanuts in cones of newspaper from Japan; I offer the ten-minute version of my life, complete with pictures of my wife and children. The boy I leave with a postcard of Arizona. He clutches it to his heart like the Hope Diamond.

A sweet acacia breeze urges me west, along the main highway to Ethiopia. The wreck has emptied the westbound lane, and I need only to watch out for the trucks coming east from Ethiopia—they cut to the inside of a corner, regardless of the lane. The drivers wave but don't honk, and I like that.

Of course I'm happy just to get through the morning without being pelted with rocks. Djibouti possesses the quiet advantage of being a country in which the worst is expected. When it fails to happen, it's easy to believe that the trip will be more than plain survival.

So when I reach the road junction heading north for Lac Assal, I instead continue west on the main road, heading for Ethiopia but planning a little detour to the town of Ali Sabieh simply to satisfy my curiosity. The skies are clean and the sun is tolerable. The locals live anywhere there's something edible for their goats and camels. Camp is a portable desert igloo: a dome of sticks knitted together with woven mats or blue plastic tarps for shade.

Little butterflies tag along. The land dries and the plants shrink until there is nothing but a desiccated lake bed, a playa called Petit Bara.

Despite my sunglasses, the zealous light off the nude earth is overwhelming. In the distance a line of camels walks across the playa with legs that
grow longer with each step. They stretch until their legs are strings holding
the balloons of their bodies high above the quicksilver earth. Then they
disappear into thick air.

At the far end of the Petit Bara the road parallels a long low ridge. My
peripheral vision begins to nag me. I've been infected with that absurd
warning: *In the rocks. Watching you.* I stop and see only a few rocks like
sentinels along the ridge.

I ride until I hear the grunting. When I stop and scan the ridge, the
sentinel rocks are gone. Then someone appears, a backlit silhouette that
walks on all fours before standing to reveal itself as a baboon.

No—baboons. At least a half-dozen, less than a hundred meters away.
They're watching me, stretching, scratching their red butts while the rest of
their clan peeks over the ridge until they, too, are overcome with curiosity.
I stop counting after forty baboons. The big boys have wild manes.

They don't follow me onto the Grand Bara. Perhaps they're put off by
fifteen miles of dried mud polygons without a speck of growth. More likely
the baboons are terrified by the sudden appearance of the French and
Djiboutian armies. Tanks and troop carriers and over a hundred jeeps and
trucks grind past Baboon Ridge, and there's really no choice but to swerve
off the road and let them pass.

That's when I discover that I can ride where I please on the lake bed.
At the same time the air force decides they can land where they please. A
big four-prop plane lands and takes off again and again. Just practicing, I
assume, but I worry that the plane may land on my head.

The monster roars aloft one last time. Meanwhile, the entire convoy
continues down a highway that now appears to be a very long diving
board over a shining pool. At the end of the board each and every vehicle
vanishes in the mirage.

The spur road to Ali Sabieh rises out of the playa and climbs a valley
between corroded hills of sandstone flecked with goats. It's late, and the
slopes of sharp-edged rubble glow orange, and so do the blond tufts of
dry grass. Then the crickets start up as the valley falls into shadow. Ladies

bent under loads of firewood drift into town. The call to prayer rings out, echoing off a mountainside ringed with concrete gun emplacements. They face south, to the border with Ethiopia and Somalia.

THE THREE-MAN STAFF of the Hotel de Palmeraie sits under the stars, enchanted by a Yemeni television show on the miracle of drilling artesian water wells. Ali Sabieh is far from the cozy balm of the Indian Ocean, and the evening temperature has already sunk to 70 degrees. To survive the near-polar conditions, the *khat*-chewing staff wear hooded sweatshirts and keep a fire blazing at their side.

"Heat hurts, but cold kills," is a Somali proverb repeated by the great wanderer Richard Burton in his *First Footsteps in East Africa*. He passed just south of Ali Sabieh in 1854 (the town did not yet exist), traveling among the Somali-speaking Issa who still live here; farther west were the Oromo, with their own quaint folklore.

> *A spear without blood is not a spear.*
> *Love without kisses is not love.*

Such bipolar sentiments thrilled Burton, who at some risk paid particular attention to the shape and habits of the local virgins. "One of their peculiar charms is a soft, low, and plaintive voice . . . whose accents sounded in my ears rather like music than mere utterance."

Burton admired the creed of the nomadic Issa ("Every free-born man holds himself equal to his ruler") although it was a recipe for both liberty and turmoil. In a land where kinship means everything, they were ungovernable by outsiders. And despite being "soft, merry, and affectionate souls, they pass without any apparent transition into a state of fury, when they are capable of terrible atrocities."

Burton eventually took a spear through his cheeks, topside. I've better luck with the Issa. Mohammed, who runs the hotel, speaks only Somali and French, but is thoughtful enough the next morning to pantomime a warning: don't go south toward the border. There is a refugee camp.

I spend the day in Ali Sabieh. The town is built of stone, usually with rough stucco but sometimes prettied up by painting the stones one color and the mortar another, for a truly stone-age look last seen in Flintstones cartoons. The feeble train from Djibouti Town to Ethiopia crawls past, with three tankers and six flatbeds piled with sacks and people, including a few candidates for amputation standing on the couplings.

It's a shy town. The people duck into mosques or slip between the tall split doors of their homes, leaving the slit-eyed glare of midday for the shadows within. The street market smells sweetly of dates and oranges. No one approaches me. I've no idea that anyone speaks English until I notice that somebody is stealing my bike.

I'd brought it into a store with me, and now a young man wearing only a skirt is wheeling it toward the door. I place myself in front of him and say, Peace be with you. He stops and glares and says something in what may be Somali. He is six feet tall, with a body that is an anatomy lesson in musculature, and finally I see that he's potentially dangerous. I nervously try a few words of explanation—bicycle, Djibouti Town, Ali Sabieh—but before I finish he yells something with a fervor that freezes everyone in the shop.

I hold out my hands, palms up, and say in English, What do you want?

A man speaks in English: "He says he is hungry. He says he is angry. He says give him money."

My natural inclination is to not give a single franc to the person who tried to make off with my bicycle. The feeling is promptly overruled by a conflicting emotion. It's not, I'm sorry to say, empathy for his situation but for my own. He looks capable of terrible atrocities.

I reach into my pocket and give him the first cash I touch: five hundred francs—about three dollars. He turns and vanishes.

"No worry," says the same man in English. "No problem."

I ride through the dirt alleys, scattering the goats, at once fearful and fuming. It's true that the actions of one can damn a nation. Now I'm sympathetic to Burton's claim that the "savages" are prone to not only robbery but all sorts of nonsense. "Those who chew coffee beans are careful not to place an even number in their mouth, and camel's milk is never heated, for fear of bewitching the animal. The mosquito bite brings on . . . deadly fevers: the superstition probably arises from. . . ."

I've got to admit that the Issa were right on the last one; they deduced the vector of malaria long before the Europeans.

I head to a gas station for stove fuel, but find only diesel. A passerby detects my disappointment and stops and asks for my pen. Drawing on his own forearm, he cleverly manages to explain that I must listen for the sound of a generator. There I will find gasoline.

His kindness begins to change my mind about Ali Sabieh. The hotel completes the process. I'm the only guest, treated to shish kebabs and spaghetti in a dining room hung with plastic garlands and year "2000" stencils. The latter are apparently left over from a millennium celebration, and perhaps saved for the Muslim millennium, which should roll around in about six hundred years.

In my room I slap mosquitoes and study the map. Lac Assal is sixty-five miles north, in the home of the Afar, also known as the Danakil, also known as the castrators. Burton cheerfully described them: "The men were wild as ourang-outangs, and the women fit only to flog cattle."

Fine: I'd rather deal with cow-floggers than refugees. I pack and retire, for a dawn departure. My sleep is interrupted, however, by the opposite of a nightmare. The dream is of a man on a flight in the not-so-distant future. He's staring at the fantastically complicated seatback of the row in front of him. Not only does it include his personal telephone, video, and computer, but also his food selection. The screen reads: "The cuisine on Flight 327 has been declared *Festive* by the Grand Prix du Chefs held annually in Akron, Ohio. To automatically sand and dip your baguette, press the # key."

The man does exactly that, creating such a grinding commotion within the device that the person sitting in the seat turns and . . .

I wake to my own laughter, rub my eyes, then realize: *Christ! I'm in Djibouti!*

I step outside to check. A rooster is crowing prematurely. The Big Dipper is rising in the east. At 3 AM comes the call to prayer, which at this hour includes the motivating chant, *Prayer is better than sleep. Prayer is better than sleep.*

The call to prayer seems unusually loud and long, and I know why. This moonless night kicks off the most holy of Muslim rituals. Of all the times to visit the slimmest nation on earth, I've chosen the month of fasting that is Ramadan.

CLUTCHING HIS PRAYER BEADS as he walks, a man with a white skullcap glances up as the sun clears the horizon over Ali Sabieh and vanquishes the possibility of eating until sundown. If he's sincere in his belief, he'll also abstain from sex, lying, and spiteful gossip. Purity of spirit, they say, allows one to draw closer to one's maker.

With the exception of my secret Ramadan food stores, I do my best to follow suit. I wheel into a desert with no hope for sex and no need for lying, and as close as I'll ever be to my maker. This slice of Africa is known to geologists and anthropologists as the Afar Triangle. Only a hundred miles west is where the bones of *Australopithecus* were first discovered—the first primate to walk on two legs. This is the only place on earth where you could ask a local how long they've called it home, and the honest answer would be, *Forever.*

The bike and I fly down the valley through the goose-bumpy chill and onto the Grand Bara. There are no mirages this morning, only a shirt-snapping headwind. I crouch lower and pedal on, backtracking to the Petit Bara. A pair of midget antelope called dik-dik bound across the road like horned jackrabbits, or perhaps the mythical jackalope.

After four more dik-dik and a panicked whirl of sandgrouse, like pigeons in desert camouflage, I reach the Lac Assal turnoff I'd passed two days earlier. There's a truck stop here, a tin-roofed patio with a ceiling of woven mats to repel the heat. The cook and the truckers are from highland Ethiopia, land of the crucifix, so I can sit down for a bowl of panting hot lentils and onions.

They speak English, so I ask what they are hauling.

"Salt from Lac Assal," says a young driver with pretty good shoes. He jots his name in my notebook, *Endalkachew Taye from Ethiopia.* "Six hundred bags, fifty-five kilos each, every three days."

Salt was the original currency of the Afar, whose homeland includes not only Djibouti's Lac Assal but also the immense below-sea-level Danakil Depression in Ethiopia and Eritrea. I'm told the Afar's territory begins just north of the truck stop, but to my eye their camps look like the Issa's—the same portable huts and yellow plastic water jugs. The ponderous camels ignore the Brownian motion of the insatiable goats. Peewee children race up to see me pass. Stopping to say hello causes them to flee in terror.

The road crests a saddle above the Gulf of Tadjoura. This forty-mile-long bay nearly slices little Djibouti in two before ending abruptly at the volcano defending Lac Assal from the sea. To reach the pit, the road must first climb the stepped plateaus whose flanks are clawed by canyons that drop 2,000 feet into the drink. At the deepest gorge I leave the bike and creep up to the verge to look straight down hundreds of feet. The moment I do, a pair of warplanes burst over the horizon and pass so low that I duck.

When the echoes subside there is nothing but the wind and the sound of falling stones. Far below the rimrock, a girl is winging rocks at a herd of goats, driving them to a waterhole that shines like a drop of mercury. She stands alone atop a pinnacle, green dress and yellow scarf flapping in the breeze, crying "*Ay! Ay! Ay!*" She is queen of her domain.

Dead ahead is Lac Assal, a bull's-eye of deepest blue ringed with purest white, sunk far below in a black spill of lavas from the volcano. At the turnoff to the pit stands a flock of Afar huts, a single sheet-metal shack painted the green and blue of the Djiboutian flag, and two open-air truck stops. I choose the one with plastic crates of empty Coke bottles forming a windbreak for the patio, and a satellite TV dish connected to nothing.

There are no customers—just me and the buzzing miasma of flies. I order a Coke and rest my eyes in the shade. When I open them I see that a lone man, whittled by the sun into a form that hardly casts a shadow, is walking toward the truck stop.

"The Danakil kill any stranger at sight," wrote L. M. Nesbitt in *Hell-Hole of Creation.* He was doubtlessly in a rotten mood after that little incident with the viper in his sun helmet. And it's true that his party, bristling with rifles, met with hostility. Nesbitt believed that only because "a white man commands a certain respect, by reason of his superior fortitude and will power," did he survive "the criminal Afars, who are easily tamed by a little tact and a few trinkets."

I offer the man a seat and a Coke. He refuses the Coke—Ramadan—but takes the seat. He does not speak English, yet his ability to communicate is without peer. Once he understands my destination is Lac Assal, he rises and points to the fresh black cone of the volcano, then pantomimes how it cut off Lac Assal from the Gulf of Tadjoura.

This much is fairly obvious. But this fellow in a purple plaid skirt and a Nike T-shirt takes the geology lecture further. He puts the sides of his hands together and says "Africa" before pulling them slowly apart. He identifies one hand as Kenya, then adds, "Seismo."

This is exactly right. The Gulf of Tadjoura is where the tectonic slash known as the Great Rift Valley enters the continent of Africa, which it is patiently ripping in two. Kenya and the Horn of Africa will ultimately raft away from the rest, although on a time scale perhaps intelligible only to the Afar.

Seismo. He carries on with pen and the back of my map, drawing a well tapping into a subterranean force that spins a little turbine. He probably wonders why I'm smiling. I'd presumed that a herder in flip-flops would know nothing of geothermal energy, and I'm happy to be wrong.

But I really wish that a goat had not snatched the Arabic notes from my handlebar bag. It's already chewed its way to the last page by the time we chase it off. The geologist laughs and shakes my hand and strolls back into the heat.

I head over to the flag shack to buy a can of "Choice Pineapple Broken Pieces," then hop on the bike for the big drop through ten miles of naked lavas. To my surprise, the road is nicely paved, and with joy I sing the geographically inappropriate "City of New Orleans" while rolling down without a turn of the pedals to the lowest point in Africa. A half hour before sundown, I'm standing on the shore of Lac Assal.

It's huge. It's whipped by a terrific wind into saltcaps. It's rimmed by plum-colored mountains and steaming hot springs. And there are no mosquitoes.

The Afar are here, salt-cutters returning from their work to a cluster of stone domes only six feet high. When one man spots me searching for a place to hide from the wind, he offers the international hands-as-pillow symbol. I accept. He further indicates, wait here.

After their prayers, three men and two women clear out an excellent little hovel, fetch a woven mat, then invite me to their hut for dinner. They break their fast with round breads and lentil stew while a tiny radio emits a faint warble of music. I exhaust my Arabic to discover that all three men are named Ali. The eldest, only twenty-five, speaks so clearly that although I don't understand the words I know what he means: if you have any trouble in the night, come here and we will help you.

I walk back under the splash of stars, and duck into my room of black rocks. It's crazy hot. One of the Alis pokes his head in to give me a candle. The men return to work, firing up a front-loader to stack the slabs of salt.

Mr. Hell-Hole didn't think much of the natives' schedule. "Then at dawn, when they ought to be doing their work, they will fall soundly asleep, and will go on snoring under the noonday sun. The glare and the flies trouble them little; only a touch of your booted toe will recall them to their duties."

Poor Mr. Nesbitt. Superior fortitude and inferior scheduling had brought him to the pits in June, when the average high is 118 degrees. The below-sea-level savages who mine the salt were nowhere to be seen.

A shame. They're actually pretty nice.

DJIBOUTI IS A PETITE REPUBLIC, about the size of New Hampshire or Sicily, and I've no intention of leaving the country after reaching its nadir. My plan is to ride back to the capital by a wholly new route.

But first I linger on the shore of Assal, riding along the salt flats in the morning sun. Crystals cling to the spinning tires, then whiz off in brief parabolas. The air tastes of salt. Like a good tourist, I take photos of the gypsum buttes rising fifty feet from the shallows like sugar-cube castles. The French and Djibouti armies, seemingly in endless pursuit of the American bicyclist, roar past without noticing me crouched with my camera.

The only salt truck stands with its hood open in distress. In the shade of its trailer sits a little nest—goatskin mat, water bottle, and a Koran—but no driver. The Alis have retired into their huts for nap time. A few half-hearted clouds drag hopeful shadows over the 6,000-foot mountain to the east, but fail to reach the pit.

On Everest it's the frozen gasp of altitude that drives humans back down; on the shore of Assal, the opposite sends me up. As usual, the unseen atoms of oxygen and nitrogen are bumping into each other and creating heat. Squeezing air with the pressure of five hundred feet below sea level is like taking a roller rink and making it half the size—a lot more collisions and sweat.

It's no surprise that the only traffic on the ride back out is the grinding military convoy. By the time I reach the truck stop, even the goats are struck down by the heat, sprawled in the shade of the big rigs. Inside sit a half-dozen Ethiopians. I slip off my shoes and pad in.

"Everybody is waiting for the salt to be ready," says a neat, balding man with good posture. His name is Sirak and his eyes are astoundingly bloodshot.

A tall, unskinny, and also balding man named Molla invites me to sit for lunch. A woman with red sparkles on her toenails holds a squirt jug over a battered aluminum bowl for hand washing. There are a few stools of cowhide, but they are reserved for the lunch platters. We sit on clean mats and wait with the patient flies.

Molla stares gloomily out at the white heat. "Nothing in Djibouti but salt."

Lunch is a two-foot-wide spongy pancake with a centerpiece slurry of chili, garlic, onions, and lentils. The men call it *injera* and *wot*. You tear off a piece of the sour *injera* and scoop up the *wot*.

Smoldering chili would not be my first choice in a café opening onto a lava field, but I admit it's pretty good. "This is the cook," says Sirak, "in the Janet Jackson shirt."

The cook bows and grins and adds, "She is my wife." Sirak translates this for the benefit of those who don't speak English. The men crack up. I ask the cook if his children look like Michael Jackson. This sets off an unanticipated discussion.

"I like his sing," says the man in a Rolex T-shirt. "No like man."

"Michael Jackson is good," says Molla with the authority of a man in a button dress shirt. "He is very intelligent man."

"But now he is a white man!" shouts Sirak, leaning forward with neck veins bulging. "He changed his color. I hate him!"

The first *injera* is demolished. A second is served.

"We love American cinema," says Sirak between mouthfuls. *"First Blood. Second Blood. Third Blood.* Action films."

"Schwarzenegger!" yells a trucker.

"And what of you?" asks Molla. "Did you like *Titanic*?"

I admit that I haven't seen it yet.

Everyone stops eating. They stare at their first living American, their hands arrested in midair, mouths agape as the *wot* slips off the *injera* and plops onto the floor. Molla shakes his head in disbelief and breaks the silence. "But *everyone* has seen *Titanic*. The Chinese president saw it fifty-one times!"

Sensing that this may be beyond the bounds of most *Titanic* fans, Molla adds, "I heard this on the radio." The truckers nod in agreement, then realize that they must eat the second *injera* before the flies carry it off. They do, and a third is served with spaghetti atop, chopped into pieces with the rim of an overturned cup.

"There is a building called the Pentagon," says Molla. "Is it true that it is very big and you need three years to walk everyplace in the Pentagon?"

I'm busy cleaning up a splosh of noodles on my pants. Molla answers the question himself. "But how could such a thing be true? It is not."

Tea is served on a blue enamel platter. The questions continue.

"My sister is in America but cannot get her green card. Why not?"

"How can I get a sponsor for a visa?"

Everyone but me is anxious to head for America. From the truck stop I turn not back to Djibouti Town but toward the port of Tadjoura, on the opposite side of the gulf. It's fifty miles. I pedal only five, to a camp on the seashore. There are Afar huts on the beach, but like the teepees along Arizona's Route 66, they're for tourists. There is only me. I prefer outside, listening to the slosh of the surf until a boat skids ashore at dusk.

Three Ramadan-famished fishermen, with droplets of sea spray clinging to their curly mops, skip through the sand and swiftly build a fire. A small shark is messily dismembered with a big knife, and tossed into a pot of rice and water. One man explores the limits of ventriloquism by holding the decapitated shark's head and working its jaws while mumbling an invitation to dinner. A funny guy, and I've the funny feeling that the talking shark routine has been performed in this spot, under these stars, for a very long time.

It's 82 DEGREES at dawn. The Great Rift Valley is blocks, slabs, pavements, waves, and curtains of frozen basalt. Nothing has coughed up since the 1978 eruption, and green combs of slender rushes have already moved in along the roadside. There are three antelope, too, with twitching ears rimmed in black and fly-swatting tails spinning like propellers. One is so terrified by the bicycle that it trips and crashes on the black rocks before bounding away.

A short hike to an Assal overlook brings me to the edge of a crevasse. It runs to the horizon, yet it's an easy hop to the other side. I drop a stone into the slit and wait a couple of seconds for the impact. It's true: Africa is coming apart.

A wobble-wheeled truck passes at 7 AM, struggling on a road that plunges and climbs and switchbacks up the lavas. Following the shoreline is impossible; cliffs drop directly into the sea. The topographic consequence is a 2,000-foot climb to reach a town on the coast, along a route that reminded the gun-running Rimbaud of "the presumed horrors of lunar landscapes."

I've five quarts of water for the forty-five-mile ride. The only shade is blocks of lava, where I devour oranges and curse God's headwind. There are no Afar to offend.

Three hours later I notice blood on my water bottle, but it's only my wind-cracked lips. Half the water is gone, and it's still over thirty miles to Tadjoura. I feel the first melodramatic stabs of self-pity, mistaking my misery for fear. Do I have enough water? I'd better, because there's nobody on the road. Like a fire lookout built where there's nothing to burn, Djibouti built a highway where there's nothing to drive.

Another hour of climbing, then hope appears as blue sky at the tip-top of a long steep shimmer of asphalt. But it's a false summit. Beyond is a canyon so deep the bottom is not visible from the rim. What *is* visible is the appalling road climbing out the far side. I slam on the brakes and stare, panting, until the shock squeezes out a panicky laugh, the hysterical cackle of a gladiator tossed into a pit with a dozen lions. I give up!

No less surprising is the slow calm that comes from realizing that there's really no choice. The hill is as terrible as it looks, but I've the road to myself and zigzag to lessen the grade. Another hour and I'm over the top and in a different world.

Low chubby clouds skid out of the gulf and are scooped up like ground balls on the slopes of a big mountain only ten miles inland. The stiff bushes and umbrella-shaped trees return—not a forest by any means, but life enough to bring the scream of cicadas and the huts of the Afar. They're not portable but thatched round houses with conical roofs drawn into a nipple at the peak. There are cows, too, and with their dung come scarab beetles, little emerald bulldozers pushing their treasure home.

There are 10,000 people in Tadjoura, and it seems most are in the streets when I roll in at sundown. With no cars to be seen, the kids are playing hopscotch where they please. The ladies, sitting on empty tins of powdered milk, are selling *khat* and goat milk and fried triangles of dough stuffed with meat or dates. *Samboussa*, they say. The houses are whitewashed cubes, shoulder to shoulder, each distinguished by slapdash additions of squat towers and oddly cantilevered constructions.

Down at the harbor, little drowsy waves collapse on black sands populated mainly by goats. The real action is on the promenade, where people are unrolling mats and setting out *samboussas* and cups of orange drink. Ancient geezers with hennaed beards watch the same old yellow sun creep toward the horizon. On the opposite side of the gulf, high on a mountaintop, the Legionnaires are finishing off their bold cheeses. Over here, it's the Ramadan countdown to chow down.

I attract little attention. Tadjoura is one of the oldest ports in East Africa, and over the last thousand years stranger things than me have walked this promenade. But I do draw a question from a man with a thin beard, toting a plastic sack.

"Can I help you find something, someplace?"

Thank you. Your English is excellent. I'm looking for a place to stay.

"I am the English teacher of Tadjoura. You can stay right here—many people sleep on the beach every night. You can leave your bicycle in one of the stores."

And can you recommend a place to eat?

"Why don't you just come with me?" He checks his digital watch. "Three to six. It is almost time to eat. Every day it is two or three minutes later." He shows me the contents of the sack—*samboussas*, crepes, and *khat*—then brings me home.

HATKE LIVES fifty yards from the sea. He shoos the goats out of an alley, opens a narrow steel door, climbs a dim flight of stairs to his apartment, and flicks on a fluorescent ceiling light. The flat is mostly empty. The walls are the color of cactus.

"I have just moved into this place. Very big, but my wife and baby are coming this weekend, from France."

Hatke, unlike his wife, is Afar. He spreads dinner out on a floor tray between big foam cushions. Through the tall windows opening onto the balcony comes the Arabic mantra that means the fast is over. Hatke fishes a Coke out of a "Nice Day" ice bucket and presents it with a flourish.

"To help you return to your environment."

We dig in. My manners belie my appearance as a simple bicycle brute, and Hatke invites me to spend the night. He's thirty-two, about the same age as the woman who walks in without a knock. "Hemeda, my housemate."

She sits with legs crossed, revealing beaded ankle bracelets on skin like polished walnut. Without a word she sets to assembling a water pipe.

Hatke says, "Ninety percent—no, 95 percent—of the ladies in Djibouti smoke the *sheesha*. It's how we keep them off the street."

I admit that I'd had no idea.

"Yes, Djibouti is anonymous." He rises to put on a Waylon Jennings cassette, then rifles through some magazines. "But look, here is a picture of a bride from Tadjoura."

It's a *National Geographic* photo of a woman behind a veil of gold bangles. Hemeda looks up while packing the *sheesha* bowl with Two Apples Tobacco. She ignites the coals that sit atop the bowl, and hands me the four-foot-long embroidered tube. The water in the glass vase bubbles and cools the sweet smoke. Hatke pulls out a bundle of *khat* wrapped in cellophane.

'How much would you like? It is for us. The women usually do not chew—they have to work! To look after the house, the children."

Hemeda doesn't know English, yet chooses this moment to look after the *khat*, covering it with a damp towel—after I'd pinched off some leaves and stuffed a fair wad in my mouth. As with espresso, it takes only a few minutes to feel the warm electric jingle. After a half hour, it seems that pedaling out of a lava pit wasn't so hard after all.

A man in a skirt limps in, a crumpled gentleman with a spot of gray in his hair.

"This is Kamil. He works at the hospital, with the microscope."

Kamil puts down his cane and makes himself comfortable on the cushions before pulling out his own *khat*. The last Coke is poured, and Hatke heads to the balcony and lowers a bucket on a rope while yelling to someone. For thirty seconds there is nothing but the sounds of Tadjoura—the *oomp!* of a kicked soccer ball, the yowl of cats, the lick of waves—then Hatke pulls up a bucket of refreshments, courtesy of a tiny store on the street below that keeps a running tab of his thirst.

Kamil offers me an especially leafy branch, and I wonder: Will *khat* keep me up at night? Hatke says, "If you believe it will, it probably will. If not, it will not."

You can't beat a drug whose effects are largely up to you. On top of that, *khat* allows me to hold two simultaneous conversations. Kamil is describing how to stain *cocci* bacteria for tuberculosis, while Hatke fills me in on *khat* delivery.

"It comes to Djibouti Town at half past eleven by plane, and reaches Tadjoura by speedboat at half past three."

Every day?

"The day there is no *khat* will be the day there is a revolution in Djibouti."

What does the Koran say about *khat*?

Hatke contemplates a response while gazing up at a ceiling papered with a psychedelic motif like a TV test pattern. "I wouldn't say the Koran *encourages khat*, but it *does* encourage spirituality, which is an effect of *khat*."

I feel the spirit—tingling, behind my ears. Hemeda demurely nibbles a modest clipping. Her thick wavy hair is uncovered. Between her bare feet and smooth ankles is a *National Geographic* opened to the ravenous jaws of a great white shark.

"In general," says Hatke, "men buy *khat* and ladies sell it. A typical day's chew runs about nine hundred francs. That's more than many people have, so the ladies sell it on credit. You must pay at the end of the month. People fall behind, but in Djibouti we always run behind. For my teaching I am only paid up to July!"

Another friend enters—in a skirt, with *khat* in hand. Nobody knocks. You simply walk in with a *Peace be with you.*

"This is Ali. I think he might be able to find you a diving mask and arrange a boat to Sables Blancs tomorrow. Unless you want to go to Dittalou. This is a very nice place. At Dittalou you will see trees. It's cold."

Dittalou is a village in the Forêt du Day, perched on the cloud mountain I'd passed this afternoon. It sounds wonderful, I say—but how are the people?

"In all the Afar region you will be welcome."

They certainly were welcoming at Lac Assal, I say—but what of the old stories of the Afar who kill any stranger?

"Yes, in the past the people were very reluctant to come under colonial power. They thought that the people coming from the outside were going to destroy their way of life. After all, they came with their armies."

With this news I understand Nesbitt's dilemma as a man who failed to see that the Afar were brutal in response to his own brutality. He could not have imagined an evening like this, when Hemeda begins singing a beautiful ditty, with eyes closed and head rocking. Kamil keeps time, slapping a box of Royals cigarettes. Meanwhile, we destroy an entire bush. The floor is littered with naked stems. Hemeda finishes her song and Hatke inserts another cassette. The tape deck wails, *Something's burning. . . . And I think it's love.*

It's the *sheesha* and the Royals. When the smokes run out the bucket goes over the side. Hatke orders the exact number of cigarettes he desires, seven. They arrive at the window in a clever origami folded from a Singapore newspaper. Another call to prayer wafts in through the same window.

More visitors: a woman, also named Hemeda, with the two-year-old nephew of Hatke, also named Hatke. The young dumpling finds and organizes a checker game into piles of red and black pieces.

"A problem in Djibouti," says Hatke, "is our failure to recognize the intelligence of small children and to help develop it." A minute later, while nobody's looking, mini-Hatke tries a suck on the *sheesha*. Although my glasses are streaked with sweat, nice-ankle Hemeda dramatically shivers and turns off the fan. Out of the blue, Kamil says, "I want a Harley-Davidson. How much do they cost?"

I say, I don't know—maybe $5,000?

"No chance." He pulls out his special bundle. "Try this. It's the bourbon of *khat*. The best. Look: you can tell by the color of the leaves."

We chew and mentally ruminate until somebody pops in and steals Kamil away. Hatke explains, "They need him at the hospital, for a blood glucose test. No matter where he is, they find him."

Nice-ankle Hemeda and I share a cushion as an armrest. She flips through a *National Geographic*—Romania, Greenland, Mummies—then stops at an advertisement and pantomimes to me, What is this?

It's a woman with her arm around her bashful yet beaming husband. The copy reads, "I'm proud of him because he asked about Viagra."

Hemeda smiles. I helplessly smile back and notice for the first time she has a lazy eye askew. It's attractive in its suggestion that parts of Hemeda are beyond her control, but a distraction, too, when I need to explain an erection drug with my Afar vocabulary of *water*, *please*, and *thank you*. I consider using my bicycle tire pump as a visual aid, but instead seek the help of Hatke. He explains. Hemeda titters and flips the page and tries another picture on me. "Amphibian Frenzy," it says. "Sex in the Mud."

I divert her attention to the toddler, who's disassembling the fan with a screwdriver. She alerts Hatke, who gently disarms the boy.

An hour passes. Maybe two.

Perhaps, says Hatke, it's time for a stroll.

It's 1 AM, and every door and shutter in Tadjoura is open to the gulf breeze. The men are slapping dominoes at coffee shops and the women are still at their *khat* tables. Ramadan is not the ritual suffering I'd imagined.

HEAVYWEIGHT CLOUDS subdue the morning sun. In the distance, a mist washes over the mountains; in the apartment, Hemeda washes my pants in a basin. I won't venture out wearing shorts, so Hatke gives me a skirt. The *futah* is breezy, better than pants, but I still feel like a Chinese in a cowboy hat when I slink out for a coffee.

I shouldn't have worried. Although it's 10 AM, the beach is littered with dozens of people still curled in sleep, under blankets and blessed by the overcast morning. Along the waterfront, every door and shutter is closed. The empty lanes are etched with hopscotch lines. No coffee.

Back at Hatke's, Ali is waiting to take me diving, but first we visit Kamil at the hospital. It's a clinic, really, just three small white buildings around a planter of periwinkle. Kamil's delighted to show off his centrifuge, refrigerator, microscope, and illustrated volume of unpleasant microbes.

"In Tadjoura," he says with understandable if misplaced enthusiasm, "we have everything!" By way of proof, he puts a stained slide on his scope.

"Look at this—woo! The red is cocci bacteria. Tuberculosis. Two people died in the last year. It is problem in Tadjoura."

That's not the only problem—there's equipment for other diseases, like the brucellosis of unpasteurized goat's milk, "but we have not the chemicals to run the machine." It sits under a dusty shroud, waiting for what may or may not come.

But Djibouti is a country of waiting. A fiberglass fishing skiff takes us to Sables Blancs, smack-smack on the waves and into a wind that has blown away most of the clouds. Lacking a diving mask, Ali plans to sit under a palm and wait for somebody better equipped to come by. I've packed a lunch, but cannot bear to eat it while Ali fasts. I silently decide that I, too, will fast. Together we wait while the sea rocks over the shadow of the reef I may or may not see. The quick clouds are very white. Nearly three hours later, a French family shows up and loans me a mask. Under the waves, big-lipped polka-dotted sea bass are waiting for me.

Shortly after our return to Tadjoura, a boat faster than ours skims into the harbor. It's 5:30 PM, and the citizens are not merely awake but surging toward the pier. They're women trotting out to take delivery of the *khat*, which apparently arrives later during Ramadan. The sedate ladies begin baying like a pack of hounds as the thirty sacks are tossed one at a time. No money is exchanged; they know who and how much. The women hustle back to their street corners, divide it among their sellers, and the rest takes care of itself.

No *khat* for me. Yet. I wander in my *futah* and made-in-China flip-flops I bought to complete my unconvincing metamorphosis. Near a waterfront mosque, a circle of men young and old sit around a blanket heaped with *samboussas*, flatbread, and empty cups. They're yakking like woodpeckers, waiting for the chant that will break their fast. For once I share their hunger, their waiting, which really isn't so different from pedaling all day with the promise of a heavenly camp in the evening.

It comes: *God is great.* The men immediately offer me a place at their sidewalk feast with a sweep of the arm that means, "What is ours, is yours." I'm dealt a sizable mound of food and served an orange drink that only later will I see is poured from an old oil jug.

The meal is a quickie, to be resumed after prayers. They rise and invite me to join them. As soon as I'm through the door my awkwardness reveals me as a non-Muslim, but instead of booting me they assign me a helper. With sign language he says: Shoes off here. Spigots for washing here. He holds up a single finger: *First*, wash the hands. Then the face. The arms. Ears, neck, mouth. While finishing up with my feet and calves, my *futah* slips up and is gently tugged back down with a finger-wag meaning: no bare knees, please.

The mosque is little more than fluorescent bulbs and ceiling fans, a wall niche indicating the direction of Mecca, and floor tiles that show where your feet go. I stand and mimic my neighbors. Arms crossed, then arms out with palms up. Drop to the knees. Then the ultimate submission: forehead to the floor. Three repetitions of this, and I give clumsy thanks not to God but to the Afar. For their kindness. With equal sincerity I pray that my *futah* doesn't fall off.

Out on the beach, the long night begins. Goats scratch their flanks against the moonlit palms. While the cats fight over the fish skeletons overflowing a dumpster, the ladies briskly bring in the cash and the men just as quickly spend it on teeny coffees and *khat*.

Back at Hatke's, I'm startled that he already knows of my visit to the mosque.

"Tomorrow, everyone will know. There are very few Americans that visit Tadjoura."

And, I add, very few Afar that visit the United States.

"I'm afraid to go to America. It seems to be a violent place. We know few American people, but many American things. Movies, videos. Even the smallest child in Tadjoura has seen the *Titanic*."

I say nothing.

"And 100 percent of the girls become romantic after this movie."

We're chewing the *khat*, naturally. I believe tonight's high-grade leaf is known as "truck-driver." I waited for the now-familiar tickle of cathinone, as welcome as sleigh bells approaching on Christmas Eve.

Ali comes by, plops down, and unwraps his *khat*. Hemeda and another Ali join us. Then another Ali. Hatke confesses that his name, too, is Ali. He's called Hatke to avoid confusion. I sense another long night, and excuse myself to shower off the day's salt. Ali number three holds up his hand: *Stop*. There are things you must know.

First, don't take a shower while chewing *khat*. The sudden change in skin temperature can cause a heart attack.

Also, don't exercise during a *khat* chew. *Relax*.

Finally, never leave home with a mouth full of *khat*—you may catch a cold.

Is there, I wonder, a bad time to chew *khat*?

The answer: No, there is no bad time. Further, don't try to kick the habit. You'll feel miserable.

This accords with the World Health Organization, which says that the primary danger of *khat* is psychological dependence—which is to say the same danger as one hundred channels of television. Some go crazy.

But, says Hatke, "These are *our* rules. Everybody has different rules. I've chewed in a *mabraze,* a special room just for *khat.* Sometimes people in a *mabraze* all fall silent after one hour. Some begin ambitious projects in their minds, projects they'll never finish, and usually never begin. Others simply try to make toy houses out of the *khat* stems."

We fall silent. Hatke casts the empty bucket over the balcony, then reels in another keeper: Cokes and smokes.

We talk of my plans to pedal to Dittalou tomorrow. "God willing," is their earnest hope. I used to believe they said as much merely as reflex. But now I've the feeling they truly believe that tomorrow is a distant and unsure future, and that everything from the miraculous appearance of a diving mask to your eternal resting place is the will of God.

Except for Hatke. He's been tainted by nearly a decade in France, where things happen because people are willing to make them happen. Tonight he moans of the utter hopelessness of getting his flat fixed up during Ramadan. I ask him why he ever left Europe.

"In France the black man is not welcome. A French wife doesn't change this. You feel it. You are always referred to as an African. But when my wife visited Tadjoura she was welcomed into the community. She felt at home, so it was decided to make our lives here."

Another cat fight starts up in the alley. Ali number one, inspired by the imminent arrival of Hatke's family, is drilling a hole for a stairwell gate meant to keep the goats out of the building.

Hatke admits that life in Tadjoura for his wife will take some getting used to. "As an Afar, you are not an individual but a member of a tribe. Your wealth is measured in how much you help other members of your tribe.

"One day we Afar will surely be more like Western countries. But then the question becomes: what of our identity? In the back of our minds there is an Afar nation. But simply to say this now makes me wonder: what is a nation?"

Exactly, I'm thinking. Although this is not a *mabraze,* I've begun an ambitious project in my mind, the exact nature of which will never be known because it seems Hemeda is again making eyes at me, in her untamed way, one eye at a time.

AS THE VULTURE FLIES, the rumpled landscape of Djibouti is only one hundred miles across. As the bicyclist rides, it seems to go on forever. It takes four and a half hours to reach Dittalou, fifteen miles and far above Tadjoura, in a dripping forest of hornbills and baboons. Along the way I dare not wander off the road. Like the man at the embassy said: land mines.

The mines are the legacy of a smallish Djiboutian civil war only ten years past, between the Afar and Issa. Since independence from France in 1977, the Issa have run Djibouti, in part because Djibouti Town is in Issa territory. The Afar would like things otherwise. Parity within Djibouti government would be a nice start. But the "Afar nation" in the back of Hatke's mind is much more: the unification of all million or so Afar. To do so would require Djibouti, Ethiopia, and Eritrea to give up large hunks of territory, a proposal to which their traditional response has been *Drop dead.*

The Afar have yet to drop dead. Like the Kurds of Asia, they occasionally lose patience and revolt, but mostly they wait. Djibouti's summer heat is not ideal for waiting, but the Afar can escape Tadjoura for Dittalou. Nearby is what Hatke called "water running over the surface." It's a creek, under big trees with flakes of bark like sycamores. Candy-red dragonflies bob and dip their tails in the water, and fat-headed tadpoles wiggle up to gobble the eggs.

It's getting late when I drop back into the slobbering-camel desert. I hurry past the soft humps of coastal dunes with their weirdly branching palms, stopping only once to let a stake-bed truck pass. In the back, standing tall among the jostle of goats, a man in a *Titanic* T-shirt yells, *Peace be with you!*

Hatke is out of town but left his flat to me, for a night under the whoosh of a ceiling fan to discourage the mosquitoes. In the morning I gulp a Malarone pill and leave most of my first-aid kit as a gift for Kamil. For Hatke I leave a fat package of Ultra Lotus Baby diapers I picked up in Tadjoura, as well as a Top Ramen noodle dinner carried all the way from cosmopolitan Djibouti Town.

That's where the lucky ones shop, and here they come now, on the twice-weekly car ferry that moors crookedly on the pier. Off the ferry comes a rush of people carrying electric fans and baby strollers, only to meet head-on a crowd of one hundred propelled by the urgent need to bring twelve sacks of charcoal, a dozen five-gallon plastic jugs, three goats, two red volcanic boulders, and one bicycle to Djibouti Town.

Moments after I board, the ferry inexplicably begins to pull away before the loading ramp is pulled up. Three policemen blow their chrome whistles and the people still on the ramp scream and jump, onto either the pier or the ferry.

The Bay of Tadjoura is deep and dark; mats of root-beer-colored seaweed are pushed away by the bow. It's time for prayer, and the passengers do their best to figure out the direction of Mecca. The water jugs come out for the ritual washing, and the prayer rugs go down.

In an apparent effort to make up for the bumbled departure from Tadjoura, our captain relies on no fewer than three crew members on the bow to guide him to the Djibouti Town pier. Sadly, all three are yelling and pointing in conflicting directions. The captain is so far off the mark that the crewmen of an anchored cargo dhow leap off their prayer rugs, unsheathe their knives, and race to the mooring lines, ready to slice them if a collision is imminent.

We slide by with twenty feet to spare. Twenty minutes later I'm riding through the Ramadan torpor of Djibouti Town. A rap on the door of the Djibouti Palace wakes Ahmed the clerk. Lucky me gets the key to room 9.

I take a nap. Everybody else is.

I wake at 4:30. Everybody else does.

After a fish dinner at the Maskali, Nasir the cook invites me to his home. It's five minutes away on the back of his 49cc motorbike, to a blue plywood box with a ceiling fan. He shares this spotless twelve square feet with two other men and a single copy of the Koran.

"This window," says Nasir, "lets in the sea breeze, so it is not so hot in the summer."

I wonder, did it get hot in your Somaliland home?

"Oh, no," says the refugee. "It is like California—very nice, all the time."

He changes into sharply creased slacks and a green button-up shirt, then takes me out on a night of endless introductions and questions. I don't mind. Everybody in Djibouti has a notion of America—very nice America, violent America—but these are merely visions that float on the horizon. Djibouti makes me extra-proud to be a real walking American. My trip is so odd—*What? You have come only to see Djibouti?*—and the country so small that it is not an exaggeration to say that by the time I leave, most of Djibouti seems to know me.

So the hookers ignore me on my last day of cruising the European Quarter. The postcard vendor says, *Hello, journalist.* The barber at Coiffures Vijay doesn't bother to demonstrate the alcohol bath for his razor.

This familiarity sharpens the bite of leaving Djibouti. After the shave I sit in Menelik Plaza and say to myself, Be reasonable. This is no paradise. The flies are awful. The plaza is pathetic. One building has collapsed for neglect and nobody bothers to haul out the rubble. Most of the town looks as if constructed by ten-year-old boys. The refugee kids stoned me. The fruit drink poisoned me.

I walk back to the hotel as the sky purples and the fast is broken. Checking out of the Palace, I notice that the Coca-Cola clock above the front desk is exactly as it was when I checked in, stuck on 2:37, the second hand struggling up, then falling back again and again.

The taxi to the airport looks capable of blinding speeds, equipped with racing spoilers and air dams and scorpion decals. The driver putt-putts at 25 mph. He practices his basic English with me, and in doing so is one of the last Djiboutians to learn that I am just a tourist, not with the embassy or on business. I came to see Djibouti.

On impulse, he makes a gift of the shiny thing that dangles from his mirror. It's a necklace, a leather thong tied to a chrome ring crudely cut with the name of Michael Jackson. It's the ugliest necklace I've ever seen, and I hold it to my heart like the Hope Diamond.

The jet noses into the night and banks over a land without lights, apparently sleeping. I know better. It's Ramadan, and the ventriloquist fisherman may well be working the jaws of his talking shark. The *khat* is surely being kept moist under wet burlap. And five hundred feet below sea level, I imagine, the flip-flop geologist is skipping stones across Lac Assal.

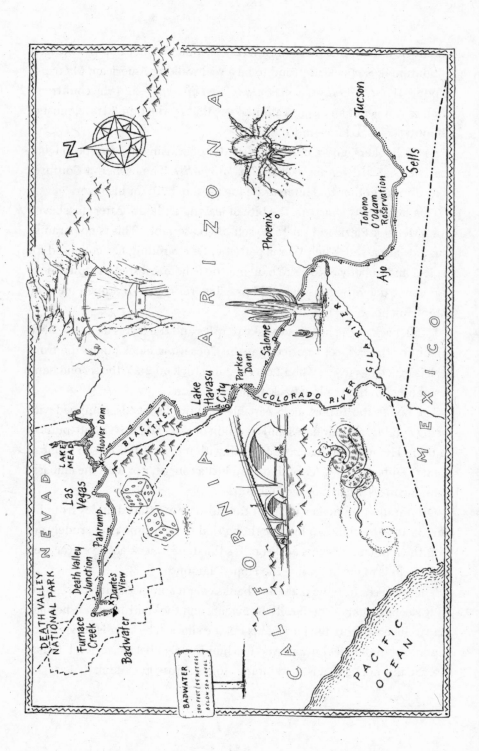

NORTH AMERICA

*Not that we set out to make some
sort of record; it was really just a
cheap vacation that got a little
out of hand.*

—Bill Beer,
"We Swam the Grand Canyon"

CHAPTER 11

Tucson
That Sounds Just Awful

IT WAS BEDTIME in Tucson. The blinds were drawn against the January cold, but they did little to muffle the sporadic yowl of sirens from the fire station. My three-year-old didn't mind. He liked disasters, and he had a very important question.

"Did the captain of the *Titanic* get in trouble for not bringing enough lifeboats?"

He was staring at a fantastically detailed illustration of the great ship in deep trouble. The bow was under and the stern lifted high above the black sea. The ship was nearly vertical, and the ranks of still-glowing portholes made the *Titanic* look like a sinking skyscraper.

I said, No, Rudy—it wasn't his fault. And now it's time for lights out. I've got to get up early to go work in the desert. I'm still making my plant map.

"How long will you go?"

Only four nights.

He considered this. "Are you going to Africa again?"

No—I promise.

Three weeks earlier, I'd returned from Africa with a mind to paint my file cabinet the colors of the Djiboutian flag, start a *khat* plantation, and finally watch *Titanic*. Not a one happened. I'd begun planning the final trip.

Driving west into the desert the next morning, I imagined myself pedaling my bike along the same road, sailing along on a smiling tailwind, bound for Death Valley, California. Fifty miles out of town, I passed a two-track off the highway that wound into the foothills of the Quinlan Mountains. At 60 mph the hills looked like nothing more than a rock pile and a bunch of well-fed saguaros, but I guessed the dirt road would lead to the perfect first camp.

With Death Valley I would end my quest for the pits in the same way I'd begun bicycle touring some twenty years earlier: alone, riding out of the only city I really knew. There would be no farewell at the airport weapons scanner, no malaria pills, and no passport. I considered myself a whiz at English. If I encountered a tribe of Harley-Davidson enthusiasts, with a glance I would know if they were lawyers in leather or true psychopaths.

All that remained was choosing the route. My thirty years of rambling around Tucson did not make this task easier, just as living in the same city as my entire extended family did not make kin relationships simpler. Familiar territory still holds wrong turns and dead ends, and among my maps I happily wallowed in the work of getting it right. While the bees were cavorting in the citrus blooms I was lingering over 1:100,000 scale topographic sheets of the Colorado River valley. By the time the summer storms rolled into town my itinerary was firmed up, and I pedaled over to the university to excuse myself from work.

I found the business manager at her desk, mousing around a spreadsheet on her monitor. Cecily was proof that you needn't be a department head to run the joint; without her, nothing happened. My request was simple: could you please hold my paychecks for three weeks?

She spun her swivel chair to ask, "Taking a trip?" She wore all-terrain office shoes, with thick soles equally capable of trotting to the printer or squashing a scorpion. "Where are you going?"

Death Valley, I said.

"For *three* weeks?"

No, I admitted, not three weeks in Death Valley—three weeks to get there. I'm riding my bike from Tucson.

"All the way?"

Sells, Ajo, Gila Bend, Parker, Lake Havasu City, Vegas—all the way.

She connected the dots and confessed, "I'm really sorry, but that sounds just awful."

I said, Cecily, I love an honest response.

Riding home, I kept an eye to the mountains ringing Tucson. Over Cathedral Rock was a whopper of a thunderhead, some 30,000 feet of vapor stacked into confections, and I thought: the desert doesn't look so awful to me. It was easy to picture myself at my first camp, alone and happy with a view of clouds glowing in the evening pink.

Of course I'd hoped for the same in Australia, and ended up pursued by imaginary crocodiles, but this time would be different. This was *my* desert. There would be no Saharan sandstorms or Patagonian pummeling. No Russian swamp, either. The list of no's grew until I reached no prostitutes and remembered that I'd be passing through Las Vegas. Once I'd driven close enough to the city to make out what resembled an art fair acrylic painting of a space colony on Venus, fed by high-voltage lines under a yellow sky. It was probably just a bad air day, but I'd turned away, thinking, *Maybe another time.*

This would be that time. It was now September, the last gasp of summer. The cicadas quit their screaming, and trusted in the next generation. Likewise, I hovered, quietly satisfied, over my sleeping children. The closer I got the better they looked, with polished skin and translucent eyelids.

One morning they woke to find my wife and me watching TV at 7:30 AM. This was extraordinary, but there was something extraordinary to see. The World Trade Center was falling. As if Channel 4 understood that I could not fathom the destruction, it played the scene again and again.

Rudy understood that something terrible had happened. He also saw a titanic slow-motion collapse that looked awfully familiar, ranks of windows vanishing into a sea of lesser buildings. He tried to cheer me by explaining the singular advantage of this disaster. "All the old disasters happened *before* I was born, so I didn't get a chance to see them."

At least I wouldn't have to worry over the psychological trauma to my son. I could fret full-time over the mood of America. Shortly after the suicide bombers were identified as Muslims, there was a revenge shooting in nearby Phoenix. The victim was a Sikh, not a Muslim, but an immigrant with a turban was close enough for the junior marksman.

I didn't relish the thought of pedaling across a United States that despised the people who had treated me so well. But every country I'd visited over the past five years had been maligned as either a disaster or a danger—the Russian Mafia, the Afar nut-whackers, the Aussie vipers. Then I'd gone and found out that, for a cyclist, all that was only muttering rumors and old fears. I figured it would be no different for this country, and there was only one way to know for sure.

Only then could I tell the story that began the last day of September, when I kissed my sleeping wife and children in the placid predawn, grabbed a banana and my maps, and headed out to the bike. The way to Death Valley was down my gravel drive, and west on Waverly Street. It was the same route I took daily, except this time I would keep moving.

CHAPTER 12

Tucson to Death Valley

Way Down in That Hole
Where There Ain't No Noise

VERY EARLY on Sunday morning, old Tucson is possessed not by cars but by dog-walkers and doves. It's quiet but not silent, and only a half mile from home I run into a real commotion, a trio of children in the street, waving feathers and yelling, "Uncle Jimmy! These are for you, so you fly like an eagle."

My sister whispers, "They're turkey feathers."

Still, I fly. The bike carries a mere fifteen pounds of gear, including a stove, pot, tent, sleeping bag, and a copy of Mary Austin's *Land of Little Rain*. Five minutes brings me to the university mall, past the fat palms and under the gothic olives; another five and I'm turning onto Fourth Avenue, where the sidewalk coffee sippers gasp whenever a cyclist wipes out on the trolley tracks.

I don't crash. Coasting down a subtle grade, I pass my unwitting sponsor, Value Village: outfitters of antiexpeditions. Their "pretested" cotton button-up shirt features a breast pocket that's handy for a spiral memo pad, pen, and aspirin in a Tic-Tac container. At speed on the bike, the shirt inflates nicely, lifting the fabric off my back.

A breezy shirt is a bonus in the heat, but today heavy clouds are spilling in from the south. Hurricane Juliette is spinning over the Gulf of California, 220 miles southwest. Luckily, the pinwheel of a hurricane rotates counterclockwise in the northern hemisphere. Relative to the eye of Juliette, I'm at two o'clock and Death Valley is noon, so counterclockwise winds should speed me on my way. There are two flaws with this scenario—Juliette will surely move, and will likely make rain—but I'd rather deal with a potential hurricane on a Sunday than certain traffic on a Monday.

Nothing's moving downtown except me and a man in a cowboy hat, rolling a smoke outside the Greyhound station. When touring in Djibouti, I was charmed to see a local in a traditional hat. In Tucson, I brand the man as a fake: he wouldn't know a steer from a heifer.

It's impossible to be a tourist at home. The Wig-o-Rama store on Congress Street, a showcase of cratered foam heads, looks doomed or perhaps already closed—but no, Wig-o-Rama is the rock of ages and has outlasted most every other downtown business. A mile farther west, A-Mountain rises four hundred feet above the sucked-dry sands of the Santa Cruz River. With a road nearly to the whitewashed "A" at its summit, it's a joyride for day cyclists, a nocturnal hotspot for eager young couples, a graffiti battleground, a dazzle of shattered Bud Light bottles, and the place I smoked my pipe with Jim Boyer two days before his climbing gear failed.

In the thirty minutes it takes to pedal another five miles, the clouds advance fifty. They soar over the pine-dark mountains, then clamp down on all horizons. Another five miles and the city ends where the road climbs over Robles Pass, a minor notch between knobby hills and a thousand or so saguaro cacti. It's easy to see why this pleated vegetable is a celebrity—it's the only plant that appears to be waving good-bye.

The wind comes up and kicks me in the rear, down Robles Pass and across Avra Valley. It's a flat and straight cruise past drought-crippled hunches of mesquite, trees that an optimist would call half-alive. There are cacti, too, the jointed spindles of chain-fruit cholla, man-high and savagely spined. But the saguaros are gone, victims of the chill that slips down to the valley bottom on winter nights and kills the seedlings with daggers of ice crystals.

Avra Valley is the Dust Belt, the creeping edge of Tucson. The pioneers live in rectangular ranch houses prettied up with split-rail fences, or in double-wide Cavco trailers on lots scattered with sun-wasted tires and pocked with dust pits dug by overheated dogs. By the time I reach the western edge of the valley, flags of dust are rising from the flats. The wind makes short work of the thousand-foot climb between the Coyote and the Roskruge Mountains, and soon I'm beyond the reach of Tucson.

Turkey vultures veer on the wind over a roadkill I easily identify as a hog-nosed skunk. The skunk's unfortunate color scheme of a single white stripe down its black back may be a benefit in the desert, but served this one poorly on the highway it very much resembles. I ride on with an ear and eye for speeding cars, but few are out this Sunday. The spoor of my fellow Americans is mostly Pennzoil jugs and Budweiser cans, and if I keep my gaze up and forward I hardly notice.

Instead I notice the mountains. This is basin and range country, all the way to Death Valley. The ranges run mostly north-south, with topographic consequences for the east-west traveler: the road and I must thread our way around the mountains. I'm moving slowly by vehicular standards, but quickly enough to entertain the illusion that it is the mountains that are moving. Mountains sink into the horizon, and mountains duck behind other mountains. What looked like a lone pyramid is actually a spine of rock twenty miles long, humped up in the center like a hissing cat. The ranges rise abruptly from the apron of eroded rubble that geologists call an alluvial fan. Locally, we're more apt to use the Spanish term, *bajada*. It's the kindest habitat for the saguaros and the foothill palo verdes, small stiff trees with a photosynthetic skin of smooth green bark.

I've driven this road a hundred times, but things look different from the seat of a bike carrying a sleeping bag with a cold beer tucked inside. For the next three weeks I'll be living mostly outside, and, as Joseph Wood Krutch wrote in *The Desert Year:* "There is all the difference in the world between looking at something and living with it. In nature, one never really sees a thing for the first time until one has seen it for the fiftieth."

So true—but not always true. It doesn't take fifty times to appreciate a hurricane.

I catch the first whiff of moisture as I near the summit of the pass. When

I look back over my shoulder I see whirling snakes of dust on the leading edge of the storm, mixed with spouts of rain close behind. It's not a squall line or a cloudburst but what looks like a vast and filthy waterfall pouring onto the horizon. The effect on my legs is immediate: faster. In the forty miles between Avra Valley and the next town is a single rest stop with a picnic bench and ramada sunshade. I reach it just as the sky lets loose.

But the wind is cutting so hard that the ramada isn't enough. The horizontal rain forces me to crawl under the concrete bench and build a little upwind barrier of my bike and cargo bags.

And still it finds me. Mesquite leaves stripped from the trees snag in the bike spokes and tremble in the gale. So do I, despite my raincoat. My usual fondness for storms is missing in action. It's not the silver whips of cold rain. It's the sound of the aluminum roof groaning as it twists and warps.

The rain quits after an hour, a long time to feel stupid and afraid. The wind still blows, flattening the tussocks of yellow grasses and taking me over the pass. I've got in mind a certain dirt track to a campsite I'd imagined many months ago.

I find it: freshly washed sands and palo verde. A slice of blue is wedging under the clouds from the south. I don't trust it; I set up the tent as close as possible to the only windbreak, a scrap-heap ridge of busted granite. The wind rolls in like heavy surf with waves that pour over the ridge and bow in the side of the tent until the fabric is three inches from my nose. When the rain returns there's really nothing to do but to stare at the ceiling and think: only 665 miles to Death Valley.

JULIETTE HOLDS HER BREATH long enough for me to shake the wet from the tent in the morning and pack quickly, under an armada of low clouds shaped like dumbbells. Forces beyond my control are tearing the clouds in two. When the wind starts to sing through the needles of the rain-swollen saguaros, I lick a finger to test its direction, smile, and get on the bike.

This is Indian land. It's a big reservation—4,500 square miles—and it's a dry reservation: no streams and no alcohol. The people call themselves the Tohono O'Odam, and their capital is the nearby town of Sells, set between stony hills the color of chocolate. The "Business District" loop runs down a street splattered with big slushy cow flops, past the razor-wire jail and a playground in primary colors. The "Planning Department" trailer is closed, the video rental trailer open. The sole human afoot is a lady with a plastic grocery sack that sags with a shape I guess to be tamales.

Every town has its warts, but Sells is all warts—except for the eucalyptus-shaded Papago Café, a crooked bungalow with a red neon OPEN. I take a picture, walk in, and a customer in a handsome velveteen blouse asks, "Are you a photographer?"

Sort of. I must explain, so naturally I end up having my eggs, refried beans, tortilla, and salsa with Rosita Ruiz. She sits with Enos Francisco and his two-year-old granddaughter, Josephine, a photogenic little flower. I ask permission to take her picture, and Enos says with a big horsey grin, "Sure, but not of us—we're fugitives."

Hardly. Enos is the former chairman of the tribe, and Rosita was secretary. Politics has made them garrulous. Most O'Odam are as quiet as the music-free Papago Café and our silent waitress. After she refills the tall glasses of ice water, Enos whispers, "I used to think her name was Mercy, but she wouldn't respond. I knew something was wrong. It's Lucy."

Josephine sucks on ice cubes. Enos cleans his thick glasses with a paper napkin. Men in uniform swagger in, freighted with handguns, GPS locators, and walkie-talkies. "Here comes Leonard and the trackers," says Enos.

The reservation's southern frontier is Mexico. The Mexicans frequently do not ask if they can visit the United States for a day or a lifetime. It's an old problem, but only recently a Mexican problem. In the 1880s it was the Chinese sneaking in to work on the railroads. In 1915, Congress created the "Mounted Guards," but they were overwhelmed by the first real border rush in 1920, when Congress passed the National Prohibition Act. By making alcohol a crime, prohibition spawned an enormous smuggling racket, run by thugs with machine guns. Congress responded in 1924 with the first 450 official Border Patrol agents. It was nice work for the adventurous: you supplied the horse and the saddle, and the government supplied the oats, a revolver, and a badge.

Nowadays the smugglers with machine guns carry marijuana and cocaine. Leonard and his all–Native American team of trackers find them, gauging the smuggler's load by the depth of the footprint. Along this piece of the Arizona/Mexico border, the "Tucson Sector," another 1,700 agents keep an eye out for the more numerous job-seekers. Last year they caught over 600,000 people heading north.

This is too much action for the locals. Rosita says with a scowl, "We've got the Border Patrol tearing up the land down by our place in New Fields. They're arrogant, insulting, intrusive—I can't find enough adjectives to describe how poorly they treat us."

I tell them that I've been working on the border, with no problems from the patrol.

"That's because you're not a minority. You've got brown skin and you've got problems," says Rosita.

Little brown Josephine warms to me and climbs onto my lap. I let her hunt through my handlebar bag and play with my flat tire kit. "Now," says Enos, "you won't be able to get rid of her." He checks out my bike outside the window. "Looks to me like there's room for Josephine."

There is, but I leave by myself. A mile west I stop at the Career Center to take a picture of its mural that faces the highway, a mural that marvelously incorporates everything from bulldozers to the holy mountain called Baboquivari. Then a door opens and a young woman asks, "Can I help you?"

Just taking a photo of this very nice mural.

"You need tribal authorization to take a picture on the reservation."

Including this building? I need a permit?

"It's sacred."

She doesn't mean the cinder block, but the mural. It depicts the O'Odam symbol of life's journey, the man in the maze.

A car pulls up—did she call for backup?—and a man in a knit polo shirt asks, "Can I help you?"

I explain—just a photo—but he says, "No, you need to ask the artist."

Who is, of course, not available. The mural is public art, but I'm not the public they had in mind.

I'm nine miles west, riding past thirty-foot-tall saguaros and squashed road-toads, before I understand: it's not the photo, but the asking.

For the longest time the O'Odam lived thinly, in a place where few others could survive. Harvesting cactus fruit, hunting rabbit and deer, and farming melons, beans, and squash, they were married to the seasons and the quick-moving summer storms they counted on to flood their fields. This kinship with the land is now an eco-fantasy of sustainable living that nobody is willing to live.

Such is the O'Odam's dilemma: to be the color of the land, but no longer of the land. They favor the Ford Taurus or the pickup truck, some of which sport a custom front plate of an air-brushed warrior on horseback against a gory sunset. They drive considerately, giving me wide berth. Still, I keep an untrusting eye on my rearview mirror. Every few miles is a roadside shrine, a wooden cross with paper flowers, to those who crashed, generally drunk. It's an unsavory consequence of the local prohibition: you've got to drive off the reservation for a drink.

The sky is black as mold, but it's not raining. A tip-toe tarantula chooses the right moment to cross the highway. The wind carries me up a long grade, the sloping *bajada* of the Quijotoa Mountains. An enormous sloppy nest of twigs is tucked between the arms of a saguaro so perfectly suited for this purpose that it's been a hawk's nest since I was a teen, peering out the window of my parent's Impala station wagon at this very cactus. A few miles beyond is the Gu-Achi Trading Post. I could buy a man-in-the-maze wristwatch, but instead I pick up a free copy of *Diabetes Forecast* magazine and learn what happens when people eat too much fried food.

America is swimming with temptations. I'd planned on another night on the reservation, in the pass where a spinning windmill promises water, but the wind is irresistible. I'll make seventy miles today, all the way to the off-reservation town of Why. The promise of a beer lands me in the XY Bar. On the tube is *Dr. Quinn, Medicine Woman.* It's set in the Old West of cowboys and Indians. Dr. Quinn is a knockout, and I join the O'Odam at the bar to watch the show.

THE ROAD TO AJO slips between a pair of plateaus, two flat-topped mountains of gray rubble stained with sulfurous yellows and poison purples. Hundreds of feet high and dramatically gullied by erosion, they might be declared a national monument if they were not mine waste.

"Ajo: World's Largest Tailings" says a postcard at the Information Center. Another card toots, "Ajo: Where Summer Spends the Winter." None say, "Ajo: Where July Is Unspeakable," but it's true. The closer to Death Valley, the meaner the desert.

Copper Hills Real Estate is next door. "We've got homes from fifty to two hundred and fifty thousand," says Edie Cargill. She's fifty-eight, speedy, in a denim dress. I ask for an overview of the town, and she shows me a wonderful aerial photo of Ajo, showing every tree and road.

"Here's the pit. They're *never* going to fill that up." She points to a grid of houses on the brink of the open pit mine. "This was Indian Town. And this was Mexican Town. The picture is from the seventies, before the mine closed, when Ajo was a very segregated town."

Presumably the rest of Ajo was Whitey Town. The old plaza of date palms and arched arcades with red tile roofs looks Spanish but was built by the Phelps Dodge Mining Company. They built the Curley School, too, with its domed bell tower. Phelps Dodge built Ajo. And after copper took a dive, they sold Ajo.

The *Ajo Copper News* survives. I read it at Don Juan's Café while my waitress Marta eyes my coffee cup and asks, "*Un poquito más?*" An ad from Edgy's Repair Service reads:

> It's too bad my competator is
> so mentally deficient as to have
> to resort to phony ads in the
> local paper. He should better
> use that money to advance his
> skills in a trade that would take
> him off the drugs.
> Written by Edgy

Small-town friendliness isn't the only reason people live in Ajo. A front-page story compares not only the lower cost of living in Ajo relative to Tucson, but the lower cost of dying. "It costs less to be buried in the Ajo Cemetery than nearly any place else in the state." Better yet, it's a classy place, with one gravestone featuring a "400-word copper wire epitaph."

The cemetery, like everything in Ajo, is only a few blocks away. It's big and barren. There are graves marked by polished granite benches, and graves marked by heaps of stones. Baby graves. His-and-hers graves. But no copper grave.

Leaving, I pass a woman tugging at a stupendous weed, a sprawling four-o'clock, beside the cemetery gate. I stop to help, but by her lonesome she rips it from the earth and heaves it into the back of a pea green 1973 Ford Ranchero.

"Been yanking since 1987, but it's God's blessing."

She's old enough to be my mother, trim in brown knit pants, nylon windbreaker, white nurse shoes, and hair by Clairol.

"The copper grave? Block 1. See that shed? Right there. Protestant blocks to one side, and the rest are Catholic. Mexicans, too, because they are most always Catholic. The copper words I thought might be interesting to put in the paper one day, but then I read them and thought, Not this crap. You're welcome to look for yourself."

I can't find it. She drives up and points it out. "People think it was his wife that made that up, but it was his secretary. My parents are over there. Husband, too. Spot for me reserved, although Phelps Dodge stopped taking reservations before I took over in 1987. *Somebody* had to take care of the place. I asked them, and they signed over the deed.

"Now I had to get someone to run it. Got one man from each church—not a woman, because I didn't want any arguing with me. Men are supposed to run it. But the president, well, he's moved off to Mexico. I'm the secretary-treasurer."

By now I've forgotten to read the copper epitaph. I ask, Secretary-treasurer of what?

"The Ajo Cemetery Association. Incorporated!"

Is it true that it's the cheapest in the state?

"I imagine it's the cheapest. It's free. We ask for a $100 fee, to help maintain the cemetery. Got two boys working for us, and the others paying off their community service. The $100 is *not* mandatory. It's so we can keep the place up—$700 a month for water! I've made a fair bit of money with my cookbook fund-raiser—sold three thousand copies, bless the Lord. I wanted to name it the Ajo Cemetery Association Cookbook, but the reaction was pretty quick: *The dead don't cook!*"

Secretary-treasurer Roberta Nixon came to Ajo in 1950, when she was twenty-one. "I didn't find out about Jesus until I was twenty-four. Didn't know who the Holy Trinity was, didn't know who was crawling around up there. My girlfriend told me. She told me, Roberta, you're going to hell. And I said, Oh I'm not without you, because you've done worse. We're all sinners."

For the first time in three days, the sun is peering through a break in the clouds, low on the western horizon. The mine tailings catch the rays and ignite in mineral colors.

"Ajo is a beautiful place. Let me show you something. Before you go."

We walk lightly among the graves. Roberta never stops talking.

"Since my husband died I've been praying for a good man I could love like my two daughters, except maybe a little more. Never would have had them if the pill had been around."

She stops at a double plot. "There's my father and mother."

The headstones are engraved with flowers, clouds, a rainbow, and the words, "Life is a rainbow of beautiful memories."

"After my father died I told my mother, That headstone doesn't remind me of you. And she said, 'We just want people to think we were happy.'"

Next door is Bill, her husband. Roberta explains how he died at home, how the last thing he asked for was a squirt of Chloraseptic Sore Throat Spray. "When I go, I want a bench here. My husband wasn't a Christian, so I want it inscribed with something for the both of us: Joy shared is doubled, sorrow shared is halved."

She waves to a passing family in a minivan. "Nice to visit. Of course the dead are gone. These are just their shells. We loved their souls, not their shells."

But Roberta misses the body, too. She hovers over her husband's grave, and for once is silent. The mine tailings glow like a sacrament in the final light.

"Hard to believe he's been gone since ninety-eight."

1998? It says 1997 here.

"Really? Why, I've never looked. You're right! Got to get that changed.

Susan, she made that. She's just a mess. Bless my soul, I've got to pray for her."

Before I leave, Roberta asks me to please send my kids to church. She's praying for me, too.

NORTH OF AJO, the saguaros are slimmer. I've dropped a thousand feet since Tucson, and lower means hotter and drier. The foothill palo verdes are not only smaller than their relatives back on the reservation, but they're farther apart from one another—say, a six-foot-tall tree every twenty feet. With their spine-tipped branches, each one bristles with a simple message for the deer and other nibblers: back off.

There is no wind this morning. The static clouds look like rolling pins. A small yellow butterfly is dead on the road, one wing inexplicably intact and looking like a Post-it note stuck to the asphalt. It's the only roadkill, so the vultures are patient, not bothering to break their huddle in a dead ironwood tree along Ten Mile Wash.

I'm weary of a desert without the sun, but there is blue hope on the northern horizon. To the east and west are barbed wire fences with the same sign posted every hundred yards:

Danger! *Peligro!*
U.S. Air Force Bombing and Gunnery Range

They mean it. A jet comes low over the volcanic knob of Hat Mountain, pulls up hard just before the highway, and releases a bomb directly overhead. I flinch and swerve, as if I can outrun the thing. But the bomb, like the jet, continues to gain elevation. Unlike the jet, it has no engine and after it reaches its zenith follows a trajectory that ends with an orange flash and a tower of dust. This rewarding bit of calculus enabled the pilot to hit a bull's-eye two miles away, without flying over it.

The desert as target: it's one way to use a land that has long been deemed useless. "A typical desert is an area of wasteland," wrote D. A. Hufford in his 1902 *Death Valley*, "whose use mankind has not yet discovered."

But mankind long ago discovered how to use the desert. The Sand People, the Hia-Ced O'Odam, lived a life of pure movement on the lands that are now the bombing range. They lived so lightly that the government did not recognize them as the rightful caretakers, and they were not granted a reservation. Landless, the Sand People now live in nearby towns, nomads no more.

Meanwhile, a combination of bombs and cholla cactus keeps out most folk. Outside the bounds of the air force range, the ranchers are reduced to a half-dozen diehards, beaten down by the facts of drought and the earnest meddling of save-the-desert folks like me. Occasionally a distressed cow wanders onto the bombing range. With joints of cholla cactus hanging from its tail, the desperate beast is looking for grass or mesquite pods but finding only creosote, the keynote shrub of the Southwest. A wispy bush with little shiny leaves as tasty and nutritious as tar tipped in turpentine, the creosote is a chemical bomb, and it's left alone.

A cow would be better off following me forty-three miles to the Gila River. With a watershed reaching into the conifer forests of Arizona, Mexico, and New Mexico, the Gila was the only perennial stream to cross this desert and reach the Colorado. That was before the canals took its water to feed the fields of dense green. Some are alfalfa, but most are cotton, being worked by green John Deere 7455 Cotton Strippers that cost over a hundred grand each. The machines steer themselves with guidance systems that follow the laser-leveled furrows. The driver's job is to turn it around at the end of the field.

I've never seen farms quite like these, all mechanics and drivers and a pilot who graciously pulls up his crop duster before its wing nozzles lay a shroud of pesticide over me. Like pennies that only a child would stoop to pick up, cotton bolls in drifts line the roadside. The air itself is cottony, plumped with moisture from the fields. The canals are filled by pumps that are run by power lines heading north to the Palo Verde Nuclear Power Plant. It's the most powerful nuclear facility in the United States, conspicuously sited on a creosote plain above the Gila River valley. Before I even contemplate a photo, a young guard behind the chain-link fence says, "Don't be taking no pictures. Not after the terrorists."

His name is Walter. His badge says, "Unarmed Security Guard," which seems an admission of vulnerability well beyond the call of honesty. If I were hired on I might have to wear a badge that says, "Ticklish Security Guard."

"Palo Verde is a no-fly zone," says Walter. A pair of fighter jets shriek overhead. "Except for the F-16s."

Only a mile north is downtown Wintersburg. It's a general store next to a large siren atop a pole. A placard reads: *What You Should Do In Case of An Emergency.* But everyone knows: if Palo Verde blows, lick your finger to test the wind, and flee upwind.

The wind is out of the southwest, at my side as I turn northwest and cross Interstate 10. On the bridge I chug the orange juice I picked up at Wintersburg and take a five-minute census of American interstate traffic. The result: fifty-two big trucks, thirty-six pickups/SUVs/vans, and twenty-four cars.

Satisfied, I take Salome Road, climbing by degrees out of the creosote and into the cactus hills. This is the old, pre-interstate route, ignored by most drivers. The greasy rumble of diesel trucks falls behind. When I'm twenty miles down the road, the sun drops behind the mountains, turning them into silhouettes like two-dimensional cutouts.

I find a track into the desert, carefully picking my way between platoons of chest-high cholla. Each is so densely spined it appears to be covered with fur, which is why some call it the teddy-bear cholla. In form it is a tussle of limbs and joints assembled with less-than-usual care, for the cholla has every intention of falling apart. Each knuckle that drops to the ground is a ticket to a new home, capable of rooting and starting anew. Gravity alone is the usual transport, but most hikers sooner or later look down to discover a clump clinging to their cuff or calf, which it seemingly leaped onto without invitation. Hence its other name: the jumping cholla. Each spine is invisibly but viciously barbed, so removal of the offending piece requires special care. Sometimes this means pliers. Always it means a vocabulary typically not used in the presence of teddy bears.

I scare off four cows—miserable scrub cattle eking by on mesquite pods and luck—with a yell, and claim as my own a smooth pavement of little stones fitted like puzzle pieces. The only big stone is actually a tortoise. Step by step it lugs its house of bone across the pavement, while chewing a leaf with the slowest mouth in the west. The moment it spots me it halts and withdraws into its shell.

The evening, the night, the sunrise: not a breeze, not a sound. In the stillness of the first light I sit up and see that the tortoise is still waiting.

"THAT'S A VERY BIG BEAR," says the bald man with a goatee. We're seated over eggs and hash browns at the breakfast counter at the Salome Café, staring at a velvet painting of a muscle-man in a feathered headdress. He clutches a rifle, poised to take action against the mythical desert grizzly. Perhaps it is a trick of perspective, but the bear appears to be an easy hundred feet tall.

The bear is a joke. So is the sign by the door, "Coffee Boiling Hot." The town of Salome is a joke, but that may be as its founder intended. His name was Dick Wick Hall, and in 1906 he bought a piece of land along the dirt road from Phoenix to Los Angeles. He liked the place and loved the desert, and his genius was in realizing that others didn't. Hall put up signs: "Smile. You Don't Have to Stay Here But We Do." He mimeographed a fake newspaper, the *Salome Sun*. By 1925 it was a nationally syndicated column, carried by twenty-eight newspapers. You can still buy the collected columns, so I do, and read about his pet rattlesnake, Lizzie.

> When the Hotel Business gets Too Quiet,
> Old Lizzie helps us to Start a Riot;
> She crawls out onto the Auto Campground
> And Sings to the Tourists sleeping around—
> And you ought to see the Tourists Flock In
> And Fight for Rooms at the Blue Rock Inne.

A framed article in the café mentions Hall's "untimely death" at age forty-nine but doesn't explain how. "They say he was shot by an irate husband," says my waitress, "but they also say that that's what Hall said."

Another joke. I ride off, to ask around. Salome is mostly an aluminum village of mobile homes, gleaming like mica under an enthusiastic sun. The lady at Outback Realty doesn't know how Hall died. She sends me down the road to a shop brimming with a hundred variations on Hall's favorite fiction: the frog who hopped around the desert in asbestos sandals, never finding water. I buy a frog postcard and a frog Styrofoam beer cooler, and ask the lady behind the register how the frog sales are going.

"To tell the truth, I'm not a frog sort of person. I felt an obligation to the town and Dick Hall."

She spies my bike. "Do you sleep outside?"

Whenever I can.

"What about the scorpions?"

I give her Mr. Hall's line: A scorpion is just a lobster who has lived in Arizona a long time.

She's heard it before. "Yes, but aren't they attracted to heat?"

No, ma'am, that's the rattlesnake. But even snakes aren't attracted to huge warm things like people—the snake can't eat them, and the huge warm thing might kill the snake. As for scorpions, they like places to hide. Like tents.

I'm not sure she believes me after I quoted Hall. But I believe her when she tells me that Dick Hall died of an infection after a pulled tooth.

Such an unfunny way to go.

Around forty miles west of Salome, over a low pass of crumbling granite and across a creosote flat, I find a dirt track leading toward the Plomosa Mountains. It's late, no longer hot, with cirrus whipping high above. The road climbs and descends the gentle swells of the nude, muscular hills. The crests are stony pavements. The troughs are veined with palo verde and ironwood along the dry watercourses called arroyos.

As is my nature, I favor the low point over the high, choosing for my camp a comfortable arroyo, six feet across. The sand is streaked with black magnetite, iron-rich grains laid down by the last flush of water. A sweep of my hand readies the sand for the ground cloth, inflatable pad, and sleeping bag. Off with the shoes and out with the sandwich and beer I picked up in town, and now I'm ready to read Dick Hall's columns from the *Salome Sun*. "Out here in the Desert," he wrote in his maddening capital letters, "you Don't Need Much—and You Don't Get Much either—and after a while you get so as you Don't Want Much—and when you get that way there ain't Much Use in going somewhere else to starve to Death . . . so we stay here."

Content in my fold in the landscape, I lie back as the sunset throws colors all around, as if I am at the center of something.

FIRST LIGHT finds me lazing about camp. My duties are few: admire the peachy sunrise, check my shoes for scorpions (none), and scribble a few notes.

Dawn, 69 degrees—SE wind—few clouds—smell of moisture. The desert is pavements of stone, sharp-edged gray limestone and deep red chert, little stones the size of my fingernail. Dune bursage and ironwood in the troughs, and creosote everywhere.

The dune bursage, *Ambrosia dumosa*, is a shin-high dome of twigs with pale ghost-green leaves. Like the creosote, the dune bursage wears no thorns; unlike the creosote, its leaves are edible. To be vulnerable and tasty seems a curse, yet the dune bursage is more common with every mile closer to Death Valley. Drawn to aridity? Not really. It's simply fond of sands and open space, and is glad as any plant can be for rain.

It's hard to say at first glance whether the ironwood is carefree or tormented. Typically a lopsided shamble, the tree is capable of fifty feet when it gets lucky, but my neighbors here aren't much taller than me. Up close it's clear that many of their limbs are dead, yet still clinging to the trunk. These badges of survival are one of the pleasing differences between plant and animal. You never see a coyote that's a head, torso, and one leg dragging around three dead limbs, but an ironwood is often three-quarters dead, with limbs polished by sun and sand.

Like many desert plants that spend much of their lives waiting for rain, the ironwood can live several hundred years. The oldest known is reckoned to have put down its roots around eight hundred years ago. In terms of current events, that's when the holy war between the Crusaders and the Muslims heated up, and the unstoppable Kurd, Saladin, declared jihad and took back Jerusalem.

Time passes, and the ironwood soldiers on. To those unfamiliar with the local seasons, its habits are baffling. It drops its leaves in April, and it refuses to unveil its pastel purple flowers until the thermometer climbs to 100. It's all about water, naturally. Over most of the ironwood's range, the seed pods split open just in time for the summer storms. In the Sonoran Desert, the summer storms are the ecological equivalent of spring. Every living thing struggles through the rainless months of May and June, counting on the bulge of heat over the drylands to suck in moisture from the Gulfs of Mexico and California. The storms erupt in July, flooding the arroyos that otherwise make the finest camps.

Despite the tinge of moisture in the air today, I don't expect rain—October is typically too late for a storm. Besides, the rains rarely penetrate west to the Colorado River, which happens to be today's destination.

The wind is a gift this morning. Back on the highway, the bike picks up speed until the breeze and I are heading west to the river together, the only sound the whiz of my tires on the pavement. The road drops out of the stony desert and slips between sand hills. It's thirty miles to the river, with traffic picking up steadily after the junction with the excessively wide but admirably smooth Highway 95. A pickup with an American flag snapping from its antenna tows a bass boat with swivel stools. A Buick slides by, towing a flatbed with a golf cart wearing a flag sticker on its bumper.

Boating and golfing in the lowest hottest desert since I rolled out of Tucson seems as strange as the ironwood's flowering in June—but this, too, is all about water. At the town of Parker, the Colorado is backed up behind Headgate Rock Dam. The slender green reservoir is called Lake Moovalya on the map, but along the shore of boat ramps and parking lots everyone calls it the Parker Strip. I test the water with a toe. Invitingly cool, yet nobody swims where the drag boats are doing 60 mph.

"This is *the* place—the Strip," says one Richard, of ample muscles. "They just motor down, turn around, come back, and go in circles all day."

He's here from California with Cassie and a pair of 951cc Bombardier Jet Skis on a trailer behind a glossy beetle-black Ford Explorer. Cassie, with a well-tanned hide and suspiciously springy breasts, sees me scribble a note. "Just don't say we're yuppies."

I promise. Instead I'll say they're a friendly couple with an expensive habit ($8,000 per machine), looking for water to play in. "The Pacific," says Cassie, "is awfully cold."

I pick up a sixteen-ounce Bud and a bag of pretzels at one of perhaps fifty liquor stores and bars, then try for a slice of pizza at a takeout. They've none ready to go, so I pick up a cheeseburger at the "country kitchen" next door, stash the lot in my handlebar bag, and confront the first steep hill of the trip.

Fifteen miles upriver of the Headgate Dam, the land humps up in a ridge of dark rock perpendicular to the Colorado. The river long ago cut a canyon through the rock. Somewhat later, in the 1930s, Parker Dam was built in the canyon, and the forty-five miles of river above the dam became Lake Havasu.

It's a short but stiff climb over the ridge. At the summit is a car with a young woman sitting on the trunk lid. She's from the pizza joint, and she bears a gift: a fresh slice on a paper plate topped with aluminum foil.

"We thought you might still like a piece of pizza."

I even have a relatively quiet place to eat, but perhaps that's because the boats of Havasu are barred from approaching the lakeside entrance to the Buckskin Tunnel. Bored through 6.8 miles of Precambrian granites and more youthful lavas, it's not for vehicles but for water. All I can see of the tunnel is what looks like a swimming pool opening onto the lake. Only the web of power lines and the thrum of electricity betray a thirst that can hardly be understood by a man who's been rationing a gallon a day.

The pumps are gulping 22,000 gallons each and every second, lifting it over 800 feet, and disgorging it into the Central Arizona Project canal that runs 330 miles to Phoenix and Tucson. Along the way the water will be raised by additional pumps another 2,100 feet. Messing with the numbers, I figure out that this distance and rise is equivalent to running a fair portion of the Colorado River backward and uphill all the way to Utah—all because of our refusal to live with aridity.

As for the natives, "The desert floras shame us with their cheerful adaptations to the seasonal limitations," wrote Mary Austin in her 1903 *The Land of Little Rain*. Cheerful is pushing it, but they certainly know how to bide their time. The hills hold mostly creosote and bouquets of thick knobby stems called brittlebush. No leaves on the latter, and it's no surprise. A survey with my binoculars confirms my suspicion: only three saguaros in the neighborhood. Although the big cactus is a canteen capable of surviving a rainless year, the saguaro's seeds cannot split open and reach for the sky without the summer rains. That they are vanishing is proof that the rains go no further.

Usually. Climate is all about statistics, not the particularly large thunderhead that hunkers over the wreck of a mountain in the west. The sun, blotted out by the cloud, looks to be down for the count—but then breaks out to burn free on the horizon with one last ferocious shaft of light. Startled but feeling lucky, I pedal on to the perfect place for the night, a clear patch of pavements atop a ridge. To the south, beyond the ragged palisade of the Buckskin Mountains, the atmosphere is boiling over. The lightning delivers simple cloud-to-ground jabs as well as cloud-to-cloud shots that spread like cracks in shattered glass.

I prepare my bed, rinse off with a liter of water, pop open a beer, and turn to see that there are now four storms, one at each cardinal point. A hoot owl tells me I'm not alone. Sitting on a warm rock, I watch, grinning goofily in anticipation. But no storm will come.

Later, I wake to thunder. I get the tent up, crawl in, and count off the seconds from flash to rumble. When it's forty-five seconds, it's like counting sheep. But when it's suddenly twenty, then four seconds, it's like my wife's labor pains, just before she yelled, "It's coming!" That's how baby Rosa was born at home, by accident. Some things are simply beyond our control.

A hot bolt turns the world from black and white to color. The wind butts the tent. And with the first heavy splats of rain, the wait is over.

RIDING INTO LAKE HAVASU CITY, I'm surprised that the first homes aren't trailers but actual houses. The gravel yards are heaped in color-coordinated mounds topped with copper cutouts of the iconic flute-playing native, Kokopelli. Electric garage doors open and close, and vehicles with tinted windows come and go. But no actual humans are about, despite the Welcome to Lake Havasu City sign (*Keep Us Drug-Free, Gang-Free, Graffiti-Free*) claiming a population of 40,000.

I ride until I find a cinder-block strip mall, but on Sunday there's nobody at Sunshine Hair Styling or the gift shop trying to unload Beanie Babies. Things liven up at the Walgreen's, with a marquee reading *Patri-*

otic T-shirts, 3 for $10. Doing my part, I buy some Made-in-America Sour Skittles.

Lake Havasu City is dense with flags. The shops have directions for "Proper Flag Display" taped to their windows. They also sell the flag decals I've seen slapped on car and truck windows. The resulting loss of visibility might explain the big wreck on Highway 95.

A man in a patriotic T-shirt and black horn-rims is reconstructing the accident for all who care to listen. He points to the filigree of skid marks and says, "Now you can see that the fifth-wheel couldn't stop—too much weight! He was *towing* an SUV *behind* his trailer. Come down the hill and round the bend and skidded into that little gray car, knocked it clear across the intersection. 'Course the fifth-wheel kept on skidding, into that Suburban towing what used to be a boat."

Sherds of fiberglass are strewn over the road. A pity, because the boat had to go only another hundred yards to reach the World Famous English Village and London Bridge. I pedal down to the channel and watch the *Dixie-Bell*, a fake steamboat, cruise under the bridge.

Unlike the *Dixie-Bell*, the bridge is the real thing. It was sinking into the Thames until Robert McCulloch, of chainsaw fame, bought it in 1968 for a mere $2.4 million (shipping and handling not included). He had a plan. In 1963 McCulloch had bought twenty-six square miles of land from the state of Arizona on the shore of Lake Havasu. It was supremely vacant of humans. Real steamboats, like the 175-foot-long *Mohave*, used to paddle the Colorado, but the dams had finished them off. Now there was nobody within forty miles.

McCulloch pitched his master-planned community on television. The curious called a number, and a man would come to your house. One came to my family's house, in a suburb of Chicago. My parents dearly wanted to escape the post-1968 desolation of the South Side. The pictures of swimming pools and palm trees looked good.

McCulloch's man flew them out for a look, and my father later recalled his impression of Lake Havasu City: "We'd just landed the astronauts on the moon—and here it was. There was nothing at all."

McCulloch needed an attraction. While my family packed up for Tucson (the Garden of Eden compared to Havasu), he had London Bridge rebuilt, stone by stone, near the lunar shore of Havasu. The completed bridge looked perfect if you didn't notice that it spanned nothing but gravel. McCulloch next sent in the heavy equipment. With 'dozers and dredgers, the lake was brought to and under London Bridge.

The year was 1972, and the effect was immediate. You could drive a boat under London Bridge, and thousands wanted to. By 1974, Lake Havasu City had seventy organizations, including the John Birch Society, Havasu Cactus Kickers, and Overeaters Anonymous.

The overeaters are still here—or are those tourists? The young men by the Old English Pub look like Maori warriors, shirtless barrels of flesh with vaguely Asian tattoos and sun-peeled noses. One is barking into a cell phone, "Bin Laden just released his latest video, and we just released our latest bombs. Did you hear? Nine-thirty this morning. Afghanistan."

I can't stop staring at these people, that bridge, those drag boats with chrome exhaust headers spitting pure noise and power. So I leave for something more familiar: breakfast at Denny's, where the coffee is hot and the air is cool.

Without air conditioning, few would live in a place where the temperature last summer reached 126 degrees. Yet air conditioning was invented in 1902 for printing, not people. Four-color printing then required four perfectly aligned runs through the press, but changes in humidity made the paper swell and shrink between runs. To keep the humidity low and constant, Willis Carrier devised the "Apparatus for Treating Air." The trick was chilled coils that cooled the air so the water vapor would condense. That's why air conditioners drip.

But the machinery was huge and unruly, and the stuff in the coils was toxic ammonia—not for the home mechanic. It wasn't until 1947 that affordable window air conditioners hit the market. It's perhaps not a coincidence that, soon afterward, Americans reversed the post–Civil War trend of moving north. They headed south.

They're still heading south, following the tanker trucks and power lines to Lake Havasu City. They pass me as I head north on Highway 95 the next day. Some are seasonal nomads in cars with North Dakota plates (*Discover the Spirit*), and others are in for the long haul, behind the wheel of U-Haul vans (*Adventure in Moving*). With looks of neighborly concern they wave to me as they pass. They're wondering, Why is that man standing by his bike in the desert?

Jotting a few botanical notes. The saguaros are truly gone. The teddy-bear cholla look scorched. It's no wonder: a typical year sees five inches of rain. Yet Lake Havasu City swells. People can live on the moon, after all.

ON THE TV at a fuel oasis called the Pilot Travel Center, a man with a beefy mustache is explaining what America is about:

"We put a human being on the moon."

He's not an historian. He's selling American cars that are superior to those from countries that haven't reached the moon.

"That's what we believe at Anderson Ford."

I share the pride in homegrown ingenuity. Nowhere but America can I buy a foam beer cooler that doubles as an insulated coffee cup. It's brilliant.

I check out the bumper stickers for sale. "God Bless America" and "Remember the Towers."

One of my high-school friends was in the South Tower. He escaped, barely. He knew of my experiences with Muslims in Djibouti, Egypt, and Jordan. Now he had his own. As he told me, with elegant economy, "They tried to kill me."

I ride north to the Black Mountains on old Route 66, across an open valley of creosote and little else, then climb slowly up the *bajada*. The closer to the mountain, the rockier the desert and the happier the arroyos, thick with tall loose switches of desert lavender. With a critical eye I judge the Black Mountains to be of questionable stability, tilted and busted into ramps and cliffs, and scabbed with old mines. Fortunately, most drivers bypass the narrow two-lane road in favor of the interstate. Along the shoulder are the hoofprints of what must be burros that outlasted the miners.

I camp high on a tree-free ridge, facing west. The Colorado River valley, now 1,500 feet below, falls into shadow, yet up here the backlit cholla are radiant with a halo of spines. I strip and pour a liter of water over my head. With a smooth boulder for a seat, I drip-dry and read the *Wall Street Journal* I picked up in Lake Havasu City.

There's a review of survival gear. A "Level-A hazmat suit" can be had for only $2,700. If you prefer to run away, you might consider "radiation-detection equipment," keeping in mind the advice of Mr. Hopkins of SurvivalLink.com: "If you've got to measure radiation levels, it's already kind of late, you know?"

Everybody is afraid of something. Desert botanists like myself fear certain plants, like the Sahara mustard I spotted down by the Parker Strip. This dreadful salad of prickles is smothering the native wildflowers. I felt the hot blush of xenophobia when I saw a big dead mustard tumbling along on the wind: nature invents the wheel, and the foreigners roll in without a visa.

This spring, while working on a map of the Sahara mustard invasion, I wrote to a botanist in Kuwait. How, I asked, to get rid of this weed? He tactfully replied that it isn't a weed in the Middle East, but welcome browse for their camels. They plant it.

In my mind the mustard remained a weed—an uninvited agent of change. I like things they way they are, or, as wilderness defender Edward Abbey liked to say, "Let's keep things the way they *were*."

The night slips in and soothes the desert. I put my shoes on and clear the sharpest rocks from a patch just big enough for my sleeping bag. So long as I keep my distance from the jumping cholla, I feel supremely safe. And it's a relief to escape the parade of flags that was Lake Havasu City. Any time more than twenty people start cheering, I feel the urge to slip into the background. Neither can I happily attend a basketball game at the University of Arizona. The crowd's enthusiasm for the home team includes a barrage of insults hurled at the opponents—as if we cannot support *us* without cursing *them*.

Now our president had struck a similar tone: if you aren't with us on the war on terror, you are helping them. This worries me. I fret over speeches in which I can no longer tell if "God Bless America" is an invocation or a battle cry. It is, after all, the same tactic used by the terrorists: you are compelled to be either for Allah or for the devil Americans that seek to destroy *our* way of life.

Disquieting thoughts in the quiet desert. Alone with my memories of tea and *khat* with the ceaselessly hospitable Muslims, I wonder if the Djiboutian bride-to-be, Roda, really did jump ship for America to escape an arranged marriage she could not abide. Not long ago she would have stayed, knowing of no other way. Now she knows, and I wonder what her family will think of America once she is gone.

The stars make themselves known, constellations appearing in concert, yet mute. There's nobody to say, How come you don't wonder about the families whose daughters were killed by these monsters?

But I do. Grief knows no flag.

THE ROAD TURNS EAST, the wrong direction, but the lay of the land forces the detour, over a 3,500-foot pass and across a valley not much lower than the pass itself. It's high desert, too cold in the winter for ironwood or palo verde but just right for the mesquite scrub bent like claws and grass that's more gray than green. It's chewed to nubs, probably by cows, although there are none to be seen. They must have moved to livelier pastures or dropped dead.

Late in the day, the valley turns northwest to Hoover Dam and Las Vegas, the big and the busy. Where the meager rains are amplified by the runoff from the pavement, a long fine yellow grass flourishes, arched by a north wind. So does a wild pea called *Senna,* with split and twisted pods rattling in the breeze.

LANDFILL 1 MILE, says a sign that is itself a kind of rubbish. There are a lot of signs in America, and not many in Djibouti. Never did I see a Djiboutian sign saying, *This Highway Adopted by the Afar Junior Salt League.*

People live here, in far-off trailers and homes among the foothills of the low dark mountains to the west. Where the map indicates "Santa Claus" there is an old tourist stop with a toy train out front. Closed, shuttered, outmoded. When I was young, places like Santa Claus were essential to a cross-country trip. Not for gas, but for the sanity of my parents in a 1968

Impala station wagon with six children. Before air-conditioning and cup holders, kids not only looked out the window, they wanted out. New cars are so sweet and comfortable there's no need to stop.

I spend the night in an arroyo no wider than myself, beside a catclaw tree—a relative of the mesquite not only in genetic terms but also in form and general fighting spirit. On the horizon hovers a great blister of light—Vegas, still seventy-five miles away.

Eleven hours later, the glow of Vegas is swallowed by the sunrise in a demonstration of who's really the boss. I rise in the 44-degree chill and dress with the speed of a fireman. Breakfast is an apple munched noisily while I poke around in the desert, hip-swiveling to avoid the big puckered pads of the beavertail prickly pear. Then it's back to the highway, where a roadkill coyote lies half-devoured by ravens that reluctantly rise with my approach.

The wind is indifferent, the sun warms my shoulders, and there's nothing I'd rather do than spend the day pedaling down the gentle slope of this valley. There are no towns, just a single café called Rosie's. There's little of what might be called scenery—the mountains are too distant, the plants too modest. Now and then I notice something extraordinary: the shining ribbon of a cassette tape stretched over what seems to be a half-mile, or the long white trumpet blooms of *Datura*, a plant sacred to some Native American peoples—the same genus of psychedelic used by the Mapuche way down in Patagonia.

But mostly I live in the ordinary, glad to be riding under the blue dazzle of the sky, through air so dry it's utterly transparent. Occasionally I suffer faint regrets and recycle old grief, generally eco-political, occasionally personal—things I should have said, or did say and said poorly. Yet, as John Van Dyke wrote in his 1901 *The Desert*, "The joy of mere animal existence, the feeling that it is good to be alive and face to face with Nature's self, drives everything else into the background."

The background stays back until the road begins the plunge to Hoover Dam. As soon as I catch a view of Lake Mead I'm stopped at a military checkpoint, where two young men from the National Guard, in camo fatigues labeled POLLICK and HOFFMAN, watch for terrorists.

"I hate to profile Arab-looking men in rental cars, but that's what it's come to," says Private Specialist Pollick. We agree that it would be easy to get through: shave, put on thirty pounds, slap a flag decal on your window, and you're an American.

It's truly easy if you're a cyclist; they don't check my bags. I ride down into Black Canyon, stopping only because it's my duty as a journalist, and I've spotted a discarded Exotic College Girls Adult Entertainment Guide for Las Vegas. Ms. Crystal says: "I'm a nineteen-year-old co-ed trying to work my way through college. Call now and I can show you how I earn Extra Credit." Crystal wears only what appear to be three targets, strategically placed by the printer.

Just before the dam is a second checkpoint, manned by Privates Pollick and Hoffman—the same two soldiers. Following orders, they've moved. Hoffman waves a car through; its bumper sticker was evidence enough of citizenship: "The only good attorney is a dead one." Next in line is a Lincoln Navigator, and Hoffman says, "Here comes an expensive bomb."

In this way they grease time and relax, for the notion of blowing up the dam with a bomb in your trunk is preposterous. The great dam will not be so easily moved. I pedal down to and atop the dam; it is a highway as well as a dam. "Please stay off the wall" is stenciled on a low barrier. No problem. But I do edge close and peer over the enormous curve of concrete that must be the most awesome skateboarding opportunity on earth.

Far below, 726 feet down, the river exits the powerhouse in a swirl of foaming whirlpools. Maybe it is the terrible height that reminds me of my fallen friend, Jim Boyer, but there is something else. Jim's great-grandfather, Godfrey Sykes—an engineer, hydrologist, geographer, and question asker—was the first to study the Colorado River below the Grand Canyon. I knew the stories. Before a single dam was built and the great floods throttled, Sykes mapped the delta. He captured and estimated the sediment load, and produced figures that allowed us to understand how this river had carried away everything you don't see when you gawk at the Grand Canyon.

In 1900, Sykes took his family down the river, and wrote in his memoir *A Westerly Trend*: "Indian family parties are what pleased my wife most.

They were often drifting downstream on balsa rafts; men, women, children, dogs, and sometimes chickens."

They pleased Godfrey, too, especially the "floaters of watermelons," cargo rafts that were no more than a triangle of willow poles with a score of melons within. "The pilot then tied his clothes, matches, and tobacco, and other effects into a compact bundle which he fastened securely upon the top of his head, took his seat in the water upon the submerged bent pole, said good-bye to his relatives and friends, kicked off from shallow water into the current and then the voyage began."

Sykes would live through the Great Depression and see Hoover Dam plug the Colorado. "Of course, as an Engineer," he wrote, "I fully appreciate the magnificent structures that have brought the lower Colorado under control . . . but I must confess that I have much the same sympathy for my old friend, the sometimes wayward, but always interesting, and still unconquered and untrammeled river of the last and preceding centuries, that I have for a bird in a cage."

The hum of electricity rises from the foot of the dam, the plainsong of a river put to work. When the sun drops behind the rimrock and the canyon falls into shadow, I ride west. The road switchbacks up the canyon wall, under the sizzle of high-voltage lines heading for Boulder City and Las Vegas.

AFTER A NIGHT behind a casino—there was no other flat spot in Black Canyon—I wake to a cold wind whipping the creosote and shivering the bursage. I warm up fast during the thousand-foot climb to Boulder City, all the while toying with the idea that I may actually like Las Vegas. Hadn't I feared Cairo, dreaded Volgograd, and fretted over Djibouti Town?

But Las Vegas seems to revel in its reputation as a den of naughtiness and icon of sprawl, growing like a tumor in a place with less natural life support than Lake Havasu City. The Chamber of Commerce boasts that "every hour 24 hours, 365 days a year, another two acres of Las Vegas land are developed for commercial or residential use."

Admittedly, this desert isn't the prettiest—no saguaros like fluted columns, no trees with green bark. It's gravel plains and the brave green leaves of creosote, which aren't much larger than a fly. When I roll into Boulder City for breakfast, I'm not surprised that most every home has a lawn. There's a prim and perfectly maintained downtown, preserved in situ since the 1930s, when it was the federal work camp for the dam.

I have a cranberry waffle at the counter of the Coffee Cup Café. A big soft guy with trusting basset-hound eyes sits next to me and orders the special, chicken-fried steak. It's a startling mountain of food, or rather a basin and range of meat and gravy. He digs in, pauses, then explains, "I only get this once a week."

Joe Fernandez is from Tucson, and he wants to go back. "A friend of mine calls this place the ashtray desert. He's right—nothing but gravel. Looks like ashes."

What about Lake Mead?

"Sure, if you want to watch kids throw rocks at the suckerfish. But there's better free stuff in Vegas. At the Bellagio you can watch a boat come out on a track, filled with those New Orleans party dancers. They throw out pearl necklaces. They're just plastic."

The man in the next seat discreetly offers a correction. "That's the Rio, not the Bellagio."

"That's right," says Fernandez. He glances at his multifunction watch on a Velcro band. "I've got to run down to the Home Depot—you could put your bike in my truck and I'll show you around."

It's a green Ford F-150. I guess the year, 1977, and Fernandez is delighted. I don't bother to ask where the Home Depot is. We head toward Vegas, down a valley like a dry lake bed, with Fernandez muttering, "Ashes, just ashes."

The city is big, and Fernandez immediately worries for me. "Just remember to get out of North Vegas before dark. It's not so bad—kind of like South Tucson—but they've got the Bloods and Crips."

The suburb of Henderson ("Where Everyone Has Fun!") is tile-roofed stucco garages with attached living quarters. We pass the Home Depot, but Fernandez is in a paternal mood and wishes to show me the bounds of safety. He drives to downtown Vegas and lays out the rules. "Don't go north of the Lady Luck. Don't go west of the freeway."

Fernandez lets me off at the Stardust Hotel and Casino, which he designates "the beginning of the safe Strip." It's an easy enough landmark to remember, with Wayne Newton permanently on its marquee. I immediately park the bike and peek inside the casino. Coming from the desert, it's like being drop-kicked into a pinball machine, a sonic stew of slot machines worked by hundreds of God Bless America shirts. I stare and think: we gave the natives trinkets and bright things, and they seemed entirely satisfied.

My free map/tourist brochure claims that there are "over 100 sharks and deadly crocs" at the Mandalay Bay, so I opt for the Somerset Motel, a couple blocks off the Strip. It's a quiet relic from the sixties, with no slot machines. Across the street is Meskerem, an Ethiopian restaurant where I feel comfortable. The clientele is entirely Ethiopian taxi drivers.

After a meal of *injera* and *wot* I head back to my room without prowling the Strip. Tomorrow. For now I open the Yellow Pages to find a bike shop. Assuming I reach Death Valley, I will thereafter ride to the closest town, catch a bus to Vegas, and fly home. I'll need a bike box, and wish to get a bike shop to hold one for me.

While doing so, I'm easily distracted by the ninety-two yellow pages devoted to Entertainment, Adult. "Bored Blonde Housewives Gone Wild (Full Service)." "Live Grateful Third World Women." "Barely Legal Secretaries in Short Skirts." Does any other industry come close to this page count? Not Automobiles, not Physicians, not Insurance. Sex is trumped only by the 147 pages of Attorneys, including, "Mainor and Harris. Putting the Personal Back into Personal Injury."

The next day I ride around non-Strip Vegas admiring the massive billboards of Wayne Newton. His teeth are so perfect that he appears to have only two very large teeth, upper and lower jaw, like a parrot fish. After I return to the Somerset, I read, write, and eat *injera* and *wot* until 8 PM. Then it's time for the Strip.

Five hours later I return. As Jimi Hendrix asked, Are you experienced?

Yes. Now I have seen gondolas with seat belts plying chlorinated canals on the second floor of a casino. I have seen very small Guatemalan women standing under bas-relief cupids, handing out pictures and phone numbers of Tender Young Girls who can be in my room in twenty minutes. I have pretended to be dismayed by the endless gimmicks, yet found myself cursing when I ran out of film as the volcano erupted in front of the Mirage. I have seen floral arrangements the size of refrigerators, casinos whose far horizon could not be discerned, and fountains with hydraulics capable of washing one hundred buses in ten seconds.

I saw them in the company of gap-toothed bikers with greasy ponytails and women dressed entirely in vinyl; Appalachian hill folk and Armani robot suits; newlywed brides still in white lace and gum-scrapers kneeling on the lovely mosaics in the Bellagio—an almost regal palace betrayed, in the end, by the blinking slot machines and legions of silent moms slipping in $10 bills.

Except for the slot machine ladies, most of them looked happy enough, as if they had discovered the poetry of Eduardo Galeano.

> The Church says: *The body is a sin.*
> Science says: *The body is a machine.*
> Advertising says: *The body is a business.*
> The body says: *I am a fiesta.*

I hope they slept as long as I do, until the phone rings at 10 AM. It's my wife, Sonya, holding the phone so I may hear Rudy say, "Where are you now, Daddy?" Sonya says the kids don't miss me. Thank goodness, because I miss them.

I shower and pack while the television tells me that I can get Cipro antibiotic for the panic price of $300, in the event that somebody sends me a letter containing anthrax. A crazy person sent such a letter, killing a man in Florida, and now 270 million Americans are very worried. Of course it's easy to worry in Las Vegas, to be suspicious. Everything for the tourist is fake, from the Eiffel Tower to the "grilled" stripes on your burger. Worse, I remember that I donated my Cipro stash—free from Dr. Pellerito—to Kamil in Djibouti. I hope he's making a killing selling them on the Internet.

I am charmed by the way the bike comes alive the moment it moves, kept upright by the blind determination of spinning wheels to maintain their vertical plane. Turning from the Strip onto Sahara is not a matter of twisting the handlebars. I merely lean, and with the slightest tilt of the front wheel the bike turns itself beneath me, then straightens as I do. Together we aim west. We've only two more mountains to cross before Death Valley, and we reach the base of the first range by dusk.

No matter what the day may bring, the bike will carry me to the place nobody's noticed, at least not from a car. This time it's an arroyo of gravel and cobble 2,000 feet above the city and 3,000 feet below a wall of white and red sandstone. It's called Calico Ridge, and it smolders in the late sun as I open my Mickey's malt liquor. Dinner's ready in ten minutes: Lipton stroganoff with an actual carrot added by the chef. Master of a minor universe, I kill the stove and listen to it ping as the metal cools and contracts. Then the sun is gone, and there is only the song of the night insects. They're not my species but still more attractive than the Las Vegas Yellow Pages. I think we'll spend the night together.

THERE ARE FEW THINGS better than waking to a sky streaked with a whiz of cirrus, getting on the bike, and aiming for a small notch in a big mountain.

The road loops south to find a break in the sandstone ramparts, a detour that is accelerated by the passing of a racing bicyclist with a scorpion on his jersey. With a flick of his wrist, he invites me to catch his slipstream for twenty miles.

The next twenty miles are up a canyon in the dense shade of cottonwoods, across a mile-high mesa of small fragrant pines weeping yellow sap, and down a *bajada* scattered with limb-waving Joshua trees like boxers with spiked gloves. Then the big plants fade away and the last twenty miles cross a plain of creosote bush, along a road as straight as a kite string in a gale. It's the sort of monotony that should drive me nuts, but doesn't. I'm only one day from Death Valley. And the primary fault of this desert—no trees—is also its virtue. With views to a horizon only slightly refracted by the ripples of heat, the eye is drawn to the mile-wide blank in the center of the valley, a patch of no plants whatsoever. It's a playa—a dry lake—the first since leaving Tucson, and the shape of things to come.

The road continues along the toe of the gray and green Spring Mountains, and into the town of Pahrump, a pair of mega-groceries with acres of parking for the 35,000 people in white houses and trailers. Propane trucks and septic-pumper trucks cruise a grid of gravel roads. It's the sort of town where folks claim to be escaping the big city—and then build their own, the spawn of Las Vegas.

Pahrump has casinos, but I've had my fill. Pahrump has an instant golf course of emerald sod and Mediterranean pines, but I've only caddied, never golfed. Pahrump has a billboard featuring a hungry blonde with arms raised above the swell of her chest, a bosom strategically cut off by the bottom of the billboard. *Venus*, it says—and suddenly I realize that this is my last day in the only state to legalize prostitution.

An arrow on the billboard points down to a little home beneath; it wears its own sign, "Adult Entertainment Information." Of course I brake to a stop. A five-second examination of my soul finds it somewhat south of its usual location, but still committed to my wife.

Inside, a lady with a French poodle greets me. Pert. Nice eyes. But she's at least sixty, raising the possibility that the prostitutes have joined the Pipefitters Union Local 211 and this lady has seniority. She's playing a crossword while the TV shows Kabul burning.

"Is there something you need?"

Suddenly shy, I mumble that I'm just passing through.

"Here's our souvenirs and novelties."

A glass case with dusty coasters and Venus bumper stickers. That's it?

"That's it."

I slip out of town at dusk, never giving Pahrump a chance. Riding west, I look for the other Venus, but fail to find her light. I do find an arroyo to call my own. The horizon is humped with hills, but not until the light of morning do I discover that they're built of cruel limestone, almost but not quite black.

So long as I avoid the many-headed barrel cactus with hooked red spines, it's an easy walk up the closest knoll to scan the coming terrain: more hills, another playa, and a sweeping rise to a fretted ridge that may be the rim of Death Valley. I jog back to camp and read the *Pahrump Valley*

Times over coffee and a pastry released from a foil packet. The newspaper I burn after breakfast, not wishing to carry an extra ounce over the pass in the Funeral Mountains. Which, I see on the map, isn't far from Hell's Gate and Coffin Peak.

The usual hints: gloom ahead. On the back page of my journal, under the heading "Cheering Descriptions of Death Valley," I've collected the impressions of others over the past century. Pit of Horrors. Creator's Dumping Place. The Smoking Furnace. Jaws of Death. More recently, Ken Kesey's *Demon Box* included a sweet little poem that goes:

> Oh, Molly, my Death Valley dolly,
> You're gone, by golly, you're dead.
> Where the scorpions hide
> and the sidewinders slide
> You lie in your alkali bed.

Yet it's not death calling this morning but the sweet trill of the phainopepla, a silky black flycatcher with a crest like a Roman helmet. The bike takes me down a dreamy road: no power line, little traffic, a stripe of asphalt. What little roadside trash exists is claimed by native squatters like the long lizard that scrambles beneath a scrap of carpet. Ten miles west, the hills are no longer malevolent. They're losing their hard limestone edges, as if melting under the fabulous sun.

An hour or two down the road and across the California state line is Death Valley Junction, the last town. From five miles off it looks terribly small, a dash of green wiggling in the heat, all alone in the center of yet another creosote valley. Up close it's still small, with a single substantial building: a big adobe built Mexican style around a courtyard of tamarisk trees drooping like desperate pines.

"Built in 1923 by Pacific Coast Borax Company," says a man slumped in a chair under the long colonnade. I wonder, did I ask? His name is Tom Willett, and he wears sandals and white socks, his long white hair in a pageboy. He faces the courtyard alone, ready to answer tourists before they get out a question.

"You can't get there from here!" Mr. Willett announces. I excuse myself and wander out of earshot—but stick to the shade. For this I should thank the Pacific Coast Borax Company, or at least thank borax, a cottony crud found on or near playas. It looks worthless, but its fibers do unexpected things, binding and strengthening, and people have long coveted those things. Since the fourth century the Chinese have known that borax makes a terrific glaze for ceramics. Marco Polo toted some home, having no idea that seven hundred years later it would be used to make Pyrex, the glass that resists the expansion and contraction of heating and cooling that would shatter ordinary glass.

Back in the 1920s, people knew something else: borax made superb soap flakes. It dissolves grease just as easily as borax itself is dissolved in water, which is why you can't find borax in most places. It runs away with rain.

So the miners came to the land of little rain. They hauled away the easy pickings, and left. Death Valley Junction persisted as a filling station until at least 1968, when a woman with presumably little interest in borax brought in her flat tire to be repaired. She's still here.

I meet her out by the mailbox. Marta Becket is seventy-six, trim as a creosote, with pancake makeup. With little prodding, she tells me that she's a "solo dance-mime," and that she can still dance on her toes. Mr. Willet is her stagehand and sidekick. What was once the headquarters of Pacific Borax is now their venue: the Amargosa Opera House.

Where? She shows me, preferring action over talk. It's not really an opera house. The flat tire gave Ms. Becket time enough to wander over to the big adobe and spy the old social hall. She peered into the shadows of Death Valley Junction, imagined a new life, and never let go.

I'm a week too early for the season. Ms. Becket compliments me on my choice of travel time: after the big heat, before the snowbird rush. "I like the visitors, too, of course—they come to my shows. But then they all leave, and in the moonlight this place is just beautiful."

I look up and down the road and notice what I'd overlooked: a stone ridge that rises from the valley floor like a fin. I imagine it in the moonlight, bid good-bye to Ms. Becket, and head west.

It's another ten miles and a thousand-foot climb to the Funeral Range, a mess of black lavas and fans of white, gray, and pink rubble that appear utterly out of place, as if they were deposited by dump trucks. I crest the pass and immediately feel the hot blast coming up Furnace Creek, the entrance to Death Valley. I'd expected as much. The Smoking Furnace. I hunker down in a wind-cheat and descend a thousand feet in elevation before halting.

"Dante's View" says the sign for a spur road leading up, not down. I take it, ignoring the warning about the 14 percent grade I'll encounter thirteen miles later, at road's end. I want to see the object of my final desire from Dante's.

Onward, past the old mines whose tailings look strangely natural. Past the black hills and desert holly, a silver-leafed saltbush looking like sprinkles on a chocolate cake. Every fifteen or thirty minutes a car passes, and the tourists grin and give me the thumbs up. Meanwhile, I weaken and stop to eat tomorrow's breakfast, another foil pastry. Another hour and I must break out the emergency food, a package of ramen noodles, and devour them uncooked. I accelerate to 4 mph, and pass a tarantula.

Just short of the summit I pass a car that could go no farther, blowing steam and gurgling wildly. The urge to walk is defeated by a feeling that I've been riding for years for this last hill. Forearms gleaming with sweat, I push on to Dante's View, park the bike, stagger to the edge of the abyss, and utter the standard Holy Smokes or whatever sums up the reaction to looking out the window of an airplane.

Exactly 5,755 feet below my feet is Badwater, the lowest point in North America. There's a road down there, my road, and the car on that road is not like a toy but like a pill bug. From this height the salt flats appear amoeboid, not a pretty word but not exactly a pretty sight, either. The broad spills of white are tenuously connected to each other with ribbons of white. The slope below me is gutted and gullied and slopped with scree all the way to the floor of Death Valley, long and narrow and bounded on the far side by the 11,000-foot-high Panamint Mountains. Here and there the range is speckled with trees, but the summits are bald fans of gray rubble.

I hobble back to the bike and find a place to lay out my bag on the rim without rolling over the edge. The few tourists climb back into their machines and leave me alone. The wind comes up and buffets my exposed position, but I will not be moved.

When I wake at 1 AM the wind has stopped. I sit up and look over the brink at the briny eye of Death Valley. Still there. The salt shines in the starlight, and I can hardly believe that I've woken to a view usually reserved for soaring birds. No wonder people climb mountains.

I lie back and look for the Big Dipper, the only constellation I'm reasonably sure of, but cannot find it. It makes no difference. I see one, then two, three, four falling stars. Five, six, seven. (And I didn't even drink a beer tonight.)

Two more flame out, leaving a brief trace in their wake—is it real, or just an afterimage? Perhaps because I am alone, I think about the first words spoken between two humans, a million years ago or so, and surmise that maybe, just maybe, they were, "Did you see *that*?"

TWENTY YEARS AGO I was a rolling penny-pincher who'd discovered that I could ride my bike from Tucson to Utah for the cost of pancakes, raisins, beans, and coffee. Now, sitting on the verge of Death Valley with a steaming cup of coffee and my pipe, I have money but nothing to eat. With map in hand I peer down into the valley and make idle calculations: Badwater is precisely 2.4 miles west by suicide leap, and 40 miles by road.

I choose the road. The gravity that was yesterday's anchor is today's catapult, and the descent is a rush of colors and wind. Delighted by the geologic wreckage on all sides, I stop to check out the half-dissolved mountains and to strip off another piece of clothing. My thermometer tells one story—58, 65, 74, 87—and my water bottle tells another: it's being squashed by the grip of increasing pressure.

Back in Furnace Creek, the road descends between ridges of yellow mud and gray ash gouged by the sort of storms that come once every hundred years. Despite the many tricks of desert plants, none have figured out a way to persist on these smooth fingers of earth.

But just when it seems that Death Valley is truly dead, a jungle of date palms and tangled mesquite rises above the shocks of arrow-weed and the springs of Furnace Creek. In 1849 an old blind man was found here. He was an Indian, buried up to his neck in sand, yet alive. The people who found him were a party of forty wagons, heading for California gold. The people who had left him had seen the wagons and abandoned their village in haste, and the old man made himself scarce in the way of a sidewinder snake.

The buried man survived, but the people and their wagons trundled down the canyon and proceeded to put the death in Death Valley. It was December, and they feared the Sierra snow more than this desert, but a subsequent three-day dry stretch made them rue the choice. Mr. Fish died, but he was old and ready to go. Young Isham somehow got separated and lost; later, they buried him where he fell. Thirst took Mr. Culverwell, and the nine men who struck off on foot may or may not have survived. Nobody's sure, but with each retelling of the story Death Valley grew more deadly. In a *Los Angeles Times* article from 1908, "The Lost Wagon Train," not a one survived after their "dreadful death march" foolishly entered the valley "in the height of summer."

Wheeling down Furnace Creek, I can see how the myth picked up momentum: the creek vanishes into the gravels. The badlands and canyon walls fall back, and the traveler loses the intimacy of shadows. Another turn, and Furnace Creek opens into Death Valley like an alley onto a great thoroughfare. The valley, sunk between two parallel ranges, runs north and south to the horizon.

The road forks: eighteen miles south to Badwater, or a few hundred yards north to the Furnace Creek Inn and food. The inn is three stories of adobe and stone under a red tile roof, buried in palms and gardens. When I pedal up and ask a man coming out if they serve breakfast, he looks at his watch and says, "It's twelve-fifteen." He checks me out. The verdict: safe, although it's clear I just descended a vertical mile on my bike. Wondering, he is, where I came from.

Likewise.

"I'm from Berkeley. I had a motorcycle dealership, but I sold it—to see the world."

Ronald Ware is not young but is nonetheless wrinkle-free; it probably helps that he's black, and needn't apply the sunscreen I loathe. Neat checkered button-down shirt, blue jeans, black leather shoes, white socks. We stand in the shade of a palm. Despite the pit in my stomach I cannot resist asking, Of all places, why Death Valley?

"I was traveling through Europe, and I was in Istanbul when I had this moment, this . . . epiphany. I'd gone to the bazaar, to the great mosques, when I realized that most of all Istanbul was a big noisy city crowded with people. I found myself thinking: I could have found this in San Francisco.

"And I said, why am I in Istanbul when I don't even know my own country? So I set out and found myself here, and I love it. The space, the quiet. I'm sixty-one and I had no idea!"

Ronald also loves desert driving. "I can go a half hour without seeing another car."

The nomad's pleasure. "Treeless spaces uncramp the soul," declared Mary Austin a hundred years ago. She liked to urge her horse along at a "jigging coyote trot" through her beloved treeless space, the Mohave desert of puckering summer droughts and zinging winter freezes. This desert.

"I'm a nice man—that's how I had a successful motorcycle business without ever having ridden a motorcycle. But now that I'm seeing my country and meeting people like you, I see that I've been an ignorant dogmatic person, too. I'm just glad that I'm getting out and learning something. About you, about me. The things I like. I've got a substantial wine collection—but I don't even like wine! Investment and prestige, I suppose. But what do I really like?"

He knows.

"Exercise, because it feels good. And soap and water and a good sleep—eight, nine hours. Reading. And this desert. I've been here three times in the last two months."

Ronald wants to know about my family, and out come my wallet photos. He's married with two children, too; he hasn't lost them but found himself. Solitary travel can do that. A man fills in the missing places in his thoughts and eases into his own skin.

I thank Ronald, who's not sure why I'm grateful, as he did most of the talking. *Just lucky,* I'm thinking as I head into the inn, into the hushed luxury of wrought-iron hanging lamps and antique ladder-back chairs.

In the bathroom I comb the twigs from my hair and use the electric shoe polisher, sending up a cloud of dust. Semitransformed, I emerge and order a focaccia and a beer. I fit right in, despite not having showered since Las Vegas.

This I remedy with a ride to the nearby Furnace Creek Ranch with its faux Old West General Store and Saloon, pool, and showers. A no-fear coyote slinks through the parking lot. A Swiss woman borrows my tire pump. At the adjacent Park Service visitor center I pay my fees and learn that the current wind speed at Badwater is a mere 0.16 knot.

But I've yakked and idled away my chance to reach the low point today. I spend the night in a canyon near Furnace Creek, munching pistachios and reading Mary Austin's account of a prospector who'd camped out so often that he "had gotten to the point where he knew no bad weather, and all places were equally happy so long as they were out of doors."

In the morning I head back to the inn for breakfast. It's just me and one other diner and Betty the hostess. She wears a bright enameled flag brooch. "I never thought I'd like living in a trailer in Death Valley, but I love it. Come by and put your feet up on the coffee table—I don't care."

I'd love to, but I'm going out to Badwater for the night.

"For the night? I met a hiker who slept out there, and he said it was so quiet that he could hear the blood pumping through him. Badwater sure is a pretty place, but I wouldn't want to sleep listening to that! Too quiet for me, way down in that hole where there ain't no noise—unh-unh."

She deftly refills my water glass and takes a seat at the table.

"I want to hear a little something—a cricket or a frog or even just the sound of a car passing, not all squealing, but just the sound of its tires, something to remind me that I'm not *all alone*."

It's already 98 degrees when I leave, all alone. The road south to Badwater is well above the salt pan, hugging the mountain front to the east. It's the shade of all colors mixed together, the unsavory brown-yellow-black that results from kneading all the Play-Doh modeling clay together. The mountain slope is amazingly steep for what appears to be rubble. Once I try to scramble up, just to see if it's somehow stuck together, like limestone, with geologic miracle glue, or if it's truly at the angle of repose. Answer:

the latter. I climb ten feet before sliding back down in a cloud of cobbles and dirt.

I won't do that again. I'm left with the impression that Death Valley is, on a grand time scale, a temporary pit. Come to think of it, so is Africa's Lac Assal. One big crack in the crust, and Assal would be flooded in the titanic rush of the Indian Ocean. When things warm up and the ice melts, South America's Salina Grande will also vanish in a flood. Asia's Dead Sea, robbed of water by ever-increasing use of the Jordan River, is sinking by several feet each year; likewise, Europe's Caspian Sea is dependent on the flow of the Volga. The only sure bet is Australia's Lake Eyre, which, like Australia itself, will probably persist in blissful geologic ignorance of the rest of the globe. Otherwise, it's safe to say that the low points will never be the same again. Neither will I, so I'm just in time.

The valley bottom, which from Dante's View appeared to be a perfectly level salt pan, is not. What looked smooth is actually blisters and little towers of salt. The farther south I ride, the closer they approach the road, until the tongue of salt reaches almost to the road and the crumbling mountain. Then the final drop, and I can go no lower. "BADWATER," says the sign, "–280 FEET": lowest point in North America. But not the least popular: there are ten cars in the lot. I peek in the windows to see their guidebooks and guess their origin from the language: Japanese, German, and Italian.

High above in the late-afternoon sun, clouds in long whips promise a show at sundown. Below sea level there's not a single puff of wind. It's the right evening for something I've been denied at every other low point for reason of wind or water: a night on the salt.

It's rough riding across the foot-wide polygons, whose borders are thickly ridged or wrecked in heaves like sea ice. I walk the bike west, toward the center, occasionally turning to watch the road and parked cars diminish with distance. Beyond the last tourists, the salt floes are much broader, three to ten feet across, with two-inch-high ridges between. The snowy surface is built of thousands of stalagmites less than a half-inch tall that crunch underfoot with a sound like knuckles popping. I could ride now, but even walking the bike leaves a track. So I carry it, not wanting to leave a mark that I myself wouldn't want to find.

If anyone ever comes out here. I'm about a mile from the road when I hear rapid crunching and turn to see two familiar faces, panting and grinning. It's my neighbors from Tucson, Rob and Jennifer. I'd forgotten that they would be returning from a Sierra hike and promised to look for me.

"We've searched half of Death Valley for you!"

After the ritual backslaps, I congratulate Rob on his remarkable tracking: You did it!

"No—you did it," says Rob. "The last pit! Now, how would you like to come back with us to our camp? We promise pasta and wine. But you'll have to pay with stories of your trip."

I tell the truth: I don't want the journey to end until I spend a night on the salt. Not that I'm sure it's legal. When I picked up my permit, the nice NPS man simply told me that I had to camp two miles off the road. At the time, I had no idea that it's against park rules to bring a bike onto Badwater—even if you carry it—or to camp there. (I've since learned better, to my sorrow, thanks to a dutiful NPS officer and my publisher, the Sierra Club.)

I promise my neighbors endless tales back in Tucson, and we part ways. The bike begins to cut into my shoulder. I pad the frame with my spare shirt. When it appears I've reached the center of the valley, I quit, lay out my ground cloth, and sit.

The sun goes down in flames without a sound. It's a good thing Betty the hostess isn't here, fidgeting in the silence. Quiet, I suppose, reminds her of death. But to be able to "hear the blood pumping" is to hear life, your own life.

I eat dinner and open a beer. Light my pipe and watch the smoke laze in blue reefs around my bag. No wind. When I stand I feel a thermocline developing: it's colder at my feet than my head. All I need now is data: my thermometer says it's 75 at my toes and 82 at eye level.

At 8 PM the moon is just a grin on the western horizon, two hours behind the sun. The cool light catches the ridges of salt that encircle my camp and extend to the mountains. A very crisp scene: the perfectly flat pure white floor of the valley, the black masses of the mountains beyond, rising 6,000 feet to the east and 11,000 feet to the west.

There goes the moon. The earth is spinning, and I'm pinned by gravity and good fortune. I think of the Seven Summits and the urge to leave Everest not long after you arrive—and how different this is, lying on a glazed sea of salt.

Everybody has a plan, something that may or may not happen—but that's really not the point. It's the plan that counts, the pleasure of possibility. You might hope to sail alone to the palm islands in a boat of your own design. To please your spouse in a remarkably athletic way or marry the right person the next time around. Or to sell your house before the plumbing goes and move to a carefree condo at the clean edge of a golf course until God's call.

As for me, I wanted to pedal my bike to the lowest points on earth. To my everlasting surprise, I did.

Epilogue

I RETURNED HOME to mild fanfare. My wife threw a party honoring me as low-rider of the decade. We provided guests with the lowest entertainment possible: a game of limbo. Some time later, my friend Mark from high school interviewed me for his website as we sat outside a Tucson coffeehouse on Speedway Boulevard. The interview went fine, but I didn't recognize my words when they appeared on the Internet. Sorry! said Mark, but the recorder had captured the sounds of Speedway, making it difficult for his mother to transcribe the tape. Much of the time she simply guessed at what I was saying.

Even so, the interview, "Adventures of the Ultimate Underachiever," generated an immediate result. A man e-mailed me an article from the journal *South American Explorer*. Authored by Victor Ponce, it began with "Recent mapping by Argentina's Instituto Geografico Militar has determined that the lowest point in the American continent is in the Grand Bajo de San Julian. . . ."

San Julian is not the low point I visited, Salina Grande, but another Patagonian pit about five hundred miles south. Before my journey, sources including the National Geographic map of South America had made the claim for Salina Grande, so there I went.

Of course, it was faintly depressing to have pedaled to the wrong depression. Once more consulting my fabulous *Times Atlas of the World*, I found the Gran Bajo de San Julian. The map indicated no point below sea level, but I'd no reason to doubt the existence of a deeper hole. Mountaineers occasionally fib about reaching a summit, but nobody bothers to lie about the pits.

I stared at the map of Patagonia. The Andes were crowned by enormous ice fields. Glaciers swept out of the mountains and calved into lakes that reached deep into Argentine Patagonia. The notion of pedaling past icebergs in the desert was alluring—but Patagonia's dripping forests and brutal winds had permanently repelled me.

Yet it couldn't hurt merely to *plan* a trip. Through no effort of my own, a logical route to the Gran Bajo presented itself: from the base of 12,700-foot Mount Fitz Roy, along the Rio Chalia and through a village with the unlikely name of Mata Amarilla, or "kill yellow."

I paused, the atlas still open to Plate 121, and considered the village. There must be another translation, or else some very strange yellow killers. I could imagine them, drinking *mate* tea as a sheep roasted in the courtyard. I could even imagine their surprise when a man and woman rolled up on bikes, an old but sturdy couple on their second honeymoon, riding to the new lowest points on the planet.

Acknowledgments

I've been lucky. I was surely the slowest bicyclist ever backed by Discovery Online, and I'm grateful for their support (while it lasted). My deepest thanks go to editor Greg Henderson—the only one of the bunch who truly wanted to join me beside a salt pit for a beer and sour Skittles.

I'm glad, too, that Stephen Vivona and Frank Cook got me hooked on bicycle riding long ago. My high school and college English teachers, Ken Wright, Jim Potts, and Ed Abbey, did a wonderful thing: they made me want to write.

I traveled to the depressions alone but with plenty of help. Discovery's Jodi Bettencourt juggled invoices and visas, and Doren Burrell assembled the traveling digital studio. Rune Eriksen of Telenor Satellite donated a phone *and* told me where to find the northernmost tree in Norway. Amina Elzeneing and Dr. Moustafa El Ghamrawy showed me the depths of Egyptian hospitality; Salim Ayoub did the same for Jordan, as well as telling me the true reason Arabs drive at night without headlights. I'm also grateful for those who took me into their homes, yet didn't get a peep in the story: Doris Soto and Fernando Jara, Delphina and Scott Knight, George and Deb the Catgirl.

My agents, Ellen Geiger and Matt McGowan, gently introduced me to the art of writing a proposal. When it came time to write the book, I often ducked into Espresso Art or Ike's until the sun went down, after which I headed for The Mint, The Surly Wench, or The Shanty. Not a one of them booted me for antisocial behavior. Peter Friederici and Mary Alice Yakutchik read parts of the manuscript and provided kind words when I needed them. Greg Henderson, Steven Hopp, and Barbara Kingsolver edited the first draft and wrote almost another book in the margins, doing their best to make it better. (They did.) Diana Landau of Sierra Club Books is the smart and patient editor I needed for the final push.

My trips and my story would have been very different if I didn't hold in mind my true home. Wherever I was in the world, I knew my children were in good hands with my sister, Sue; the Black family next door; my tireless mother-in-law, Rosa; and my wife, Sonya—the grand prize winner for my warmest thanks. The pits are pretty nice, but I know where my heart belongs.

Bicycle Touring and Books

My touring bicycle, a hybrid, has drop handlebars and 700 x 47 road tires. It's a 21-speed with a 13-30 rear cluster, a 26-42-45 crankset, bar-end shifters, front and rear racks, panniers, handlebar bag, and a kickstand (in the desert there's not much to lean your bike against). I can carry up to two gallons in triple frame-mounted water bottles, various loose bottles, and a water bag.

A Japanese touring bicyclist I met near my home in Tucson in the 1980s had a "ready-for-anything" tool kit that included a foot-long crescent wrench and a hundred feet of rope. This seemed to me excessive, and apparently he had come to agree—I still have the rope today.

This is noteworthy because it's best to bring less and prepare more for your trip. A good bike is fantastically reliable, so long as it's ready for the road with an overhaul, new cables, and new or at least not-old tires. If you feel up to the task, try taking your bike apart and putting it back together again at least a couple of months before your trip, so you'll understand how it all works. You don't want to pedal a mystery.

Even on long trips like those described in the book, I don't bring special tools for the bottom bracket, headset, or wheel bearings. I do bring extra spokes (including a "fiber-fix" spoke) and a spoke wrench, a screwdriver, a six-inch crescent wrench, several Allen (hex) wrenches, a spare tube (but not a tire), a tube repair kit, an air pump, some odd nuts and bolts in case a rack loosens, a bit of baling wire, and duct tape. I also carry a pair of disposable latex gloves such as medical folk use, in case I have a greasy job to do. I'd rather drink the water I have than wash my hands with it.

Spontaneous omnivory is one of the pleasures of bike touring. For emergency food, I bring a few packs of ramen noodles (in a pinch, they're edible without cooking), and otherwise rely on whatever the locals are eating. You'll be surprised how good fried gristle tastes after a day of pedaling.

If you're keen on hitting the road, here are my recommendations for a bike trip abroad. First get an atlas; get the best one you can afford, look at the maps, and dream about baguettes or tortillas—or, if you're going to Australia, white bread and Vegemite. You'll want a good atlas also to find out a few things about when it rains and which way the wind blows. If the information is lacking, you might as well pedal with the sun at your back (south in the southern hemisphere, north in the northern) so you have a pleasing, glare-free view. And drivers coming up behind you can see you better without the sun in their eyes.

You might follow my pretrip training regime: riding or at least sitting on the bike long enough so it doesn't hurt the butt, and a pedal to the drugstore to buy a big bottle of aspirin. Next, pack all the things you think you'll need, then repack and leave half of it behind. You can always buy something you later deem essential. Then fly away (a bike in a box is free on international flights), land, assemble your bike, and pedal away. Not too far at first. After a week you'll be feeling better, or you'll hate me.

Either way, you'll want something to read, like this book. Or perhaps one of the titles in the list below, all of which I've read, enjoyed, and now recommend. Original publication dates are given; check your library or bookstore for available editions.

AUSTRALIA

The Future Eaters: An Ecological History of the Australasian Lands and People,
by Tim Flannery, 1995

> Why slow and tasty animals tend to vanish after humans arrive on an island,
> even a very big island like Australia.

The Fatal Shore, by Robert Hughes, 1987
> Eighteenth-century British authorities, looking to offload their less desirable citizens in a natural prison, give Australia a try—and never leave.

Cooper's Creek, by Alan Moorehead, 1963
> Pride, excess baggage, and drunken camels foil the 1860 Burke and Wills Expedition, the first attempt by non-Aborigines to cross the continent.

ASIA

Cairo, edited by John and Kirsten Miller (in the Chronicles Abroad series), 1994
> A collection of excepts from novels, essays, and letters whose authors range from Naguib Mahfouz to Michael Palin.

Baghdad without a Map, by Tony Horwitz, 1991
> A journalist is caught in the whirlpool of bottomless hospitality that is the Middle East.

Sinai: The Great and Terrible Wilderness, by Burton Bernstein, 1979
> Travels among the Bedouin during the Egypt–Israel war(s) of the 1970s.

Notes on the Bedouins and Wahabys, by John Lewis Burckhardt, 1831
> Burckhardt, a Swiss, reveals the tradition-bound habits of the Bedouin. In doing so, he discovers their disgust with the fundamentalist Wahaby, who "propagates his religion with the sword."

EUROPE

Imperium, by Ryzard Kapuscinski, 1994
> A bitter recollection of the Soviet empire in the direct prose of this Polish journalist.

Proletarian Science? The Case of Lysenko, by Dominique Lecourt, 1978
> The terrible story of how Trofim Lysenko crippled Soviet biology.

The Unknown Civil War in Soviet Russia, by Oliver Radley, 1976
> An account by an English law professor of the Bolshevik crackdown on the peasant revolt in Tambov province.

The Russian Revolution, by Alan Moorehead, 1958
> The Bolsheviks triumph—barely—after Lenin's return from exile. Moorehead's a good storyteller, and remarkably fair for a man writing during the height of anticommunism.

Early Voyages and Travels to Russia and Persia, by Anthony Jenkinson, 1877
> Very early travels (1557–72) by Elizabeth I's ambassador to the court of Ivan the Terrible; by turns breathless and amusing. Jenkinson reports: "They have many sorts of meats and drinks when they banquet, and delight in the eating of gross meats and stinking fish."

SOUTH AMERICA

Attending Marvels: A Patagonia Journal, by George G. Simpson, 1934
> During a 1930 paleontology expedition, Simpson's truck is constantly getting stuck; his cook wants to murder a crew member who foolishly complains of too much garlic; and the camp pet, a rhea, drinks kerosene and croaks—yet Simpson seems to enjoy both fossils and Patagonia.

The Voyage of the Beagle, by Charles Darwin, 1839
> The twenty-two-year-old biologist joins Captain Fitz Roy for a five-year trip around the world that will change all of science. A quarter of the book is devoted to Patagonia.

AFRICA

Somebody Else: Arthur Rimbaud in Africa, by Charles Nicholl, 1997
> A nice bit of research and personal travelogue that attempts to explain the young poet's self-exile, and succeeds. "At dawn Djibouti is like a half-lit shower room. The steam condenses on you as you walk down the stairs. . . . You would do better, as usual, to follow the local example and dedicate the afternoon to khat."

The Danakil Diary, by Wilfred Thesiger, 1996
> Summarizing his 1930 expedition into what is now Djibouti, Mr. Thesiger writes that the Afar "were a cheerful, happy people despite the incessant killing."

Hell-Hole of Creation, by L. M. Nesbitt, 1934
> The lurid account of a 1928 expedition into "that black and savage country."

First Footsteps in East Africa, by Richard Burton, 1856
> The polyglot Burton delivers on any subject, from how to kill an elephant with only a knife (cut the Achilles tendon) to the sexual habits of the residents of Harar: "Both sexes are celebrated for laxity of morals."

NORTH AMERICA

Killing the Hidden Waters, by Charles Bowden, 1977
> Bowden takes the long view, back to when the Spaniards came to the desert of the Tohono O'Odam Indians, and "the cow looted the vegetation, the horse shattered ancient tribal boundaries." When the pump arrives in the desert, something is lost as well as gained.

The Desert Year, by Joseph Wood Krutch, 1952
> Krutch serves up biology and philosophy in a way that captures the spirit of the Sonoran Desert without resorting to spiritualism. "What I am after is less to meet God face to face than to take in a beetle, a frog, or a mountain when I meet one." Amen.

The Land of Little Rain, by Mary Austin, 1903
> In the desert she adored, the Mohave, Austin bravely wanders alone and in the company of herders, miners, and Indians. "For all the tolls a desert takes of a man it gives compensations, deep breaths, deep sleeps, and the communion of the stars."

The Desert, by John Van Dyke, 1901
> An art professor from New Jersey, Van Dyke wanted a good look at the air and light of the desert Southwest. After three years of wandering about on a pony, with a fox terrier for company, he wrote, "The desert has gone a-begging for a word of praise these many years. It never had a sacred poet; it has in me only a lover."

About the Author

After graduating from Catalina High School in Tucson, Arizona, Jim Malusa worked as fry-vat lid opener at Kentucky Fried Chicken, a steel bender at A&J Sheet Metal, and a deconstructionist at Cro-Magnon Demolition. He later attended the University of Arizona, which eventually granted him a degree in biology.

As a botanist, Malusa has published in academic journals such as *Systematic Botany*. He is proudest of his five-year effort to map the vegetation of Arizona's Cabeza Prieta Wildlife Refuge. As an author, he has ranged far and wide for *Natural History* magazine and The Discovery Channel, whose assignments included Mount Pinatubo in the Philippines, the Atacama Desert in Chile, carnivorous flies in Panama, and Three Gorges Dam in China.

Malusa still lives in Tucson with his wife, Sonya, and their two children—neither of whom has yet shown an unusual fondness for caves, pits, or other depressions. Find out more about Malusa's anti-expeditions—and view pictures—at *www.IntoThickAir.com*.